# The
# Passionate
# Mind

# Books by Robin Fox

*The Keresan Bridge:*
*A Problem in Pueblo Ethnology*

*Kinship and Marriage:*
*An Anthropological Perspective*

*The Imperial Animal* (with Lionel Tiger)

*Encounter with Anthropology*

*Biosocial Anthropology* (editor)

*The Tory Islanders:*
*A People of the Celtic Fringe*

*The Red Lamp of Incest:*
*A Study in the Origins of Mind and Society*

*Neonate Cognition:*
*Beyond the Blooming Buzzing Confusion*
(editor with Jacques Mehler)

*The Violent Imagination*

*The Search for Society:*
*Quest for a Biosocial Science and Morality*

*Reproduction and Succession:*
*Studies in Anthropology, Law and Society*

*The Challenge of Anthropology:*
*Old Encounters and New Excursions*

*Conjectures and Confrontations:*
*Science, Evolution, Social Concern*

*The Passionate Mind:*
*Sources of Destruction and Creativity*

# The Passionate Mind

## Sources of Destruction & Creativity

# Robin Fox

with a foreword by Ashley Montagu

Transaction Publishers
New Brunswick (U.S.A.) and London (U.K.)

Copyright © 2000 by Transaction Publishers, New Brunswick, New Jersey.

All rights reserved under International and Pan-American Copyright Conventions. No part of this book may be reproduced or transmitted in any form or by any means, electronic or mechanical, including photocopy, recording, or any information storage and retrieval system, without prior permission in writing from the publisher. All inquiries should be addressed to Transaction Publishers, Rutgers—The State University, 35 Berrue Circle, Piscataway, New Jersey 08854-8042.

This book is printed on acid-free paper that meets the American National Standard for Permanence of Paper for Printed Library Materials.

Library of Congress Catalog Number: 99-40000
ISBN: 0-7658-0632-0
Printed in the United States of America

Library of Congress Cataloging-in-Publication Data

Fox, Robin, 1934-
    The passionate mind : sources of destruction and creativity /
    Robin Fox ; with a new introduction by the author and a foreword by
    Ashley Montagu
        p.   cm.
        ISBN 0-7658-0632-0 (alk. paper)
        1. Title.
    PS3556.0948P37   1999
    811'.54—dc21                                             99-40000
                                                                    CIP

for Lin

# Contents

**Seven: Epilogue: Fire of Sense/Smoke of Thought**

*About the Author*
*About Ashley Montagu*

# Introduction to the Transaction Edition

This is a much expanded and revised version of my earlier experiment in multi-media expression, *The Violent Imagination.* The reception given that small and slim edition was suffiently enthusiatic by those who  read it—across a wide range of disciplines, styles and schools of thought and criticism—that I was encouraged to expand it, to make its point more pointed, and to introduce completely new kinds of material, although within the same kind of framework that critics had liked in the original. What perhaps surprised me most was the friendly reaction of colleagues in humanistic anthropology since I had been pretty merciless in teasing them about the science-phobia from which I reckoned they suffered. But they are cultivated and forgiving people, and once they discovered I was a closet versifier—even if my verse was not their idea of truly current poetry—they welcomed me to their bosom as a fellow "postmodernist," praised my effort as a "new way to 'say' anthropology" (Ivan Brady in the *American Anthropologist),* and even got together to nominate me for the Victor Turner Prize in Ethnographic Writing of the Society for Humanistic Anthropology.

I was touched since Vic was a friend (a fellow brain-drainer) and something of a hero of mine, who, despite his leadership of the "symbolic anthropology" school, had come round late in life to repudiating its basic anti-reductionist premises and embracing an anthropology based on a firm acceptance of man's biological make-up and evolutionary past, quoting me as one of his sources of conversion.  It has been a lasting delight to me that his son Fred, one of our leading poets and literary critics, is wholly on the side of the angels (i.e., me and my like-thinking colleagues) in this, even if Vic's wife Edie (who edits the *Anthropology and Humanism Quarterly* ) continues to spar delightfully with the pair of us in defense of a "pure" anthropological humanism untainted by murky biology. I didn't get the prize, of course. I am, by the standards of the now almost wholly ideologized anthropology profession, hopelessly politically incorrect. Too bad. I was more than a little embarassed anyway, since I did not consider this as a contribution to anthropology per se. I agreed that it was a "commentary on the human condition" but couldn't see that this, except in a sense so broad as to be meaningless, made it anthropology, which for me is still "The Science of Man." (How un-PC can you get?) But I agree the distinction is not a hard and fast one. Great poets like Sophocles, or fabulists like Golding, seem able to look right into the heart of the human condition in a way that all the careful science of anthropology manages to miss. (I try to give Sophocles and the Theban Cycle their due in chap. three of *Reproduction and Succession*, Transaction, 1993, while Golding permeates *The Red Lamp of Incest*, Notre Dame, 1983.)

I believe these approaches—the scientific and humanistic—to be complementary and not necessarily in conflict, and make some noises in this direction in the original introduction, even to the point of somewhat pompously calling for a "raised consciousness" that would erase the distinction—eventually. But I was still taken aback by the insistence of my humanist friends that I was one of them—even some kind of paradigm of what a humanist anthropology might look like. But they know what they think about what they are doing and I am not going to argue with them. Certainly there is a heavy anthropological content here. How could that be avoided? I am commenting on the human condition and I am a lifelong anthropologist. This is going to color my commentary whatever form it might take. If the result is a kind of anthropology in and of itself, so be it. One is not always the best judge of the significance of one's own efforts. I defer to my colleagues on this one.

As to the extended material, some critics have seen it as more "personal" than the original. I have, they say, stepped out from behind the "personae"—Yeats's poetic masks—and told it more straight from the shoulder. Perhaps. But the distinction is fuzzy to me. Some of the truly most "personal" items have to be told from behind a mask anyway. The Rev. Patrick Brontë (in whose Parish I was born and lived my early years in the 1930s—he was of course long gone by then, but I knew old people who remembered him) understood this very well. He made his children

(Branwell, Maria, Charlotte, Emily and Anne) stand before him wearing home-made masks when they wanted to convey deeply personal things. I heard that story from villagers before I ever read about it in Mrs Gaskell. It stuck very deep in my subconscious, obviously, and I have been hiding behind a variety of masks in order to say personal things ever since.

Where the mask stops and the face begins is often therefore hard for me to say. Some of the earlier things (the poem for my daughters on Kent State, for example) are straight from the heart. Other things that sound confessional are pure fictions. But if a poet is after anything it is the general in the particular and vice-versa. (Unless the poet be one of the free-verse narcissistic lyrical confessional know-nothings who dominate today's poetic scene by the grace of Amy Lowell and Creative Writing Departments and university patronage of contemporary poetasters.) I think the same mixture is there in the new stuff. Zygon Y and the Shaman of Lascaux, as well as the Dream-Man, are pure masks, while the poet of the New Jersey Landscapes and some of the "New Songs of Innocence and Experience," is as close as I might ever come to emotional directness. I was not raised to be emotionally direct, I admit, and the mask comes more easily. Zygon Y delivers a Browningesque dramatic monologue. But then Browning often revealed more of himself in these than in his straight "confessions." (For further ruminations on Browning the reader might want to look in *The Challenge of Anthropology*, Transaction, 1994.)

I think though, that the critics may be right to some extent. In the new material I have perhaps been less worried about the need to be constantly making some general point in order to escape the narcissistic trap that puts me off most contemporary verse. (Like Auberon Waugh I like poetry that "rhymes, scans and makes sense" but also that stands up and says something about the world, not just about the poet.) One of my critical friends had in fact said: "Let more of your own voice come through directly." And one, a little more toughly: "Preach less, reveal more." (How hopeless. I am, like Coleridge, an inveterate sermonizer.) However, since I gained confidence from having done it at all, I guess I found the confidence to do just that. In all my books I have been shamelessly autobiographical—letting the reader in behind the scenes as it were; not pretending that the ideas were somehow pristinely arrived at by a disembodied processs of reasoning, but were embedded in the turmoil of a real and often confusing life. (See, e.g. *Conjectures and Confrontations*, Transaction, 1997.) Consequently the hectoring by the new wunderkinder of anthropology on "reflexivity" leaves me cold. How much more was this personal approach justified in a book that was avowedly a personal statement from the outset? So I let my life creep into this one more boldly.

One usually starts life at the beginning—with the possible exception of Merlin, so I went back and looked at some youthful things, and am not surprised to see that—apart from some uneasy experiments with "free verse" quickly and mercifully abandoned (I leave one surrealistic, Eliotic exercise as a sample)—a style, a voice, was already in place. One's subject matter expands, but at least in my case, I don't think one gets any better. Poets, like mathematicians, are at their best early, and should die young. In my case however, in an excess of revulsion against the life of the feelings and a fanatical embrace of the life of the mind, when I decided to become a scientist in my early twenties I destroyed all the poetry and music I had written to date and did not write any more until well into my thirties. It was, in fact, coming to the United States that once again liberated the poet who had been buried under the mountain of scientific career greed. (I was also put off publishing since tastes in poetry, as in most other things, changed, probably post-*Howl* and the late 50s and 60s when I wasn't paying much attention). A few of the early things survived in student publications, and I have used this opportunity to revive them since they have a nice period flavor (the mid-fifties), just as those of part three are saturated with the seventies. The sixties remain a poetic blank for me.

The rest I was tempted to call "American Encounters" since it was those encounters (I've always used the "encounter" motif since *Encounter with Anthropology* in 1973) that gave rise to most of it, but I would have had to add "and other excursions" since there are obviously other points of stimulation—the Alps for example (shades of the Romantics!). Those who think it worth the time may try matching up some of the later poems with their obvious earlier counterparts, and indeed some *are* obvious as with the Shaman who partners the Hunter, the Hippie Girl who is Isis, and the daughters who get something more gentle and personal here than the rumination on Kent State. The impossibility of poetry continues to get its due. But this is not a quiz and there will be no exam. The general theme of the paradox of human existence—that what exhalts us (the ability to order our lives according to our ideas) just as surely brings us down—remains thoroughly intact. Some things are in there just for fun of course, redolent with memories of Chesterton and Gilbert, Belloc and Lear and the marvellous tradition of English absurd verse so obviously mysterious to foreigners. Even it is making the point about humor and survival I suppose, but as I grow older and look hard at the world, I see less and less chance of our laughing our way out of our problems. But the gentle reader, who is asked to work hard enough, deserves the occasional coffee break.

Speaking of growing older, if there is a new "theme" in the new material, then it is about going far from gentle into that good night, and while looking the horror in the face, having a good laugh at it and at oneself: the surest way to tame at least one's personal violent imagination. Poets were once expected to do everything for us: both to illuminate and to amuse. They have become so deathly serious (and lamely trivial) of late. Perhaps this little volume will help redress the balance. That is why I am delighted to accept the offer of my old friend and antagonist Ashley Montagu to use his charming review as a foreward. We shall perhaps never agree on the innateness of human aggressiveness, but we have managed to maintain a civilized disagreement over more than three decades now. Does that say something to the general theme? I hope so. Here let me just thank my friend for the benefits of his erudition, wit, kindness and unfailing good counsel over the years, and Marjorie for putting up, in her gentle but wise and funny way, with a lot of nonsense from the two posturing males.

I did ask Ashley whether he thought I should include so much about love and sex. "The real question," he answered, "is why you should include anything else." As the anthropologist of Kinship and Marriage and the Evolutionary Process, I should have known that. We are in the business of contributing our genes to the genepool of the species (although we often forget this in the pursuit of more proximate ends) and anything else, in the long view, is merely contributory to this. Love, courtship, sex, childbirth and death are the wheel on which it all turns (see the "Ode to the Selfish Gene"), and if they were not heavily represented then the driving force of evolution would be missing and this would not be anthropology at all. Voltaire said something to the effect that love was a canvass given by nature and embroidered by imagination. The anthropologist in us should insist on always seeing the canvass through the embroidery. Too many cannot see through the embroidery at all, or even proclaim that there is no canvass. I embroider with the best of them, but my fingers bleed from the resistance of the stubborn canvass.

The title—an obvious echo of Lévi-Strauss's *The Savage Mind*—is borrowed from a previous article, "The Passionate Mind" which appeared originally in *Zygon: The Journal Of Science And Religion* (appropriately as a tribute to the then recently deceased Victor Turner). This was reprinted as a chapter in *The Search For Society* (1989). If my original scheme had not terrified publishers generally, it would have appeared here among the poetry and drama along with other scientific and academic articles. But that was obviously asking too much, so I have simply appropriated the title, with the implicit suggestion that readers might look at the chapter in *Search* to help complete the picture. (The article on "Conciousness out of Context" also originally destined for this volume, became itself the last chapter of the same book, and the original article—or sermon—"The Violent Imagination" is in there too.)

Some Acknowledgements

For encouragement (and one needs a lot when one is bucking orthodoxies) over the last decade or so, may I thank, in no particular order but Fred Turner above all: Dudley Young, Dana Gioia, Robert Storey, David Perkins, Dame Iris Murdoch (RIP), Doris Lessing, Lionel Tiger, Iain Prattis, Ray Smith, Joyce Carol Oates, Micheline Herz (RIP), Joseph Carroll, Edie Turner, Roy Wagner, Ed. Wilmsen and Jane Greer (the loss of her *Plains Poetry Journal* was a tragedy for the real poets; the "New Jersey Landscapes" sequence was slated for publication there when her illness forced its discontinuance); to the *American Arts Quarterly* and James F. Cooper for permission to reprint "Snowflakes and Similes" and to *World and I* for permission to use the Ashley Montagu material. And as always to Kate, Ellie and Anne: my best readers, and my best friends. Anne's adventures in bookselling had her producing the *Bay Books News* (California, Maryland) where some of the shorter verses had their first outing on her poetry page. Some of the "Undergraduate Poems" appeared in *Beaver,* the student newspaper of the London School of Economics. They tell me I don't need permission since I own the copyright anyway, but I acknowledge—with nostalgic fondness for my days as an assistant editor—the source. "The Conference of Foules" first appeared in *The Cambridge Revue,* 103, #2270, 1982; "Image de la Comtesse" in *Bulletin de la Société des Professeurs Francais en Amérique,* 1978-79; and "What the Hunter Saw" in Iain Prattis, ed., *Reflections: The Anthropological Muse,* American Anthropological Association, 1985. I should like to thank Derek Brewer, Master of Emmanuel College, and then editor of *The Cambridge Review* for much stimulating correspondence on the role of evolution and archetypes in creating our stock of meaningful symbols.

For encouragement and help during the early days of my personal poetic revival, I would like to thank Paul Friedrich, Howard Moss (RIP), Nathaniel Tarn, Enid Countess of Hardwicke, Bob and Berdine Ardrey, Elsbeth Monod, and Karyl Roosevelt. Tony Cattaneo did fantasic illustrations for "Alpindians" which is not included here since it is too long. It may never find a publisher, hanging as it does in that unpublishable void of what appears to be children's verse but which requires an adult audience (and one that knows some French to boot.) The loss is not so much the over-clever doggerel verse, but the marvellous color cartoons from the man who gave us Tony the Tiger (and also the terrific Peter who directed that definitive essay on the declining male, *The Full Monty.*)

The great fabulist William Golding encouraged me to cross the boundary from science to the humanities, at a time when his own search was taking him in the opposite direction. His death robbed us of the fruits of that endeavour, but I am eternally grateful for his words of support, and to Virginia Tiger for the introduction. ("What the Hunter Saw" was written for him.) Suzanne Grossman, actress, screenwriter and brilliant translator of Feydeau, is duly acknowledged in the proper place. My original editor, Becky Staples, turned out to be one of my best critics. My current editor, Laurence Mintz, continues to be not only a good editor but a literary and musical friend of the kind I thought had disappeared with the Bloomsbury Group and the Left Bank. His total devotion to English poetry and music puts me, a native son, to shame, but is something I can always draw on when I need a nostalgic Anglo-fix. As always my undying thanks to Irving Louis Horowitz, Mary Curtis, and Transaction Publishers. They are unique in my experience among publishers in letting an author do what he wants to do without undue interference. Only fellow authors will appreciate this happy landing in publishing nirvana. The dedication is to my wife, Lin, for her loving optimism (the poem "Last Request" is specifically for her.) We can only hope that she is right, and I am wrong, and take heart that this is usually the case.

R. F.
Princeton, N.J.
February 1999

# Foreword

# Origin of the Specious

*Ashley Montagu*

Man is the only 150–pound nonlinear servomechanism that can be wholly reproduced by unskilled labor. Add to this the grim fact that he is wholly without those determinants of behavior called instincts, and therefore has to learn everything he comes to know and do as a *human being* from other human beings, and you have quite a problem: a helpless creature who is in danger from the moment he is born, and even before. We, of course, share a great many traits with other living creatures, but as human beings we are unique in our incomparable ability to learn, to think, and to speak. In short, we are the most educable of all creatures. Indeed, the dimensions of our educability together constitute, beyond all else, the trait that distinguishes us as a species from everything else on this earth.

The evolution of that unique educability has a history of several million years. During most of that time, humans lived in small bands of between thirty and fifty people, half of whom were children, much, indeed, as do the few remaining hunter-gatherer peoples: the pygmies of the Ituri Forest of Zaire, the Bushmen of the Kalahari, the Australian aborigines, the Andaman Islanders, the newly authenticated Tasaday of Mindanao, and others. Under such conditions the challenges of life are simpler, less complex, and more manageable, if not less strenuous and demanding, than those characterizing more technologically advanced societies. The number and complexity of the challenges in highly civilized societies are vastly greater, more complicated, compelling, and stressful, to the point that humankind is now the most endangered—in fact, the most self-endangered—species on this planet.

The threat of extinction hangs over us all like a dark cloud in the sunlight. And the threat comes not from nuclear weapons but from man-made folly, a folly that is the result of the abuse of that very educability with which we are so generously endowed. For that capacity to learn not only enables us to be taught what is sound but also what is unsound, not only what is true but also what is false; and what is worse, not to be able to distinguish the one from the other. Even more alarming is the ensuing worship of the false and meretricious as if it were true, the acceptance of what is unsound as if it were sound and, by the next easy step, the celebration of evil as if it were good, leading finally to the embrace of the ugly, the mindless, and the brutish, as if they were beautiful.

In such a society, confusion replaces intelligence, and success is measured by specious external validations; the success that becomes the dominant value of the culture usurps the place of the inner values of the True, the Good, and the Beautiful. Education largely ceases to exist in such a society; it is replaced by instruction, the training in technics and skills, so that there is hardly anyone left who knows the difference between education and instruction. From the earliest ages the child is taught not *how* to think, but *what* to think.

Since hardly anyone understands what a child is and what its basic behavioral needs are, great violence is done to the child by a socialization process that consists largely in the disregard of the child's needs for healthy growth and development; that is to say, of his or her need to grow and develop in the ability to love, to work, to play, and to think soundly—the four great chords of mental health. What is customarily done is to impose upon the child the traditional ways of child rearing, instead of encouraging the child's own needs for behavioral development. This approach precludes the development of an authentic self, producing instead a mosaic of segments and pieces of selves derived from the child's socializers. This mosaic becomes the inauthentic self that each of us wears, uncomfortably and awkwardly, like an ill-fitting garment, vaguely aware that something is not quite right with us but unaware of what it might be. As a result, most of us have been turned into impediments to our own completion. As Willy Loman says in *Death of a Salesman,* "I feel kind of temporary." The tragedy for most of us lies in the difference between what we were capable of becoming and what the socialization process has caused us to become.

So much then by way of prologue to an extraordinary book, one I expect that readers who are looking for solace and enlightenment in this cubistically dilapidated world will enjoy as much as I have.

The book is *The Passionate Mind* by Robin Fox. The author, who is a University Professor at Rutgers University, is an anthropologist of wit and distinction who writes good prose and equally good verse with verve and éclat, all of which is abundantly displayed in this highly original romp through the labyrinths and jungles of the human condition. Darwin was interested in the origin of species. Fox is interested in the origin of the specious, how we got to be the way we now so unwittingly and suicidally are.

Many writers before have attempted a similar anatomy (or is "autopsy" the better word?), but no one, to my knowledge, has done so in as original and diverting a style as has Fox. His book is structurally unique in my experience, combining as it does prose, poetry, meditative musings, raucous diatribes, snippets of observed reality, overheard conversations, dramatic scenarios, delightfully unpunctuated blank verse ruminations, and much-weathered wisdom to offer a well-rehearsed accounting of the present state of that tragic figure so prematurely, oafishly, and arrogantly self-defined as *Homo sapiens,* who in his present sorry state deserves no better appellation than *Homo sap.*

Not that the potentiality for sapience isn't there. It is. But it is yet to be earned. As Fox says, it is a sad irony that the crucial knowledge which promises to transform our ideas of what we are and what we can hope for in the future has been acquired at almost exactly the time when we are threatening to make that future impossible. In his words, "We are like someone who has been handed a great fortune along with instructions to commit suicide."

Fox goes on to remark that

> Reason, imagination, and violence today coexist in a way we can only try to analyze or express, [as] we can't seem to do much about them. But the two cultures of Reason and Imagination-the wrong basis for the antagonism between the humanities and the sciences-do not exist out there in the world; they only exist in our cognitive reconstruction of it.

Precisely. It is in keeping with the Platonic dichotomy demoting emotion to a much inferior status to reason. But was it not Pascal who opined that the heart has its reasons of which reason knows not? And was it not the poet Ralph Hodgson who so luminously wrote

> Reason has moons, but moons not hers
> Lie mirrored on her sea,
> Confusing her astronomers,
> But O! delighting me.

And is it not true that our feelings more often than not influence, and frequently determine, what we think and, for the most part, perceive? And tell me, where has the fancy fled? What of imagination, perhaps man's greatest triumph? It was Einstein who said that his ability to fantasize was his most valuable trait, and that imagination is more important than knowledge. Reason, of course, is important, but secondary. But where, alas, for the greater part of humankind, has the ability to think soundly fled?

The fact seems to be that it hasn't fled: For most people, it never was; or for the children who were once capable of it, it has been corrupted and replaced by an inability to think except in the form of a debasing stereotypy of various kinds, which is as far removed from thinking as the pleasure of challenging hard work is from an incorrigible laziness. Apropos of that, it was the wonderful English author Jane Taylor (1783–1824) who said it all beautifully, long, long ago:

> Though man a thinking being is defined,
> Few use the grand prerogative of mind.
> How few think justly of the thinking few!
> How many never think, who think they do!

The ignorance of what has been called "the masses" in so-called civilized societies is frightening, for it is they, the ignorant, who, in the vanity of their ignorance and in their trained incapacity to think, place us all in deadly jeopardy.

As Witold Gombrowicz put it in his recently published *Diary* (vol. 1, Evanston, Illinois: Northwestern University Press, 1988): "We were horrified to see that we were surrounded by an abyss made of millions of ignorant minds, which steal away our truths in order to pervert, diminish, and transform them into instruments of their passions."

It is a discovery that some of us, especially those living in a democracy in which the most liberal orders of freedom prevail, are rather late in making. Equally late comes the discovery that freedom is the greatest of all responsibilities, and one that too many, especially in this land of liberty, are only too happy to evade. Most Americans, for example, interpret freedom to mean the right to be able to do what they like, rather than the obligation to do what they ought. For them, liberty only too often is identified with libertinism. A society characterized by such an ethos is doomed to extinction.

That education should have become what it is, that the greatest educational medium ever devised, namely television, should have become a corrupting agency for the habituation to violence and similar choice "enchantments"—to brutishness and deviance of every kind—is commentary enough upon the sorry slough of despond into which we have fallen. Deviants, perhaps, should serve the purpose of indicating what a society should be, by being what society isn't.

As Fox says, the world we inhabit—what we call history—is an aberration. How right H.G. Wells was when, in 1922, in his *Outline of History,* he wrote that history is a race between education and catastrophe. Since prehistoric times, when our consciousness, including our violences, were in balance with our environment and society, we have become a "superfluous race" hopelessly trying to justify a way of life we cannot sustain and from which we cannot escape. We are in thrall to illusions about ourselves, mostly illusions of progress. The harmony between our environment and our evolved attributes as a species—our intelligence, imagination, our tendencies to violence (Fox, in my view erroneously, regards them as innate), our reason, and our passions—which existed up to some ten thousand years before the present, has been lost: "This harmony," he writes,

> did not mean peace, love, and justice for all, but rather that the pieces
> fit together in a way that served to further the interests of the species
> directly, and above all did not threaten its existence as a species. This is
> no longer true....Partly it is simply a matter of scale and complexity,
> but with these goes fragmentation.

The harmony that once existed no longer seems possible to our fragmented consciousness, "where every frenetic addition to our already overburdened civilization seems to produce a...disaster...whose 'specialization' brings short-term benefits and long-term destruction."

In which connection I cannot help recalling the occasion when a reporter asked Mohandas Gandhi what he thought of Western civilization; whereupon, lowering his head for a moment, he smiled and replied, "You know, I don't think it would be such a bad idea."

Early on, Fox declares that he

> really doesn't have any solutions, only hints and guesses: perhaps only the cries and whimpers of an animal trapped in the awful circum-stances of its own success—a situation to which it will not admit because it is too terrifying to face. We have met The Enemy, as Pogo declared, and He is Us. All our efforts to improve the deteriorating situation seem to backfire.

Because, says Fox, one of these backfiring efforts seems to be the academic/scientific mode itself, he has deliberately avoided that approach to the discussion of our sorry fragmented condi-tion by trying a kind of "theme and variations" approach. The themes are rehearsed from a variety of angles and through differ-ent modes of expression, and are mixed and mingled every which way, in anything, Fox hopes, but a boring manner. As I have al-ready indicated, he has nothing to fear on that or any other score, for he has scintillatingly succeeded in his splendidly original, nour-ishing performance.

I say "Performance," because this very serious and important book is also delightfully entertaining. Far from being depressing, it is full of witty sallies that will keep the reader in a risible as well as a reflective state. I suppose that is why in our tragicomic world we value comedians rather more highly than we do tragedians.

Fox makes no explicit plea for entertainment, though he ad-mits that appeal would follow from his generous approach. His plea rather is for a new kind of consciousness that will transcend the fragmentation of our times. He confesses that he doesn't know yet what that will be, so he pleads for an exploration of the possibilities, and for us to face up to not only the dangers, but the virtues, of the violent imagination, as opposed to those of reason, intelligence, culture, or especially "artificial intelligence." He veers, he tells us, between mild optimism and total pessimism, hoping that his pessimism may alarm and alert and so serve a useful purpose.

We devoutly pray, and at the same time remark, that the only philosophically tenable position for a pessimist in a time of crisis is optimism—not a "mild" optimism, but a profound conviction that if enough people were prepared, and had the courage, to do what they ought, we might yet save the human enterprise for its birth-right: the pleasure of learning to live and love as if to live and love were one. This may sound like a good theme for a Sunday-morning sermon, but it happens to be perfectly good social biology.

If there is one criticism that I have to make of Fox's extended feuilleton, it is that he omits any reference to the most promising area of social and human reform revealed by scientific studies of interaction between genetically based potentialities or predispositions and their actualization in behavior under differing environmental conditions. It is there, it seems clear to me, that we can learn what we need to know in setting the agenda for rescuing our species from the disaster into which it has fallen, to provide more than the clue that Fox and others seek toward establishing the harmony of the lost past and the possibilities of the almost lost future. Fox, I am sure, is acquainted with the work on behavioral human development, but somehow unaccountably fails to give even so much as a nod in its direction.

On the few occasions Fox quotes from a foreign language, he leaves it in the original. It might have been more helpful to provide even the educated reader, for whom the book is mainly intended, with a translation into English. Long experience has taught me that while most educated readers may be able to manage one foreign language, few are able to deal with two or more. Of course it is true, as Goethe once said, that he who knows only his own language knows not even that.

Goethe also makes Mephistopheles say that where an idea is wanting, a word can always be found to take its place—and a whole system of philosophy erected thereon. Form, as Fox says, imprisons function; and, he might have added, most of us remain all our lives prisoners of our vocabularies. It may be that in the beginning was the word. It would have been far better if things had started off on the right foot with an idea rather than a word. As Léon-Paul Fargue put it:

> The idea is that which exists, but has no
> form,
> It is art not yet realized.
> The idea is a point of departure,
> The lifting of a veil's edge,
> A faint stirring,
> Or like the leap of a violin
> In a moment of despairing gloom.

Beautifully true; but alas, ideas are not only what they are but also what they are not. The most powerful of all the conditions that produce mental incompetence even to the point of insanity (insanity being defined as the inability to govern one's affairs in a responsible manner), or the appearance of sanity, are not genes, but a social and so-called educational system that makes such incompetence inevitable and destructive. Physical and genetic factors are real enough, and they are capable of producing mental defects in various degrees, but such factors do not compare with the damage done by social conditions. The greatest damage done to the mental health of the individual and society is effected by the diffusion of unsound, indeed *pathogenic,* ideas concerning the nature of human nature and of human needs, especially those of children. Such pathogenic ideas—the idea of "race," for example—are at least as dangerous as the worst of disease-producing organisms.

Fuzzy ideas can be just as bad. In the latter connection, Fox starts off in his "Diary of a Superfluous Race" with a sort of cross between Bernard de Mandeville's *Fable of the Bees* and George Orwell's *Animal Farm.* Titled "The Conference of Foules" (by way of Chaucer), it is a piece that would have delighted John Maynard Keynes, and will annoy economists in general and divert some social scientists and anthropologists. This amusing cautionary tale contains a great deal more wisdom than is to be found in most treatises on the relation between social organization, economics, power, and politics. Which reminds me that politicians seriously interested in the welfare of their country might also benefit from reading this sparkling romp.

As I read Fox, I could not help but think of the lines

> Would we could start again whence we began,
> And go to school to prehistoric man.

Yes, but...would we not end up as we have done, once again, we who greeted the dawn like cocks, and now threaten to depart at sundown like capons? That, however, is not a judgment, but a cautionary *aide-mémoire* for us all as we work in the present to pass into the future. Good luck, *Homo sap.*

In the last stanza of "The Fool Sings of His Skull and its Contents," Fox writes:

> But of all the things that go on—
> that leak in through the ears—
> that jump in through the eyes—
> the things I mostly fears
> are the things that were always there.
> What they are you never know
> but they've got you trapped in the bony cage
> and though you argue plead and rage—
> they'll never let you go.

But Fox is not really that pessimistic. He is merely (I expect) describing a common mood. I wish I could quote his poem "What the Hunter Saw," but it is too long for quotation. If someone doesn't anthologize it, I shall be surprised. It is enchanting anthropology, a dramatic event both dramatically and beautifully retold. I shall reread it often, for Fox is a genuine poet.

The sequence of poems on the evolution of man is very good reading, and just the right length. Possibly Fox will here have started a trend that will result in most anthropology textbooks being written in verse rather than in their customary prosaic style. After all, Lucretius (c. 90–55 B.C.) did it two thousand years ago in his great philosophical-anthropological epic, written in magnificent hexameters, *De rerum natura* (On the nature of things), a modern work in the best sense of the word, and a scientifically prophetic one. Anyone who has had the misfortune of having missed it should repair at once to the nearest dispenser of civilization, a good bookseller, and procure a copy.

Lucretius was a genius, and not all anthropologists should be expected to go and do likewise, but they could strive to be poets in Wordsworth's sense, when he described the poet as a man speaking to men: a man, it is true, endued with a more lively sensibility, more enthusiasm and tenderness, who has a greater knowledge

of human nature, and a more comprehensive soul than are supposed to be *common* among mankind.

I happen to know that many anthropologists, and a rather larger
percentage than I suspect is to be found in most other profes-
sions, past or present, have written good poetry. This is no accident, for the qualities that attract a person to poetry are much the
same as those that draw him/her to anthropology. Over a long
life, I have found also that anthropologists generally are good,
literate writers. I used to attribute this to the fact that they often
came to anthropology by way of the humanities. It may still be
true, whether they have formally studied them or not.

Fox's series of poems on the social evolution of humanity are
alone worth the price of the volume and again suggest that anthropology is written best when it is written in poetic form. Pas-
sages such as this one on the population explosion must serve as
typical:

> We were enough  We didn't
> need so many  What do more mouths add
> but hunger?  We are too alike each other
> for numbers to do more than multiply
> monotony  But given all that went
> before it was inexorable.

The chapter following, titled "Violence : Ritual :: Power : Authority," really presents the essence of the book. It is magnificent.
And the same is true of the next entertainment, "The Interroga-
tion: A Nightmare," written in a Kafkaesque style. It is riotously
funny and a marvelous commentary both on the law and civilization, and it is also very tragic. It would make a delightful one-act
play. Another, this time longer, play, which I hope may sometime
find a producer, is entitled "The Trial of George Washington."
With its star-studded cast, including Thomas Jefferson, John
Adams, Jonathan Sewall, and Benedict Arnold, it convincingly
dramatizes what would have happened had the rebels lost the War
of Independence. The verdict goes against Washington, and he is
sentenced to be cruelly and viciously executed.

It is all admirably done. Reading the play, one breathes a deep
sigh of relief that the court of law did not have it in its power to
decide whether the rebels' cause was just.

In the fourth and fifth sections of the book are a dozen enchanting poems on contemporary themes, the most powerful of which, "Liberated Woman," shows Fox at his poetic best. This is followed by a skit on "overdevelopment," with Sweden as the alleged victim. Here Fox repeats the theme of "The Conference of Foules," and again asks whether in our passion for "progress," "modernization," and ultimate perfection, we are not in fact destroying ourselves? Are we our own battery of hens, building our own cages? With tongue in cheek and strictly by way of not-so-oblique commentary, Fox suggests that what is required by way of remedy is "the introduction of a sufficient measure of social injustice and communal chaos to restore normal human functionings." Toward this end, ten specific recommendations are made, running all the way from the introduction of the Mafia, gambling casinos, corrupt bankers, and the bribing of judges and ministers, to Ingmar Bergman's being allowed to make a staggeringly boring, highly symbolic movie of the results—with Spanish subtitles.

Four sonnets of real skill, one of which is of great beauty, return us to humanity. The first is about intuition; the second gently parodies the "structuralism" lying behind such formulas and their impossible rationalism; the third harks directly back to an episode in an earlier poem; and the last invokes through music the clash of reason and passion and the failure to find a compromise. In "Design Failure: A Post-Tutorial Dialogue," Fox brilliantly returns to his main theme: the effect of a too-powerful intelligence upon a creature unable to handle such a responsibility.

In part four Fox continues the themes of the futility of progress and the tyranny of the idea in a section aptly titled "Toward a More Perfect Dissolution." Here the possibilities of "salvation through romantic eros" are exhausted in a series of poems on "the female enigma." "Psalm 151," a longish poem, concludes Fox's soliloquy. Beginning with an ominous Latin epigraph derived from Catullus' little epic "The Marriage of Peleus and Thetis" (which remains untranslated and unreferenced), it rings out the very knell of doom:

> escape there is none, hope none; voiceless all,
> desert is all, all covers the face of doom.

Is man really at the end of his tether? The answer, in keeping with a theme H.G. Wells sounded shortly before his death in his last book, *Man at the End of his Tether* (1945), is perhaps best expressed in the words I once heard from a cynical hippie: "If you're travelin' on the *Titanic,* you might as well go first class." Wells asked himself whether, for all one's efforts, one could ever do better than slightly improve the lot of some people and add to their happiness by giving them the stature and the vision of a world in which there is less frustration, and more opportunity of appreciating the beauty of the sparks as they pass by. To the last he thought it possible, and this gave him some comfort.

"Psalm 151," in a combination of Whitmanesque lists, Blakean declamation, Nietzsche, and Ecclesiastes, half savagely, half wistfully addresses the child of Kent State/the holy fool/the innocent/the believer-in-causes, and speaks plainly: Everything we create adds another "idea," and the tyranny of the idea, without which we cannot act at all, will in the end kill us all: a reprise of the themes of many of the pieces throughout the book. Our very creativity, says Fox, is the source of our ultimate destruction. Once we could die for a cause knowing that we died for better things to come. Now, he concludes, with nothing left to come, "we have left thee with nothing worthy of thy death"—the worst blow of all, since in the end, a worthy death is all we have to make life mean anything.

I continue to be skeptical of the usefulness of Fox's use of untranslated quotations in foreign languages as epigraphs, but it should perhaps be pointed out how they sometimes add a second dimension to a poem. Thus the Greek quote from Medea at the head of the "daughter poems" (in Part Five) is not so much important for its substance as for the fact that it is the epigraph Elizabeth Barrett Browning used for one of the most moving social protest poems of the nineteenth century—a poem of protest against child labor called "The Cry of the Children." Again, as in the Kent State poem, Fox sees his particular fears about protecting his own children as an exemplar of a more universal problem of protecting the innocent young from the inadequacies or predations of the old.

"The Dream-Man" he writes in an alliterative style based on Anglo-Saxon verse. While he spares us a quote in that language it is obvious that he has in mind the greatest Anglo-Saxon poem of all, and his dream-man is surely Beowulf contemplating Grendel. The human hero looks into himself and sees reflected the reptilian-amphibian thing he is trying to exterminate, but which is also part of him—which is part of us all. The prescient "Beowulf" protagonist then expands this insight into a vision of what we now know has gone into the making of man. It is worth comparing this with another poem that deliberately echoes an ancient original. "Amergin's Song About Ireland" is by Ireland's first recorded Bardic poet, and is obviously a ritual incantation or riddle delivered in the first person:

> I am a stag of seven tines
> I am a flood across a plain
> I am a wind on a deep lake
> I am a tear the sun lets fall

and so on in the same vein. Fox uses the same first-person device—the same identification of the poet himself with nature including human nature, to satirize the current state of public morality and, in a sense, to show how far we have fallen from the supposedly "primitive" Celtic original.

It is said that all Western poets have a "Jesus poem" in them that has to get out (but mercifully rarely does!). Fox is no different. He has already in Part Two tried to come to terms with the great secular revolutions, through the American version. He now tries (in Part Six) to tackle the great religious revolutions through, obviously, the one he knows best. His way of doing so, however, is typically eccentric. He uses an extensive knowledge of material on the "historical Jesus" to comment once again on the human condition; but he uses the neat device of turning the modernist, de-mythologizing critics on their heads, and making the miracles central to the conception of Jesus as a purely spiritual alien entity trapped in the horror—to him—of a human body with its feeble excuse for a mind. This certainly helps him make his point about the tyranny of the passionate mind, but it is fair to say that there has never been a Jesus like this one!

Perhaps most unusual, though, in view of his usual style which is witty and epigrammatic (perhaps best exemplified in the hilarious but bitingly satirical "Where Have the Heroes Gone?") is the "New Jersey Landscapes" series. Here he is almost the Robert Frost of the pastoral-narrative style, but with a pastoralism that has a harsh background: a struggle for existence against what Darwin chose to call "the hostile forces of nature." Fox and his local farmer friends pit themselves against cunning crows, voracious seagulls, sinister vultures and vicious winters, as well as uncomprehending yuppies in the new developments. Even here, though, he cannot resist shifting levels. In the poem about the death of the crow, via a wickedly clever parody of the late poet laureate Ted Hughes's *Crow* poems, he announces the death of Hughes's style of imagist free verse, and appropriately in traditional rhyming couplets! The reader, although able to take the poems at face value and derive pleasure and insight from them, has always to be on the lookout for such switches of register, as the linguists would put it.

Perhaps the ultimate judgment he renders on "the human condition" is that of the somewhat bewildered hedgehog in his fable of "The Hedgehog and the Fox" (again redolent with overtones from the original famous essay of that title by Isaiah Berlin). We humans act according to our nature which is the end product of many millions of years of evolution. This is, for Fox, no cause for complacency, because the combination of "the passionate mind" and "the violent imagination" with our rather feeble efforts at reason, makes us an unfinished amalgam of a creature which cannot be depended on to act in its own best interests. We are, for him, constantly at war with ourselves, with usually disastrous results, even when we are acting according to our highest ideals and from our purest motives (perhaps most particularly when that is what we are doing.) And so it will remain, despite our capacity for love and laughter, which are our only, very slender hope for some kind of mitigation from the ravages of the passionate mind. For me the key essay is "Design Failure", and while I realize that Fox intends to lead his readers up to and then away from this central, rational, statement through the thickets of his "inventions," I will risk his wrath by suggesting that the reader who perhaps lacks the time to be puzzled read it first, and then deal with the rest. For here he makes his key paradox: without attachment to ideas we cannot function, but once attached to them we become their prisoners and hence cannot function intelligently.

This is not necessarily a view of mankind that I share. I am more optimistic, perhaps, regarding the possible effects of better and better education (if these can be achieved) on improving human understanding, especially of the right way to rear children in security and love so that they do not need to resort to violence. But it is a view that Fox has distilled from a lifetime of distinguished work in anthropology, and that he argues forcefully with wit and elegance, and we should pay attention to it. For there is no question that we do seem easily to hitch our creativity to destructiveness, and it is no bad thing to be constantly reminded of this so that we may be on our guard. The tender and humorous side of Fox's nature as revealed here in so many poems is a constant reminder of what we should be aiming for, while at the same time we listen seriously to his warnings about what is the worst in us.

Lucretius' great epic was unfinished when he died. While *The Passionate Mind* is a finished work, Fox, happily, has many years before him, during the course of which we may look forward to further contributions from his pen, to the enlightenment and entertainment of *Homo* sap*iens*. In the interim, his book deserves accolades, attention, and a wide readership.

# INTRODUCTION

*I think it is likely that our view of ourselves as a
species on this planet now is inaccurate, and will
strike those who come after us as inadequate as the
world view of, let's say, the inhabitants of New Guinea
seems to us. That our current view of ourselves as a
species is wrong. That we know very little about what
is going on.*
    Doris Lessing, *The Sirian Experiments*

*What is your opinion of progress? Does it, for example,
Exist? Is there ever progression without retrogression?
Therefore is it not true that mankind
Can more justly be said increasingly to Gress?*
    Christopher Fry, *A Phoenix Too Frequent*

*—History, Stephen said, is a nightmare from which I
am trying to awake.*
    James Joyce, *Ulysses*

Yes, Virginia, this is yet another "commentary on the human
condition." Despite the ponderous overtones, this is really a
serious tradition and one I am glad to belong to. But the conditions under which we now have to write such commentaries
have drastically changed. Two things have altered our sense of
ourselves radically: the daily prospect of total annihilation for
our species and our very recent awareness of our ancientness as
a species (with all the implications this has for an understanding of ourselves).

It is a sad irony that this latter crucial knowledge, which promises to transform our ideas of what we are and what we can hope for in the future, has been acquired at almost exactly the time when we are threatening to make that future impossible. We are like someone who has been handed a great fortune along with instructions to commit suicide.

Reason, imagination, and violence today coexist in a way we can only try to analyze or express; we can't seem to do much about them. But the two cultures of Reason and Imagination—the wrong basis for the antagonism between the humanities and the sciences—do not exist out there in the world; they only exist in our cognitive reconstruction of it. Before Plato they were not sundered, but before Plato there was not much science either. Yet Plato wanted the poets and artists out of the Republic because, as Eric Havelock rightly observes, they laid claim to a rival method for arriving at the truth, not just a superior capacity for entertainment. So Plato argues for their banishment.

This perhaps necessary divorce, however, like so much of the Platonic heritage, may yet cost us dearly. It may yet cost us everything. As Voltaire, in 1770, passionately declaimed:

O Platon tant admiré, j'ai peur que vous ne vous ayez conté que des fables, et que vous n'ayez jamais parlé qu'en sophismes. O Platon! vous avez fait bien plus de mal que vous ne croyez. Comment cela? me demandera-t-on: je ne le dirai pas. (*Dictionnaire Philosophique*)

Why wouldn't he say what the damage was? Perhaps because at that time it had not been fully assessed. Perhaps because Voltaire sensed the dangerous fragmentation that Plato had wrought, but had not seen its full effects. If that is the case, then Voltaire was truly prophetic. And again there is a real irony, because when Plato wanted to express the great truth of truths, in the *Timaeus,* he resorted to the language of myth and poetry, and obviously meant us to take him seriously. (Which leads me to wonder if the mass of the Socratic dialogues are not perhaps some kind of send up: a vast satire on the misuse of reason.)

But the reintegration that our condition cries out for cannot be on a pre-Platonic basis: a tribal, heroic, oral basis. Our capacity for literate communication and self-annihilation has outrun that possibility. Yet we do not seem able to make the imaginative/ rational leap into the state of consciousness needed to handle this monstrous situation that we have ourselves created out of the Platonic sundering of reason and imagination. Where must we start in trying to re-understand ourselves?

The foregoing is set off because it is the beginning of another academic, argumentative piece of writing, but it serves just as well as the opening blast of this book. Indeed, when this project first thought itself through me, such pieces were included in it. There was this one, ponderously titled "Consciousness Out of Context: History, Progress, Evolution, and the Post-post-industrial Society." (Well, that's the way we do things in our little world: first stun 'em with a title, then wow 'em with an argument.) Another piece, already published, would have been "The Violent Imagination" (P. Marsh and A. Campbell, eds., *Violence and Aggression* [Oxford: Blackwell, 1982]). The third heavy would have been "On Inhuman Nature and Unnatural Rights" *(Encounter* 58, no. 4 [1982]). Its original title was "Rational Ethics and Human Nature," but Mel Lasky, the wise and cunning editor of that remarkable magazine, thought up the new one as both smarter and more to the point. The point? The point of all these pieces is that we are indeed living in a state of "consciousness out of context"; that the true context of our consciousness was the upper-paleolithic (our "environment of evolutionary adaptedness" as the jargon has it); that in this environment there was a harmony of our evolved attributes as a species, including our intelligence, our imagination, our violence, (and hence our violent imagination), our reason and our passions—a harmony that has been lost; that this harmony did not mean peace, love, and justice for all, but rather simply that the pieces fit together in a way that served to further the interests of the species directly, and above all not to threaten its existence as a species.

This is no longer true. Partly it is simply a matter of scale and complexity, but with these goes fragmentation. T.S. Eliot and Henry Adams among others deplored the fragmentation as much as I do, but from a very different perspective and a different sense of our species' history. Eliot could take us as far back as the sensibilities of the Metaphysical poets (late seventeenth century) for his time of harmony; Adams could go back to the eleventh century and Mont St. Michel and Chartres. But in the evolutionary per-

spective these were sadly fragmented times in which reason, imagination, violence, and curiosity were all working against each other,
and passion was deeply suspect unless it was religious passion, and
even then (and perhaps even more.) The basics remained the
same: zealotry, xenophobia, greed, lust, gullibility of the many,
and power hunger of the few; the evil dominance of the idea by
which we live and for which we will die and which is wrong; the
search for meaning that is our original sin and that either elevates
us to godhead, or reduces us to foaming fanatics when our answer
is threatened. All these were surely there from the start of our
humanity. But what we find hard to imagine is that they could
work together and harmonize and produce, for the species, a
positive result.

This does not seem possible to our modern fragmented consciousness, where every frenetic addition to our already overburdened civilization seems to produce an unsought disaster. "Modern" in this view means after ten thousand years before the present
(B.P.) for most societies; and today even those that retained the
harmony are not untouched by the easy if short-lived triumph of
the fragmented civilizations, whose "specialization" brings short-
term benefits and long-term destruction.

So that's what is in the heavy articles that were originally to
have appeared in this book; at least those are the conclusions. I
wanted to include them as part of my plea to reverse the fragmentation. But the tyranny of the idea is implacable. (See "Design
Failure," in Part Four). Such a product was impossible: it was a
denial of established and sacred categories; it was more than error, it was witchcraft. (The social anthropologists have analyzed
this very well—the fact that the unclean, polluted, and dangerous
is that which offends the established system of categories.) So I
took them out, and the result is different, but still makes its point
especially if taken with the heavies as a chaser. Here, rather than
rubbing the readers' noses in "the message," I have sketched it,
hinted at it, approached it obliquely through themes and variations, made it implicit in the very structure and content of what
follows, and even introduced a fashionable air of "metalogue,"
insofar as the total structure of the effort (including the real presence of the absent articles) makes its own point about the sources
and dangers of, and maybe even solutions to, the fragmentation.
But I really don't have any solutions, only hints and guesses: per-

haps only the cries and whimpers of an animal trapped in the awful consequences of its own success—a situation to which it will not admit because it is too terrifying to face. We have met The Enemy, as Pogo declared, and He is Us. All our efforts to improve the deteriorating situation seem to backfire.

One of these backfiring efforts appears to be the academic/ scientific mode itself. One fears to abandon it much as true believers fear to abandon their religions, but one fears equally to get stuck in it and thus perpetuate the already unsatisfactory situation. So here I try another way: a kind of "theme and variations" approach. Such academic-style argument as tries to rear its head is quickly turned into a parody of itself. The themes are approached from a variety of angles, and through different modes of expression, and are differently mixed and mingled; every which way, one hopes, but boring. And the "metalogical" scheme, which has started with a plea to reject Plato's banishment of the artists from the Republic of Science and Virtue, then tries to illustrate some of the consequences of letting them back in. ("Putting the poetry back into politics," as E. P. Thompson has recently argued and demonstrated.) Indeed, if the whole thing could be set to music and staged it would perhaps make this point more effectively. It is hard to make the right impact with a purely linear medium like a "book."

And this is not a plea for entertainment—although that would follow—but for a new kind of consciousness that will transcend the fragmentation of our times (if you'll forgive the pomposity.) I don't know yet what that will be, so I can only plead for an exploration of it, and for us to face up to not only the dangers, but the virtues, of the violent imagination, as opposed to those of reason, intelligence, culture, or especially "artificial intelligence." I veer between mild optimism and total pessimism; but the pessimism may alarm and alert and so serve a useful purpose. The implicit cynicism (of course the last, battered refuge of an idealist) is more troubling; but again, the fear of being driven to it is perhaps a healthy fear.

I have resisted demands to supply "linking material"; the whole point here is to keep the readers off guard so they have constantly to be making the links themselves: between the dilemmas of the battery hens and those of the moral relativists; between the condition of Sweden and the fallacy of historical progress; between the author's implicit plea for a total society and his totally contradictory defense of individualism when faced with the inquisitorial consequences of one (despite his cynicism over the insects); between the estimation of the imaginative (cultural) transformation of power by authority, and the role of violence in ritual and sexual passion; between the art of the paleolithic, the symbolism of the bullfight, the basic human design failure, and the psalm's "tumor" and despair at wasted consciousness and meaningless death; between the nightmare of history from which we all, like Stephen Daedalus, are trying to awake, and the author's nightmare about history, which is itself part of Vishnu's world dream—the maya in which we are entrapped, or, if the intrusive philosopher of mind is correct, in which we entrap ourselves, and of which Vishnu (Christ/God) is himself a product; between the rationalizations of violence by the highly rational purveyors of a national revolution, and the fantasy salvation-by-sexual-violence of two latter-day products of that enterprise; between a provincial Colombian bullfight with its search for meaningful death as a response to an existence without meaning, and the contrivance of a bizarre death-through-sex by a contemporary New Yorker, itself linked to the paleolithic cult of the bear sacrifice; between the vision of the hunter before his xenophobic murder, and that of George Washington before his terrifying sentence; always between the highly general and argumentative (and usually blank verse) ruminations, and the lyrics (some of which are indeed words for songs) that pull the questions down to the most painful and comic intimacies of personal lives while constantly questioning the doubtful possibility of salvation through eros—the Romantic solution; and sometimes a mixture of elements that looks for the general in the particular, and vice versa. But I've already preempted too much of what I have declared to be the reader's privilege. The sheer complexity of the possibilities, once grasped, should convey to the reader why logical academic argument with its own linear limitations cannot sustain the themes, and why they so easily tip over into poetry and myth. Perhaps this itself is the clue to the harmony of the lost past and the possibilities of the almost lost future.

In any case, my hermeneutic colleagues tell me, the text, now written and out there in the world, isn't mine any more. So go to it. The links I make may not be yours at all. Stephen Spender told me that Eliot told him that what was uppermost in his mind during the writing of *The Waste Land* was Wagner's *Ring.* Despite the wailing of the Rhine Maidens, I would never have guessed this. The whole poem looks different to me now, but this does not invalidate the "linking themes" that we had seen in it before this revelation of the poet's preoccupation.

Some readers, while grasping the point of Part Two, have nevertheless asked why I particularly chose George Washington, and why the American Revolution, rather than the Russian, French, or English. (How easily people forget that there was an English revolution.) As it happens, my first choice was the English fracas, and an original sketch has this as the trial of Oliver Cromwell. But as Part Three shows, I have spent most of my adult life trying to come to terms with the puzzling consequences of the Anglo-American civil war. As the bicentennial came and went, I was driven more and more to thinking about the Revolt of the Rationalists, and the Utopian hopes that were its consequence. What appears here is really an extract with adaptations from an epic intended for the bicentennial. While well regarded—as they say—it was never produced, if only because agonizing reappraisal had gone out of fashion and no one wanted a play in which George Washington gets hung, drawn, and quartered. Understandably, it lost out to the super patriotic if dreadfully dull *Valley Forge* in the Hallmark Hall of Fame Television Theater Stakes. The attempted television version was written in collaboration with Suzanne Grossman, since I had no idea how to adapt for television. While what I use here is dialogue that I wrote myself (except for a few words of Washington's final address to the court), Suzanne did a lot of the research with me and her notion of the whole undoubtedly had an influence on shaping the parts, so her indispensable collaboration is gratefully acknowledged.

This book is very much work in progress. It has to be seen as part of the larger scheme. Nothing is settled here; it is mostly hinted at. But nothing is particularly obscure either except the odd literary joke. We pedants are incorrigible jokesters with a particular fondness for bad puns. It is what separates us from mere intellectuals. The scepticism over the liberal version of optimism is real. But while the "message" (God help us!) is serious enough, it is also playful. So let us remember Huizinga: "The play-concept as such is of a higher order than seriousness. For seriousness seeks to exclude play, whereas play can well include seriousness." Or hear the 2,000-year-old Mel Brooks: "The greatest comedy plays against the greatest tragedy. Comedy is a red-rubber ball and if you throw it against a soft, funny wall, it will not come back. But if you throw it against the hard wall of ultimate reality it will bounce back and be very lively." In the end, perhaps, we must laugh one another, or die.

In token whereof I give you the following as an appetizer:

## RESEARCH REPORT: CONVERSATION AFTER A SABBATICAL

"So you've written a new book?"

"Yes"

"Tell us then

the number of the pages   publication
date and price   the publisher   and yes
the subject matter   theme   that sort of thing"

"The subject matter is intact   The book—
well   it was written in a different way
I wrote in sometimes with my fingers dry
and sometimes wet with wine or honey on
an undulating   brown   and scented body

I wrote a lot—a thousand words a day
for—well—a hundred days   A lot of words
At each day's end we would make love   and I
would lick them off   or scented sweat would smudge
the wine-dark prose   But every day the parchment
would be there fresh and clear   and I would write"

"But then you have..."

"No book?   But don't you see
I still have her body there to read
and when I'm finished reading   then to write
It is my book   And now I must go work
Work   Work   Work   I'm such a puritan"

# One

Diary of a Superfluous Race

*. . . only make no laws, no fine theories,
no judgements, and the people may love,
but give them one theory, let them invent
one slogan, and the game begins.*
— John Le Carré, *Call for the Dead*

# THREE BASIC LYRICS
## (to establish some basic things)

*It is because of the difficulty of translating right-hemispherical processes into the logical, verbal formulations of the left brain that some emissions into ego consciousness of archetypal images are perceived as numinous, awesome, and mysterious, or uncanny, preternaturally strange. They seem to be clad in primordial authority undetermined by anything known or learned.*

Victor Turner, *Body, Brain, and Culture*

CAROUSEL
*(Asbury Park, Summer)*

I smile indulgently to see
the carousel go spinning by—
the children calling out to me
to get aboard   at least to try

I shake my head   demur   decline
I'm too old for the roundabout
Those screaming joys are yours not mine
I'll look on while you wave and shout

But then I am afraid to look
afraid because I know I'll see
the phantom from the story book
the ghostly child who looks like me

Staring from his painted horse
he smiles his never changing smile
and whirls precisely on his course
mile after jangling   dizzy mile

11

He nods with every rise and fall
he beckons me at every turn
he never speaks   but seems to call
his eyes are cold   but seem to burn

When to the phantom spinning by
I whisper   (not to seem absurd)
"Are you the phantom or am I?"
he spins and smiles without a word

It stops   he goes   the children call
"Daddy you look so unwell"
"It makes me dizzy   that is all—
just looking at the carousel"


## THE FOOL SINGS OF HIS SKULL AND ITS CONTENTS

*Nun sag'! Nichts weißt du, was ich dich frage:*
*jetzt meld', was du weißt;*
*denn etwas mußt du doch wissen.*
Wagner, *Parsifal*

Oh the queer things that go on
under this bony cap
they makes me want to sing
and dance and curse and clap
they makes me want to laugh
and cry and storm and shout—
but most of all they makes me want
to shake the thing about

Oh the odd things that go on
inside this bony bowl
they calls 'em mind and thought
they calls 'em spirit and soul
they calls 'em moods and states
and other fancy names—
but nobody ever found the rules
for their funny little games

Oh the strange things that go on
and on and on and on
things that are always there
things that have come and gone
things that confuse the day
things that disturb the night—
all those puzzles and problems
and nobody gets 'em right

But of all the things that go on—
that leak in through the ears
that jump in through the eyes—
the things I mostly fears
are the things that were always there
What they are you never know
but they've got you trapped in the bony cage
and though you argue plead and rage—
they'll never let you go


## HE APOLOGIZES TO HER FOR COMPARING HER EYES TO THE WINGS OF CAPTIVE HUMMINGBIRDS USED IN NAVAHO RITUALS

Forget the hummingbirds   I didn't mean
to make you pretty speeches   but your eyes
demanded metaphors   and I have seen
the captive bird and all that it implies

That's no excuse for rhetoric   I know—
but form imprisons function like a child
enmeshed in discipline   It should be so
else childish function   wordlike   would run wild

The bird   when free   is but another bird—
a formless phrase   a brief emotion spent
a frozen movement   fluttering unheard—
captive it's a magic argument

So I have no excuse my love but this—
a need to capture   in my cage of words
a meaning deeper than a formless kiss
on eyelids brushing me like frightened birds

Forgive me my formality   my speech—
my futile effort at control—unwise
because it will not last   We cannot each
escape the consequences of our eyes

*THE PARADOX OF CONSCIOUSNESS (O Muse*
*I sing) as such is not confined to man*
*If we define it as a minimum*
*"Matter aware of its own existence" then*
*we cannot be sure that animals do not*
*possess a rudimentary form of it*

*Full consciousness is a unique event*
*in earthly history   We can be sure*
*our solar system lacks it   but about*
*the universe we cannot be so certain*
*If there is organic life there is*
*the possibility of consciousness*
*The very number of the galaxies*
*makes the existence of it probable*

# THE CONFERENCE OF FOULES

*La turba che rimase li, selvaggia*
*parea del loco, rimirando intorno*
*come colui che nove cose assaggia*
Dante, *Divina Commedia: Purgatorio*, Canto II.52

The Cities of the Battery Hens were in trouble, and the Guardians, knowing that the trouble was endogenous, had cunningly assembled what they thought to be the cleverest and wisest of the hens in the same place to see if they could come up with their own solutions. The hens had no idea there were Guardians at all (they never saw them) and were under the impression that they were responsible for their own lives. Some rather daring intellects among them had suggested that "the forces of history" or "the species struggle" or something such was responsible—but the pragmatists paid them little heed.

So they sat there, one hen to a tiny cage, immobile, beaks plucked out, their legs bred away, their feathers reduced, their bodies flooded with hormones and chemicals, clucking and producing, clucking and laying, laying, laying. A conveyor belt took away the eggs, they knew not where or why. But the eggs were tasteless, the hens listless. They died easily from contagious diseases that racked the cities despite the massive sanitary precautions of the Guardians. Mostly they sickened from mysterious maladies that no one could diagnose; they simply gave up laying, gave up clucking, became glassy-eyed, and eventually died.

The wise ones, however, clucking and swallowing their uniform, vitamin-rich, hormone-treated food pellets, were busy analyzing the situation.

The first to speak was the wise old economist. She was very insistent. "Facts, facts, facts," she said, "and then models, models, models." She continued—to a chorus of approving clucks—"We need the finest input output model of the Battery World Economy (BWE); we need to feed it with the richest information from every possible source; we must analyze the flow of pellets, the state of sanitation, the infrastructure of the cages, the gross world product (GWP) of eggs, the huge differential between the advanced battery economies (ABE) and the underdeveloped barnyard economies (UBE), the problems of barnyard to battery transition, and why huge transfers of cages to the barnyard won't work." There was tumultuous applause. "Give that hen a prize," they said, and they did give her a prize. "How decidedly post-Keynesian," they said, and felt a lot had been achieved. They adjourned to sip at their sugar water (also laced with hormones, of course, and vitamins, of course), then resumed.

The political scientist hen was not so sure. "It is not clear," she said sagely, "that the question is fundamentally economic. The question is one of power: who controls the economy? Our problem is that we do not know. There are many assumptions, some of which can be dismissed as purely supernatural, like the theory of the Guardians" (much clucking and chuckling and even outright laughter), "but the question remains—who controls the pellets?" (much muttering and head wagging). "If only this question could be settled," she said, "perhaps we could regulate our own lives better and cure the terrible malaise. It will, of course, require massive research, since the source of power over the pellets is obviously multifactoral, multifunctional, and multidimensional."

There was much agreement—if not much enthusiasm. The hens were uneasy at the thought that they were not the masters of their fate. They accepted it intellectually—after all, they were intellectuals, and if things were indeed entirely as they seemed to be, then there would be no mysteries to solve, and they would have no excuse for being. But "mysterious" problems of "power" bothered them.

It was with great relief, therefore, that they turned to the famous architect, praised for the "near mystical" beauty of her vision and her compassion for the beings who inhabited her structures. "The problem seems to me," she said, "to be one of vision—literally." They were intrigued. "We are so restricted in our ability to *see* each other because of the structure of the cages." The excitement was palpable. "If we cannot see each other properly, how can we effectively communicate?" True, true, they clucked, how indeed? "My solution, my architectural solution, is to redesign the cages with rods of mirror glass. Bank upon bank of reflecting cages with slender mirror-glass rods, stacked in quadrangles rather than aisles. We could not only communicate more readily, but live within a vision of shining—but utilitarian—beauty."

The applause was deafening. The clucking uncontrollable. "Mystical," they said; "visionary," they said; "astounding genius— give that hen a medal." And they did give her a medal. When the noise died down, the psychiatric hen (socially oriented) could only come as an anticlimax, but she did her best.

"Our problem lies at the psychosomatic interface," she said (groans, yawns—insofar as beakless mouths can yawn). "Basically, the hens lack a sense of *personal well-being*. This leads to stress and breakdown. Redesigning the cages is all very well, but without massive research into the *attitudes* and *motivations* of our fellow egg-producing persons, we shall never understand our malaise. The essential problem is one of *adequate adjustment*. Given the perfect environment, why do the organisms not adjust perfectly? They are free from want, free from disease, free from fear of predators, free from all needs—but they are *not well adjusted*. We need massive research—multifactoral, multifunctional, and multidimensional—to discover how we can manipulate the cage environment and how we can *remotivate* the inhabitants to achieve well-being and health."

"Yes," interjected the political scientist, "but that doesn't solve the problem of who controls the pellets—you merely divert us from the real problem."

"Nonsense," said the great economist, "the real problem is with the productive infrastructure."

"Now, now," said the great architect, "all we need is vision and compassion."

"What price vision without power!" shouted the political scientist—and things looked like they were getting out of hand. The philosopher saved the day by turning the discussion to the semantics of the question, and everyone became totally engrossed in the business of the difference between "power *to* control" and "power *for* control"—except the political scientist. Everyone suspected her of prejudiced political leanings anyway. The sociologist then spoke, but no one understood her. It had something to do with the inevitability of the whole world of hendom converting to batteryism because of changed social consciousness consequent upon the social revolution in the imperialist battery cities, which itself was an epiphenomenon of the interaction between the rise of battery technology and the ideology of Persistent Egg Production (PEP) transformed into an imperialistic world battery economy in which...Everyone was clucking away to her neighbor by now and someone called for a sugar-water break, which, to everyone's relief, was agreed on.

Except by the Still Small Voice that had not spoken, interjected or even clucked during the above. "But you don't understand," it now interposed desperately. "We're asking the wrong questions."

Everyone looked amazed. Weren't they the best brains in the battery? How could they be asking the wrong questions? "Enlighten us, SSV," they said, sarcastically, while paying more attention to their sugar-water.

The Still Small Voice cocked her head as far sideways as the restrictions of the cage allowed. "Out there," she indicated, "is the barnyard whence, very recently, we came. Most chickens in the world live like that, and most have for most of their known existence." There were rumbles of obvious distaste at this indelicate topic, but the SSV persisted. "They live in the open except for roughly constructed roosts. They live in polygamous families, and the cock fertilizes their eggs. They have little nests of straw where they incubate their eggs and raise fluffy chicks who follow them about and peck and peep. They don't lay nearly as many eggs as we do, and the eggs are small and brown, but the chicks grow legs and feathers and peck at the ground for their food (more murmurs of distaste). It's true," said the SSV plaintively, "that they don't have our advantages—totally controlled environments with sanitation, food pellets with vitamins, scientifically designed cages, and high egg production. It's true the cocks fight among themselves and the hens are submissive to the cocks and have their own pecking order (clucks of horror), and it's true they peck in the dirt with real beaks for their food (more horror), but they don't die glassy-eyed, from unknown causes, and they see the sun and feel the wind and they survive. And that's what we did for most of our chicken history. Perhaps something went wrong?"

The chorus of abuse, sarcasm, and scorn that followed drowned out the odd cluck of agreement here and there.

The sociologist said that she would never have imagined that Narodniks were still flourishing, much less daring to express opinions. Everyone knew that the transition to batteryism was inevitable and this was just romantic populism.

The great economist complained that this kind of consideration could not be put into her input-output model—and how did knowing about the barnyard help improve the cages?

Or, for that matter, said the political scientist, solve the problem of who had power over the pellets and how to get it.

There was really no future, said the socially oriented psychiatrist, in a back-to-the-barnyard philosophy. The problem was with adjustment to the cages. The economist and the sociologist chorused together that all the barnyard hens were rushing to get into the battery cities anyway, and this trend was irreversible. So the issue could only be how to improve the cages and get more pellets. ("Power over the pellets," corrected the political scientist, but she was beginning to be ignored.)

The great architect was more constructive, more visionary, more compassionate. It was perfectly true, she said, that the barnyard-to-battery transition was inevitable, but the SSV had a point. The truly visionary and compassionate way to deal with this was to build cages that were aesthetically in tune with the indigenous barnyard culture—not to force our steel and concrete (or even glass) notions onto them (laughter) but to design cages from their own materials and in their own traditions. She proposed, therefore, that the cages be made of firm rods of twisted straw—the natural material of the barnyard—but of course beautifully braided, and the floors of the cages could be made of compacted dirt with a suitable polyurethane covering. The de-beaked, de-feathered, and de-legged hens would then feel less alienated from their traditional settings. We should not, she repeated, force our notions of the perfect cage upon them. Let the cage arise out of their own traditions and their "well-being" would be more certain.

The applause was again tumultuous. "Constructive," they said; "compassionate," they said; "give that hen another medal." Of course, the diehards quibbled. "Infrastructure, infrastructure," said the economist. "No barnyards exist without massive subsidies." "Power—who builds the cages, is there a wings deal?" said the political scientist. "Romantic piffle," said the sociologist—but she was cut short by the general applause.

The Still Small Voice, however, was quite agitated by now. She became a Still Large Voice and heckled the multitude. "You still don't understand. Sure, the barnyard wasn't paradise—it isn't clear we should have been living in barnyards either, but we did, and we survived, and somehow it worked, and we still had our beaks and legs." ("Reactionary," they said, "romantic piffle.") The SSV (or SLV) continued above the hubbub: "But I'm not saying the barnyard was *the* answer—I'm saying it was about the best we could do. We're here to discuss why all the hens in the cages are failing over dead, damn it. Perhaps we shouldn't be in cages, or barnyards."

There was a shocked silence, broken when, with something between sadness and sarcasm, a querant demanded, "But how would they get the pellets to us?"

"Who," asked the political scientist, "are *they?*" But the Still Small Voice was insistent. "The battery cities, with all their technological wonders, are a few decades old; even the barnyards are only a few thousand years old. We were meant for neither. For millions of years our ancestors (groans) lived in the jungles. They only laid one or at most two clutches of eggs a year. But they kept their chicks around, and the chicks imprinted on their mothers and stayed in little families. They roamed the jungle for food in small territories, and groups of mothers were guarded by great cocks with brilliant combs and plumage that was always luxuriant with the greens of the forest and the oranges, reds, and purples of their arrogant displays. And they had great beaks, talons, and flashing spurs on their ankles, and they fought for territories and females and crowed defiance to their rivals at dawn. The rain rained on them and they snuggled in their nests; the sun warmed them and they strutted and pecked in the open places. They were killed by snakes and birds of prey; their eggs were eaten by reptiles and primitive mammals, but they hung on and flourished. There never was such fierce beauty in any ground birds as in their cocks, or such broody sexiness as in their hens. And they made eggs to make more chickens—not for its own sake as we do (or for whatever purposes the conveyor belt has for them—we don't know). They lived for themselves without the help of scientists and scholars and technicians. And this, my poor companions, was for millions and millions of years. This is what we are. What have we done to ourselves? That is what we should be asking, not how to get more artificial pellets and how to design better cages."

The sheer length of the speech had stilled them to silence. The sociologist broke it. "Brilliant," she said, "but I have only one question." "What is that?" asked the philosopher (who was happier with questions than with answers). "How do we get more pellets and how do we design better cages?"

They all broke up in laughter and resumed serious discussion.

One morning the Guardians came to the battery city at dawn and found all the hens had died of stress and boredom. Out in the barnyard a hen cocked her head on one side as she pecked among the gravel for specks of corn. "Quiet in there, isn't it?" she said. Somewhere, out in the primeval forest, a splendidly colored cock rose on his talons, flapped his wings, stretched his strong neck and fiercely crowned head to the sky, and crowed three times to greet the sun. No one heard.

## ACKNOWLEDGMENTS

I could not have written the above without the kind assistance of the Nobel Foundation, the Gulbenkian Foundation, the H. F. Guggenheim Foundation, the Rockefeller Brothers Foundation, the International Federation of Institutes for Advanced Study, and numerous other generous and well-meaning organizations dedicated to understanding "modernization."

## POSTLUDE: CONFERENCE ODE

We had this conference   you see
to set the sorry world to rights—
to frame a new philosophy
It lasted thirteen days and nights

Exhausted   in our final round
officially we failed to find
a single plot of common ground
We were of a divided mind

We sought the one eternal truth
on which to base our polity
We slowly passed from age to youth
from wisdom to frivolity

Our days   so boring   soon became
merely a prelude to our nights
Sagacity served to inflame
a lust for frivolous delights

The darkness   brighter than the day—
while not producing something new—
had   Mr. Chairman   this to say
One thing is certain: People screw

# WHAT THE HUNTER SAW

*In a Shanidar occupation level fifty feet below the cave floor, in a niche of stones, lies the skeleton of a young man, and around the skeleton clusters of more than 2,000 grains of fossil pollen. One late spring or early summer day, people had lain him to rest on a bed of yellow, red, white, and blue flowers, grape hyacinth, rose mallow, hollyhock, bachelor's button, groundsel.*
John Pfeiffer, *The Creative Explosion*

*Clearly, when a royal person died, he or she was accompanied to the grave by all the members of the court: the king had at least three people with him in his chamber and sixty-two in the death-pit; the queen was content with some twenty-five in all.....It is safe to assume that those who were to be sacrificed went down alive into the pit.*
Sir Leonard Wooley, *Ur of the Chaldees*

How could they be so slender   men and girls?
Breeders yes   but breasts so small   high pointed
child sucks on what   swinging at waist   how feed?

Dragging spear butt   keeping low   in the juniper
bushes   mouth open   thirst   tangled greasy hair
flecking his eyes   raw dried meat
sundried   dirty   hanging at waist
eyes flicker to berries   question   habit
dying hard   like him   near death resisting

NOTE: I have cheated here since Shanidar dates from approximately sixty-thousand years ago and the young man in question could not therefore have seen Ur or any of the early neolithic towns. But it is the contrast that matters, and that is still valid. Fables do not have to respect chronology.

Last run   last rains   last hunt   kin dead
leg useless   blood dried   days gone   pain
loss   rains   no stars   rains   then heat   scorch
lost   more pain

       How could they?   Girls like
unblooded boys   How could they be so slender?
Buttocks shrunk smooth   no use for child work
not the making or releasing   hips
chipped down like flints   brittle sounds
like falling ice at ankles and wrists   pieces
of shining ice   Men and girls   slender like
gazelles

       All senses leap now   tell   urge
get up-wind   keep low   let Morg and Gmask
creep   creep deep in dust behind   then rise
and yell and watch the sentinel stot   stot
his up-and-down   useless   brave signal   Then
throw   stop the grace dead there in dust
grace into meat   young fed   mate pleased   night good
All lost   Morg to the tusks   Gmask in the rain

These human graciles laugh   move hand in hand
half naked   yes skins   not wearing skins
cobwebs   from spider   giant   in their cave
spinning out the purple   violet cobwebs
And the ice that tinkled   tinkled   how
did it stay whole in heat of summer   how?
Laughter like breaking ice and song and
bird sounds   mating bird calls   coming
from beaks of males but not like beaks
moved from mouths to laugh and kiss the
slender girls

       Moving now towards their
cliff   square   regular with square holes
in its sides   and trees   regular trees
two-sided   linking branches   leaning against
cliff

Moving slowly through high yellow grasses
passing smaller   heavier   men and girls
cutting   stooping   curved knives   flint yes
but curved like new moon   useless for killing
brittle for hunt   break in flesh
Why hunt
the yellow   tall   seed-heavy   waving grass?

Stopping   all stopping   quiet eyes turned down
presence of power sensed strain   see a straggle
no   too regular   lines and lines these graciles
lines and lines   song   all regular   all
shaman chant   but hundreds   hundreds   how
to feed so many?
Cobwebs   white   on old males
of herd   yellow   glinting like the grasses
round necks and foreheads   Green   yellow knives
at waist   Smooth lines   not gut   not creeper
dragging beasts   White bull   black ram   fat
clumsy   smooth   easy kill   one thrust   Chant
low   long   nearer   now in circle at flat rock
All eyes down   the graciles kneel   unknown
fear   bull   ram   but not of hills   plains   smooth
fat   people slender   beasts smooth   fat   stupid

Blurs now   not clear   sweat   tiredness   stay
hidden   hide spear   leg dead   body dying
but the hunt   hunt was good   Morg died well
Gmask lost in rains   Women   women heavy bellies
long breasts   huge buttocks   good women   waiting
at cliff base   wet   afraid   some others   yes
perhaps   women fertile   would be taken
Mnag's clan perhaps   too late

Look   look again
last look   how did they stay so slender
the young ones   and their cliff   blurring out there
sticking like outcrop from dry plain
regular like leaning trees   like slender
lines of water through the grass   There were
no lines like that but men made them   yes
and white beasts   they made them   yes
and yellow grass   they made it   yes
and cut it down and made what?   what
did it matter now world was theirs
now

Hills blur   hills theirs too in time
water for the grass comes from the hills
White bull dies from yellow knife
Fat ram dies from knife of ice
Graciles sigh together like lovers   mutter
one response to bloody shaman's cry
Then the stench   burning   flesh burning blood
not for food   burn to burn   blood   flesh   fire

In all that death he felt his own   began
to sing his death song   nasal high   sending
to hills   sky   plain   herds   all the listeners
beyond   beneath

The graciles hear   freeze
horror   surround   horror   hiss   sacrilege
surround

Feral one   hill brute   filthy thing
surround   close   stab   crawl   stab   roll   stab
Blood closes eyes   laughter   clinking ice
How could they be so slender   still give birth?

They left him for the buzzards   but at dusk
the women came and took him to the hills

*Human self awareness is unique*
*in that we give voice to it through speech*
*Animals communicate but not*
*on existential questions   Language is*
*more than mere communication   it*
*admits of self reflection...*

*...not enough*
*to be a creature conscious of one's own*
*existence   one must be aware of one's*
*awareness and articulate the same*

# OVERHEARD IN THE PUB

"We'd start wi' the Jews   because they ask for it
I mean   if they'd shut up about themselves
and keep out of the way   they'd be alright"

"Yer right mate   First the Jews   Another pint?"

"Thanks mate   and then the Krauts   because they done
the Jews—which was their right—but still
they're dangerous bastards   so we'll do them next"

"Who then mate?"

                    "Well   I think the bloody Frogs
because they're bloody awful and because
they'd do us all if they 'ad 'arf a chance"

"Quite right mate   Get the filthy Frogs   Who then?"

"The blacks of course   the bloody lot because
they're   well   a bloody big embarrassment
worse than the Yids   They clutter up the place
You don't know where you are"

                        " Right mate   Not like
the old days eh?  'Ere  'ave another pint"

"Good on yer cobber   Then we'll get the Yanks
the fuckin' know-alls   serve 'em right   and then
the bleedin' A-rabs and the little Chinks
and all the nasty little yellow men
What fuckin' use are they?"

                    "Right on mate—what?
That's what I asks myself   what fuckin' use?"

"No use at all   They hate our bloody guts
So we'll do them   and then the Indians
No more stupid voices serving chips
We'll choke 'em on their own chapatis   then
we'll finish off the Russkies before they
blow us to bloody bits"

                    "The bloody bastards   right
An' all their pals   They would   Another pint?"

"Right 'o   Then all the Spicks and Wogs and Turks
and all the bloody rest   The Irish first"

"Right   Get them murderin' bastards right up front
Who's left?"

                'The friggin' upper classes mate"

"That's right   the bleedin' middle classes too"

"And all the prolo-bloody-tariat
The lazy bleedin' bastards"

                    "Right That's them
Who's left?"

            Just you and me mate   and I'm not
all that bloody certain about you."

# EVOLUTIONARY POETICS

*It's all too much.*
The Beatles, *Yellow Submarine*


Consciousness out of context   (Muse I sing)
The point's been made before   change is too fast
The Neolithic revolution was
somewhat too fast for hunters   but they coped
The urban revolution was a jolt
but one that was absorbed and staggered by
with mere elaborations   nothing new
(Unless the sinister emergence of
a literate class which soon began to take
its literacy further than the lists
of punishments and tribute and supplies
and valedictions of pathetic kings
into the exploration of itself—
the fascination of the words and wordy
that was a revolution in itself
but did not make its impact fully felt
until the mass of men caught the disease)

But noting this and passing on we find
th'industrial revolution in degree
more of a jolt   even a jolt in kind
A rebirth   sudden   from the chrysalis
of mercantile and feudal caterpillar
into the fragile butterfly of steam
of coal and iron   capital and wealth
drawn not from land but from the sweated arms
of proletarians— peasants without land
and lacking all the certainty that dirt
between the fingers gives if it's *your* dirt
and not the filth that cannot be removed

because the skin is stained in laboring
for surplus value
       That was change enough
into a different kind of slavery
But there had been so many slaves before
Why was this worse?   Because it held the seed
of anger different from a slave revolt
of possibilities beyond the dreams
of Spartacus or Christ—the dreams of Marx

(Continuing the theme of consciousness
out of context  but reflecting on
its wobbly route to this plateau  herewith
reflections on the crucial stages of
hominid history  Thus each stage produced
a curious "surplus" which somehow became
the basis  accidentally  for the next
"Preadaptation" in the jargon but
that hints of teleology  far too
deliberate a process  this is not
even a hint at dialectic  there
is struggle but no synthesis  At best
it's happy accident  So sorry Karl)

## TREES

CIRCA 72<br>MILLION<br>YEARS B.P.

Imagine if the rudimentary
primates had not made *that* cute excursion
Then goodbye grasping hand   binocular
vision   diminution of the sense
of smell etcetera*
   *Surplus:* "Intelligence surplus"
You didn't have to be that smart
to live in trees   It came in handy though


* By this time there had been a revolution
unseen yet terrible   the creatures dreamed

REM sleep is something unreptilian
it comes with mammals   With it comes the chance
of long-term storage in the memory
and hence the freeing of cells cortical
for other and more sinister endeavors
In lower mammals dreaming is enslaved
to theta rhythms   keeping it on rein
to those activities the species has
found useful in survival   But comes man
and like the other higher primates frees
his dreams from theta and dependency
on mere survival...

BIPEDALISM

and the striding walk
converted shambling brutes into efficient
machines for covering long distances
with minimal effort  You could not outrun
the prey  but you could walk the buggers down
What's more it freed the hands from locomotion
and hating idle digits as he does
Lord Belial quickly found them other work*
*Surplus*:  "Energy surplus"
You didn't have to be quite that efficient
to get by in the scramble for the meat
But what a great stride forward for mankind!

*and from this work man made himself  at least
so Engels would maintain  *The Part Played by
Labor in the Transition from Ape to Man*
(written in 1876 but only
published in 1896  those hands
were busy keeping Karl from penury)

## HUNTING

CIRCA 2
MILLION
YEARS B.P.

I mean in earnest   Kill the beast
and organize the hunt and distribution
of meat within the horde   It came on slowly
perhaps at first   but once they got the point
then they were off and running   Yet the hunt
itself was maybe less important than
the organizing and the sharing   but
the meat made all the difference at that*
      *Surplus:* "Protein surplus"
You don't need the massive   (not that massive)
input of protein—those amino acids
that niacin   that vitamin $B_{12}$
But once you've got them then the bulging brain
and even more efficient striding walk
are poised for takeoff scarcely dreaming where

---

*A lot of effort currently is put
into the proof that "man the hunter" was
" man the scavenger"—a lazy lout
a carrion eater   robber of the kills
of more efficient carnivores   But think
the great decani of the hunt   the wolves
only attack the young   the old the maimed
and lions steal from other hunter's kills
Now would our enterprising ancestors
have been less capable than wolves or dogs?
So if they drive these hunters from their prey
garnering a banquet second hand
they only imitate the lion   One small step
and they too could be pulling down the sick
A scavenger by any other name...

## LANGUAGE

? PERHAPS
CIRCA 1
MILLION
YEARS B.P.


Above all the talk
and permanent attachment of the memories
that could then be transmitted and preserved
passed slowly   surely on through song and verse
and myth mnemonics   proverb   formula
    *Surplus*:   "Information surplus"
You didn't need that massive a change
in information processing   But on came speech
and names and sentences*   The angular
gyrus has a lot to answer for
But once you had   the brain was off and running
in circles more and more of its devising
Not circles in the world but strange recursive
pathways inside thought itself   thought about
thought about the thought of thought—the prospects
were alarming   This was the mother lode


*There are thase wha say Neanderthals
cannet he credeted weth "lengage" Wha?
Thar laranxes cad enle farm twa vawels
What thenk ye ef thes nefty argament?

## AGRICULTURE

CIRCA 7-10
THOUSAND
YEARS B.P.

    Why bother? No one's yet explained
why happy hunters having so much fun
would willingly exchange their affluence
for dawn to dusk back-breaking servitude
to mutant grasses  cultivated roots
The entire episode makes little sense*
Don't blame the brain  we had that long before
Some blame the women  (others think to credit
the female sex with this "great innovation")
Chacun à son goût  I'm with the hunt
      *Surplus*: "Food surplus"
and all its charming consequences
including leisure classes creaming off
their very own dear surplus from the mob
Chiefs  states  empires  wars and tyrannies
but above all...

*One theory that I like is that this step
was taken by the *least successful hunters*
Driven from the choicest hunting grounds
they turned to seeds and roots extensively
and since they were dependent found a way
to make their vegetarian supply
a great deal more reliable than that
of simple gatherers  If this isn't true
it ought to be  the irony is perfect

## POPULATION EXPLOSION*

We were enough   We didn't
need so many   What do more mouths add
but hunger?   We are too alike each other
for numbers to do more than multiply
monotony   But given all that went
before it was inexorable
                    *Surplus*: "Labor surplus"
Once you've got 'em keep 'em all employed
If worst to worst should come they can construct
your tombs and pyramids and temple courts
(after they've fought your wars and tilled your fields)
where that surplus information can
find outlet through the excess energy
and so to further cumulation…

*The human population had been stable
throughout the paleolithic at about
a million   Come the neolithic then
it shot up to a hundred million
Five billion later that might not seem much
but then it was a crowded little world
to those who had to cope so suddenly

## WRITING

CIRCA 3-5<br>THOUSAND<br>YEARS B.P.

Not enough to have
the language that you did not need   you choose
to make the symbols permanent and join
vision and speech in altering the brain
which surely had enough to occupy it*
*Surplus*: "Concept surplus"
Goodbye old oral world for now we have
the anal institution of the pen
Science mathematics measurement
and records—above all those wretched files
And so to that appalling consummation
the growth of rational bureaucracy

(Between the first city states and the late
eighteenth century nothing happened.   Then...)

*Thus literate aphasics rarely make
more than a small recovery of speech
while their illiterate counterparts do well
and often speak as well as ever since
their brains are not encumbered with the need
to make the auditory-visual
connection   Literacy we take too much
for granted in its benefits   Why not
let's wait and see...

INDUSTRY

   So we return to where we are
and pick up the crazy unforeseen
consequences patchworks bits and pieces
serendipitous and accidental
cumulation of surplus upon surplus
rolling like a golem to its end
  *Surplus*: "Physical energy surplus"
leading God knows where
If we didn't need the brain the hands
the walk the meat the words the weeds the crowds
the letters surely we don't need the power
to exploit the energy of energy itself
Unhappy ape You know not what you do
But driven from one surplus to another
you pile up problems that your cunning brain
was never meant to solve however well
it handles things mechanical*

So what? This latest surplus helps you churn
the rate of change beyond the brain's capacity
to comprehend much less control
The paradox of...
To say nothing of computers and nuclear
weapons We could go on about those too
But I don't want to go on
I want to hear the Beatles singing
"It's all too much"

*  a surplus too
another preadaptive accident
that came from some severe selection for
manipulative skills The brain is quite
obsessed with hands and feet as much as words

This was to have been a learned article
("…should like to introduce the concept
of the 'preadaptive surplus' as a useful
analytical tool which…)
It was all about how NATURE must win in the end
That's the way to bet but
I won't be around to collect

# TWO MORE LYRICS
(to explore a few more things)

*nempe aliae quoque sunt; nempe hac sine viximus ante;*
Lucretius, *De Rerum Natura* 4.1173

## THE SPIDER AND THE HAWK

I had not thought that it would end like this
And will I ever learn from my mistake?
Or learn from everyman's mistake—that bliss
is just for sleepers    pity those who wake?

For sleep of love is sleep of reason too
where dreamy madness weaves a dusty web
And therein I was trapped for love of you
watching the sluggish tide of wisdom ebb

Such sweet exhaustion   rocking in the wind
of all our fantasies each cloying hour
while madness   smiling like a saint that sinned
stared at the love-meal   waiting to devour

The fierce arachnoid pleasure of the bite
that sent the poison singing through my veins
I loved   as Tristan and Isolde might
have loved the potion surging to their brains

If only madness were complete I'd stay
asleep from reason   but in dreams a crack
of fretted logic filtering in the day
shows nightmare reason poised for the attack

He hovers with his cold hard empty eyes
(for reason takes no pleasure in his task)
and draws me from the web of my demise
until   awake   I see you in the mask

The multi-featured mask that madness makes
that once in dreams was love personified
but grins its vampire grin when one awakes
and screams the message   "Fool   your dreams have lied"

That sad old king was wise who never drank
and who was never mad because he knew
what I now know   with only dreams to thank—
I must love reason as I once loved you

## LE PRINCE COCHON

I did not really want to be a beast
a prisoner in this skin against my will
yet when my long imprisonment has ceased
a beast I will be   and imprisoned still

You tell me that true love is my release
and I will love you true to gain reprieve
but time will come when truest love will cease
when I shall not rejoice   but you will grieve

My love is true   but not eternal truth
if what is finite ends is that a sin?
Your love will last   mine not outlive its youth
I did not cheat   but still you cannot win

Your one true love will fade as you grow old
my love will be renewed at every feast
I shall grow sleek   emancipated   bold
and frightened as a poor imprisoned beast

Which of us suffers most is hard to tell
you reap a hard reward you did not earn
but each time Love unlocks my bestial cell
She leaves the door ajar for my return

NOTE:  Stories of the pig prince (or Marcasin) flourished towards the close of the seventeenth century in France. I am thinking in particular of those by the Comtesse de Murat, and the Comtesse d'Aulnoye.

43

*Human consciousness is then defined*
*as consciousness of being conscious couched*
*in Language   The articulation of*
*awareness of awareness*

                        *This release*
*from our entrapment in the material base*
*is our first paradox   For the release*
*results in a more baffling enslavement*
*to language   in itself no less material*
*since anything expressed in it becomes*
*an object in the world incorporated*
*into the tissue of the brain through memory*
*What is expressed in language thus becomes*
*an object of the thought that's born of speech*
*Thus the expression of consciousness becomes*
*an object of that consciousness.*

# VIOLENCE:RITUAL::POWER:AUTHORITY

*How many divisions has the Pope?*
Joseph Stalin

Who would question that Man is the most intelligent of animals? No sensible person given Man's own definition of his intelligence.

Who would question that Man is the only animal with culture? None save those who regard potato washing or termite picking as cultural activities, which is simply to confuse "learned" with "cultural" (i.e. couched and transmitted in symbols). Even pigeons, tape worms and blood cells can learn.

Who would question that only Man has the necessary ingredient for this high intelligence and culture— language? None save those who play the Clever Hans with puzzled chimps.

No. We are the epitome, and though, in academic circles, souls are suspect, culture, language and intelligence are safe. What totters, teeters, and reels under the impact of modern science, though, is the nineteenth-century certainty that these automatically meant progress: inevitable, upward and onward, to the empyrean of utopian perfectibility in technologically superior, socially harmonious societies. Somehow the old Adam seems to have the last laugh and all these vaunted attributes are more easily put to the service, it seems, of the lesser instincts, the "animal" passions. The dinosaurs could no doubt have used their size for noble purposes had they known what these were. They did not, and they died out: we do, and are in danger of extinction.

The dismal truth has slowly dawned during the terrible twentieth century—the century of mechanized, bureaucratized extermination—that culture, language, symbolic thought, intelligence, and the perfection of reason lead only to the technology of destruction, the cultivation of genocide, the intelligent organization

**45**

of mass hysteria, and the rationality of cold war politics and hot war deaths.

So where's the catch? Must we drag in metaphors? Weight and size were perfect for the dinosaurs, until conditions changed and they fell over and died.* Culture and reason have worked beautifully for us—but we changed our own conditions, and we totter toward destruction. Reason does not motivate, and we do not understand our motivations—we follow them. Reason is the handmaiden of the passions: cold and indifferent in her servitude. The flaw is that we cannot reason well. We fear a slave revolt. The handmaiden must grovel.

But to what? To fanaticism, to conviction, to outrage, to righteousness, to the conviction of truth, to moral certainty. Those who cry against the curse of conviction piss into the wind of certitude. We are the best, but lack all conviction—since to be convinced would be to be fanatic. So we encompass our own demise.

So this is the catch? Yes, simply this. And now, to demonstrate its ultimate futility, I shall embark on a rational enterprise. Unlike the dinosaurs, we know what we are doing. So why don't we do something constructive? Well, we've really only just found out. Since Darwin. And we don't like what we know. For what we know is this: all that exalts us above the animal state is a superior capacity for self-deception. We call this culture, reason, intelligence, foresight, symbolic communication, etc., etc. We are born, digest, reproduce, grow old, and die like animals. And that of course is all there is to it. But the animals get on with it. A cruel God gave us only one thing more: the capacity to ask why, knowing there was no answer, but knowing that this capacity to ask for one would keep us busy and drive us crazy.

We invent incredible fantasy structures to justify our getting on with it (in one way rather than another) and call these cultures. We have even taken to inventing armies of people to investigate these alternative delusions and rationalize them. We are the masters of illusion. Magicians fascinate us; our hero is the con man. We invent the great con man in the sky to mastermind the greatest illusion of all: that we need not die. And aiding and abetting

---

* O.K. So they died from a nuclear winter following a meteorite strike. The principle is the same. Pick another extinct species. Ninety percent of all that have ever existed are extinct.

all this is the prime agent of rationality, the brain, whose major function is to protect us from reality so that we might act and not drown in endless processes of unresolvable decision-making.

Well, now, the enigmatic title of this piece of self-destructive rationality is of course a take off on Lévi-Strauss's formula for formulas .* Violence is to Ritual as Power is to Authority. It isn't even true, but these two dimensions are part of a multifunctional, multidimensional, multifactorial analysis I choose to make so the hell with it. The problem is that violence and ritual are both found in nature; power and authority fall on another dimension that corresponds to nature and culture. But we started this whole game with violence, so reason demanded continuity and got her own unfortunate way. Try it again:

Nature: Culture:: Power: Authority

Better. Violence and ritual cut across; they are yet another dimension/ factor. We can plot, as Lévi-Strauss saw, most things against the Nature:Culture dimension because it is our basic intellectual dichotomy and intellectual dilemma. Thus, for example:

Nature: Culture:: Reality: Fantasy

makes good sense. Nature knows no fantasy. Of course for us fantasy becomes reality because our intelligence can make it such by restructuring reality according to our fantasies, as the sociologists of knowledge tell us at length.

To what should we oppose intelligence? Like Bergson I choose intuition, although this could be seen as intelligence working at high speed: computerized intelligence. But I will take it in a more old-fashioned sense and use intelligence to equal "reason" as opposed to "just knowing." But does:

Natural: Cultural:: Intuition: Intelligence

really work? I think so, but a two-hundred page footnote on Bergson would be needed to justify it and that's another book, so

*Actually, I think it was Kant's in his *Prolegomena to Every Future System of Metaphysics that May Ever Arise in the Way of a Science* (1783). It is, of course, simply the formula for ratios borrowed from mathematics.

let it pass. "Intelligence—intuition" is a continuum anyway, not an opposition, but the curious mix in us of both makes me think they are functions of the same process only seemingly different in their operation—and often not different at all in their outcome (viz the human versus the computer at chess). Leave it. But it matters. It is somewhere at the crux, for our central idea—our mother goddess—is imagination, which is the ultimate marriage of intelligence and intuition somewhere at the intersection of all these operations.

Let's try a few more since we still have space on our three-dimensional diagram. (I have to give this away: we are leading up to a diagram—the pictorially minded can take comfort.) Ritual and violence have to be a prime axis. Ritual is violence tamed, turned into fantasy: the rules of war at every level from domestic quarrels to SALT II agreements. Men love the diplomacy as much as the combat. The war of words is what matters for that is where true mastery lies in the realm of fantasy. And crossing this main axis is its equivalent at a more abstract level, for it represents how we interpret what is happening in a primate pack or a Versailles Conference: Power and Authority. Primates (and I single them out for snobbish reasons—they are well-connected) have Power: We have Authority. (Power is the ability to enforce one's will on others: authority is the right to do so. The ability is real: The right must be invented.) It is the supreme con game, authority. It is power either with or without force; an option no animal would understand. Those in authority often lack power completely. (Hence Stalin's sarcasm at the expense of the Pope.) Those in power often lack all authority: but they will kill you if you resist them. Democracies count heads and hand power to the numerical winner—he has no other. And this, among the other forms delineated so well by Max Weber, we call "authority" and we obey—more or less. No animal would be so riddled with reason, fantasy, intelligence, and culture. Tell him some small male has the vote and he will swipe the little animal aside. This done, a ritual baring of the gums will suffice to keep the upstart in his place. The ritual is a reminder of the reality of the swipe—of power. But authority is ritual fantasized: a game of rational make-believe. And because of this it is most fragile. There are those whose business is or can become the effective use of power, and for them authority lacks all authority if it is not enforced by bayonets or terror. Generals and Mafias overturn authority like the house of cards it is. But then they reinvent it: they claim the "people," or "respect" for cosa nostra, or the "public good," or whatever. They always had ritual—that goes with violence and really differs not that much from its animal counterpart: it is the reminder of the gun behind the smile. But authority they have to claim on some basis other than power. Even here though, "right of conquest" has been recognized as a basis for authority. But the heirs of the conquerors claim by right of inheritance, and so once again we are in the land of make-believe. And always out of the desert there is the possibility of the hairy figure with the staff striding in to claim his share of power on the authority of the God that speaks to him and not to priests and kings or elected representatives. "Zadok the priest *and* Nathan the prophet anointed Solomon king." (Italics mine.) Our willingness to submit to authority is purely human. Our pleasure and terror in seeing it overthrown by power, and the exercise of power through force itself, is part of the pre-cultural heritage that knew no fantasy and had only ritual to curb the excesses of power.

I throw in Hedonic:Agonistic. Why? Because Michael Chance's distinction serves, as does the one between ritual and violence, to show the mechanisms that lie behind our capacity for far-reaching self-deception. It is a dimension that suggests that even in the chimps (for example) the capacity for authoritarian delusion must exist. Dominance is agonistic (among baboons for example) when society is maintained by brute force translated into ritual. The hedonic society on the other hand can make pure display a mode of seizure of power—I almost said authority and there's the point. The animal with the most spectacular and effective display need not be the one that could, in open combat, lick the others. But they defer to what appears to be a demonstration of superior might. Reality: Fantasy begins here. We are its supreme elaborators. No kings, no mandarins (for all their poems), no aristocrats had authority without force in the last analysis. Yet for centuries they could wield authority with only a minimal show of force in many cases and virtually none in others. A fantasy of "superior birth" was enough. Other fantasies have succeeded, but they are fantasies none the less.

No analysis of modes of production, ecological adaptations, culture change, or social functions even gets to the starting gate unless it can deal with this primitive given about the human being: its capacity to accept authority however bizarre; its willingness to play out the make-believe, its weakness for the con man and his game.

And for the paradox: we have no option. We can only live by self-delusion. And by it we must perish. It is, in evolutionary terms, the size of the dinosaurs. And yet we call it reason.

I throw in Primate: Human for obvious reasons (using primate again to mean "non-human primate"). The glimmerings of our own idiocy are there in primates. But the primates escape the worst ravages. (They mostly encounter these at our hands.) And, courting screams of outrage, I offer Female: Male. Yet consider. This puts the female (human) close to nature where she obviously belongs. it makes her hedonic, realistic, powerful, intuitive, and natural by definition. Oppose her to the male whose intelligence is used for fantasy, authority, culture, agonistic struggle, and the dubiously human. What woman would wish to ape a man? Forgive my puzzlement at those who claim that all they want is to be better at the games of self-delusion than the illusion-riddled males. They can do better than that surely. Am I the last romantic feminist? But where is imagination? Somewhere hidden in the hinterland between intuition and fantasy, violence and culture, hedonic display and the pretensions of intelligence. Imagination is dead center and is ignored mostly because people fly to the poles, and polar opposites attract.

My Egri Bikaver is finished. All I can leave you is the multidimensional (inadequately represented in three) and multi-factorial (work out the factors for yourselves) diagram. And these few thoughts.

*On the human existential predicament.* Very simple: it is this animal's capacity to imagine a predicament. It is the problem of being able to ask, "why?" about existence. The existence is no problem. We exist in the same way all other animals exist and we do not ask why *they* exist. Nor do they ask it of themselves. We can ask *how* they— or we—came to exist, and the question is in principle answerable. But neither we nor they ask *why* they exist, because they cannot ask it of themselves, and only an animal that can ask the question qualifies for it. Even of so close a cousin as the chimp—very intelligent, very human—we do not ask it. Chimps are born, grow, eat, cavort, struggle, mate, make little chimp replicas, and die. This makes them no different from any other animal (at base than any

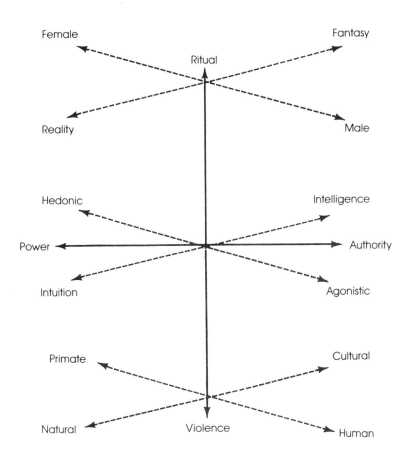

Imagination is the (potential) integrating force of all these factors

other organism). The chimp does not ask why it exists, neither should we. We too are born, grow, eat, cavort, struggle, mate, make little human replicas, and die. We are no different. But consider: endow the chimp with one extra capacity—the capacity to ask why it exists? To ask what is its purpose? To ask how should it live? In other words to question its existence: its manner of existing. Nothing has changed. It is born, grows, etc., etc., and eventually dies. Nothing has changed. There is no more meaning now than before. But now it can ask "Why do I die? Why am I alive at all?" That is all. No more meaning. No change in its life—other than the questioning.

And that is us: chimps with existential questions. And yet the change is radical, because we then devote as much of our energy to answering or avoiding the question as the chimp did to eating, mating, etc. (Even those existentialists who agree that there is no meaning—for whatever reason—agree equally that we should hurry to invent some of our own.) If there is an answer to such a non-question as "Why do I exist?" perhaps it should be, "to ask that question." For that is all that has been added to the tedious list—the capacity to ask why the list should be there at all. It does not supply the answer. Without the capacity to ask we would still exist; go through the paces as our ancestors did before they could ask it. And we would likely survive and replicate well enough. (Or not; nature is careless of species.)

So much for the human existential predicament.

O philosopher! O theologian! Try looking an intelligent chimp in the eye and asking "Why do you exist?" You will receive the only appropriate answer; your indifferent respondent will go off to eat, struggle, mate, make little chimp replicas, and die.

*On the end of civilization.* When civilization ends it will be the work of crazed saints and sober scientists; it cannot be saved by spaced-out musicians or drunken poets.

The violent imagination will triumph and will fail at one and the same time; we have no choice but to be human.

> And did some sly malicious god
> when an ape first stood and faced the sky
> prepare a two-edged gift  a rod
> it thought to cure this hubris by?
> It did  and so the creature choked
> then straining through its tears it croaked
> the first  pathetic  "why?"

# TWO (More) GHOSTS ARE INVOKED

## LOVE AMONG THE PLANETS: BALLAD FOR THE GHOST OF YEATS

Where does love go in autumn
remembering the spring?
To the inner rings of Saturn
where no songs are sung

Where does love go in winter
yearning for summers gone?
Where all lost lovely things must go—
the dark side of the moon

Where does love go at midnight
with thoughts of golden dawn?
To Jupiter's cold darkness
where tired souls lie down

Where does love go at twilight
with memories of noon?
To Mercury's cruel surface
where all hopes burn

Where does love go forever
when planets cease to spin?
Where all things shall end their sorrow—
the deathfire of the sun

## DIVINA COMMEDIA
## FOR BYRON'S GHOST

The saga of belonging
is a comic tale of grief
where the days are full of longing
but the nights bring no relief

Where the dread of deep desiring
makes indifference a gain
but where loss and love conspiring
make the victory seem in vain

Where the tyranny of needing
makes parting a reprieve
but has separation feeding
a hunger to retrieve

Where the fierceness of possession
makes losing a release
but provokes an intercession
to restore possessive peace

Where the thousand ways of holding
are the shackles forged from greed
and the arms that are enfolding
do not strengthen but impede

Where every tense restriction
is a necessary theme
and each tedious interdiction
sets the limits of the dream

Where imprisoned in the dreaming
we are nervous but secure
and escape is but the scheming
to make surety more sure

For the tragedy of passion
is a comedy of fear
which the gods delight to fashion
in which mortals can appear

Where the gaining or the losing
leaves us weeping on the stage
in confusion freely choosing
both the exit and the cage

>...*recursive*
>*Consider that for Hegel God was thought*
>*thinking about itself\*   For us then God*
>*and human consciousness are one    This is*
>*paradox the second    it makes God*
>*an accidental consequence of His*
>*creation*

\*As it was for that matter with Aristotle and Aquinas, the latter writing "Est in Deo intelligente seipsum Verbum Dei quasi intellectus."

*   *   *

>*If recursive consciousness*
>*depends on language as a necessary*
>*condition of existence    then the same*
>*is a contingent product    It need not*
>*—like language—ever have evolved at all\**

\*The empirical issue here is not our concern. All we need to know is that language occurred late in hominid evolution as a result of structural developments in the left temporal lobe, the angular gyrus, and the pre-frontal cortex. These, like any other evolved features, need not have occurred. The rest of the animal kingdom exists well enough without them, and the plant and inorganic kingdoms lack them—even the rudiments of them—and survive very well indeed. Or did so until the superior hominids took over.

# THE INTERROGATION:
## A Nightmare

*You must remember that in these proceedings things are*
*always coming up that are simply beyond reason, people*
*are too tired and distracted to think and so they take*
*refuge in superstition. I'm as bad as anyone myself.*
*And one of the superstitions is that you're supposed to*
*tell from a man's face, especially the line of his lips, how*
*his case is going to turn out. Well, people declared that*
*judging from the expression of your lips you would be*
*found guilty, and in the near future too.*
Franz Kafka, *The Trial*

*Standard scene. Court in session. At a long, raised table the inquisitors in*
*dark suits and darker shadow. In front of them the prisoner in a harsh*
*spotlight. Behind, coughs and mutterings indicate a small audience. One*
*black—suited figure in a large chair at the center of the table speaks.*

COURT: Have you anything to say before we pass judgment?

PRISONER: But there hasn't been a trial yet, has there?

COURT: (*Surprised*) You do not think that the evidence of your
life, work, and opinions is enough to condemn you?

PRISONER: Maybe. But doesn't justice have to be seen to be
done—or something like that?

COURT: (*Sighs*) Very well. We must go through with a formal trial
if the prisoner wishes it.

PRISONER: He sure as hell does. Of what is he accused?

COURT: There is no accusation. This is an enquiry into your
fitness to be a member of society. There is a prima facie case
that you are not. We shall question you.

PRISONER: This court is, I hope, ruled by arbitrary standards of
law and procedure?

COURT: Why do you ask that?

PRISONER: Because, if so, this trial becomes a game with rules
and I stand a chance.

COURT: No. Your answers will be judged solely on truth or falsity.

PRISONER: Then I am doomed, for no man knows the truth.

COURT: Indeed he does; the truth speaks for itself.

PRISONER: On the contrary, someone always speaks for it, and whoever has the voice has the veracity.

COURT: Be assured The People will recognize the truth, for, by definition, what the will of The People recognizes is true, and we are the representatives of the will of The People.

PRISONER: No. The truth resides outside us. It is a small cruel eye that will not release us from its gaze—not you, not me, not The People, not their representatives.

COURT: You are doing your case no good by speaking blasphemy in your defense. The People will ignore your remarks. The inquisition will begin as of now. You will be asked questions about the epochs of Man's history and you will reply what you believe to be the truth. We shall question you in turn.

*(He nods to the first dark figure at the far end of the line and the question and answer session begins. It is all quiet and reasonable. Almost a conversation.)*

Q. Describe the Age of Innocence.

A. The Age of Innocence was when man killed without guilt, copulated without shame, and got drunk without either.

Q. What of the Dawn of Civilization?

A. This was when man left the State of Nature and discovered the Nature of the State. After which life became nasty, brutish, and short.

Q. Before this was Man a noble savage?

A. He was a human savage—noble and ignoble by turns.

Q. And the Rise of the State?

A. Was when man invented his most potent chain: the chain of office.

Q. And the Age of Matriarchy?

A. It was, by definition, the age when mothers ruled. Two other types were automatically killed: men. once their useful breeding life was over; women who were not mothers, and who aspired to be like men.

*(This next came from an inquisitor who had a beard and deep-set eyes, but the light was not good enough to make out more than a faint Viennese accent.)*

Q. What does a woman want?

A. A god to be the father of her children.

Q. What does she get?

A. Constant frustration when this has not materialized, or complete self-deception when she believes it has.

Q. Should men avoid investigation of this issue?

A. Certainly not. The unexamined wife is not worth loving.

Q. Will men ever be as gods?

A. Not while sober women make the assessment.

Q. And what of God?

A. One thing is certain: God cannot be as bad as his believers make him out to be.

Q. Is God dead?

A. More probably bored into silence.

Q. How then should men rid themselves of God?

A. Those gods whom men would destroy, they first make sad.

Q. And what do the gods do then?

A. They leave in the intermission.

Q. What is the greatest of man's gifts?

A. Self-deception: the power of delusion.

Q. Not reason?

A. Reason is its own kind of deception: all the more deluding since it claims the opposite.

Q. Does not reason control the emotions?

A. Reason is an emotion; an excess of emotion is madness; excessive ratiocination is its own kind of lunacy.

Q. Does not reason arbitrate among the emotions?

A. The emotions, of which reason is one, are not subject to arbitration. It is the war of all against all. The triumph of one emotion is madness.

Q. And if reason triumphs?

A. Then its form of madness will prevail.

Q. Which is?

A. Ratiocinosis: the delusion that reason is not an emotion and therefore can save us from the emotions.

Q. Are we all doomed to self-deception?

A. Yes, but we need not all work at it: we can delegate delusion.

Q. Must some of us always lie then on behalf of others?

A. As for lying, our savants can do that for us.

Q. What cure is there for the madness of reason?

A. For ratiocinosis? Only an inoculation by some other form of emotional madness.

Q. What do you suggest?

A. Imaginative compassion.

Q. Is that not rather terse?

A. Very well. If civilization as we know it should end it will be the work of crazed saints and sober scientists; it cannot be saved by spaced-out musicians and drunken poets. The violent imagination . . .

Q. Have we not heard all this before?

A. You should have listened the first time.

Q. To what end if reason is futile?

A. To the end of preventing boring repetition.

Q. Are you not being frivolous with the court?

A. The court is frivolous to start with since the verdict is prede-termined.

Q. Do you accuse the court of prejudice?

A. No. Simply of mean-mindedness and murderous intent.

Q. Do you think that is our purpose?

A. The end justifies the meanness.

Q. Does anything justify bad puns?

A. Frivolous litigation might. Serious litigation certainly would.

Q. On what grounds?

A. Litigation is reason used to perverse ends—puns are the subversion of reason by using a rational linguistic process to make nonsense of the process itself. Therefore to use bad puns to annoy judges is to use reason to combat reason and provoke unreasonable outbursts.

INQUISITION IN CHORUS: Absolute bullshit!

PRISONER: Thank you for making my point.

JUDGE: The questioning is no longer serving any useful purpose

PRISONER: I couldn't agree more.

JUDGE: Let us stay within our mandate to ask of the epochs of history. Continue.

Q. What was the Age of Enlightenment?

A. When reason was exalted over fact with a resulting constipa-tion of the intellect.

Q. And the Age of Science?

A. When fact triumphed over reason and produced a diarrhea of the mind.

Q. What was the distinctive feature of the Age of Faith?

A. Hundreds of cathedrals claimed to have the phallus of Christ.

Q. Have we improved on the Age of Faith?

A. We no longer treasure the phallus of Christ; we promote the female orgasm.

Q. Do these have something in common?

A. They are both relics.

Q. What of the Age of the Common Man?

A. The age of the common man has only one notable achievement, the invention of new tort: Invasion of dignity.

Q. And the Technological Age?

A. When faith and reason will combine to destroy the fruits of their own folly.

Q. What then of the Age of the Individual?

A. It has witnessed the most obscene acts ever of collective violence and tyranny.

Q. Who shall inherit the Earth?

A. The Insects; they had the wisdom to abolish the individual will as a social force. We try hard to do so, but we have gone too far. We are like insects who behave as such except that we can be swayed by individual wills.

Q. What of the Age of Aristocracy?

A. When we ensured the incompetent would govern by reason of superior birth.

Q. And the Age of Democracy?

A. When we ensured that the mediocre would govern by reason of popular choice.

Q. And the Age of Socialism?

A. When we ensured that the unimaginative would govern by reason of their ideological purity and complete lack of scruple.

Q. What prevents the best from governing?

A. They lack the energy of will and singleness of purpose.

Q. Why do they lack this?

A. The best have only many good questions; the governors have a few bad answers; people prefer answers to questions.

Q. What of the Rise of Bureaucracy?

A. It ensures its own failure. It is intended for the governance of human beings, but the qualities demanded of a bureaucrat are of their nature inhuman.

Q. And the Age of the Proletariat?

A. The proletarian is a peasant without land. Deprived of land he lapses into a predatory existence. The proletariat is a pack.

Q. And the Capitalist?

A. is the hunter who has become the hunted—even by his hounds, the bourgeoisie.

Q. And his response?

A. To form his own packs.

Q. And the Silent Majority?

A. Their silence is ignorance multiplied by fear and divided by indifference. They will fall between the packs—noisily.

Q. What of the Age of Revolution?

A. Revolutions cannot succeed, for if they do they are no longer revolutions.

Q. Even the Sexual Revolution?

A. It is the ultimate triumph of male chauvinism: countless females available with whom men can copulate while assuming no responsibilities whatsoever.

Q. What then of We, The People?

A. You are a pool of sulking sharks. Greed has you rending each other in short order.

*(Much buzzing and consternation. The judges confer briefly with much nodding. They sit back.)*

COURT: We declare that you have failed.

PRISONER: May I know the reason?

COURT: You have attempted to be too clever in order to demonstrate individual superiority. The People's truth being collective, it cannot allow assumptions of individual superiority, and so finds your testimonial untruthful.

PRISONER: But in so condemning me The People surely tries to show its superiority to me?

COURT: No. The People simply declares you its equal, and its condemnation is not superiority, merely justice.

PRISONER: Justice is man's easiest excuse...

COURT: You will not be allowed further testimony...excuse for what?

PRISONER: I was going to say for oppression, but that is so weak I risk a just condemnation.

COURT: You are in any case condemned. You will be taken from this place to a place of lawful reeducation where you will be washed by the brain until you be humble, and when you are in full possession of your popular senses you will be released to do useful work in a capacity that will fit your pleasant mediocrity: a mediocrity all the more worthy for having been achieved. The case is closed. The People will retire.

*(One judge demurs and asks that the prisoner be recalled for an extra question. The court is annoyed but agrees.)*

Q. Why do you despise The People?

A. I do not despise The People—rather people. I simply do not recognize a category of The People. The People is a mistake.

Q. Then whom do we represent?

A. You are people who probably represent other people. But not The People.

Q. What of the Historic Destiny of The People?

A. A collective delusion of some people.

Q. As with the so-called Chosen People?

A. One of the greatest collective delusions of all time, for of all people they are surely the most obviously abandoned.

Q. But do they not survive despite all persecution?

A. They do. But so do the Irish and they certainly don't think they were chosen.

Q. What have the Irish and the Jews in common?

A. They both believe that reality is chaos—only narrowly kept at bay.

Q. And how do they differ?

A. The Jews think they can do something about it.

JUDGE: I see no point in further questions.

*(But the bearded one leans forward and asks one anyway.)*

Q. We asked you what a woman wanted. What does a man want?

A. Someone to fuck, something to hate, and some way to forget.

Q. But what of...

A. Anything you want to add comes under the third head.

Q. To forget what?

A. Whatever.

Q. A strange answer from one who has not, as he expected, been sentenced to die but to live.

A. A sentence of life dissipates the mind abominably.

JUDGE: He is incorrigible. Remove him.

*(All nod, All leave. Lights dim. Figures move...)*

Vishnu in his lotus-dreaming groaned
and moved one shoulder slightly   Mountains fell
Continents shifted   Empires collapsed
Received ideas appeared ridiculous

*To say full consciousness is accidental is*
*only to say it is a product of*
*natural selection   Everything*
*is such a product   This is not to say*
*that it is inexplicable   there must*
*have been selection pressures favoring it*
*most likely by the preservation of*
*those organs that had generated speech*
*Occurring as mutations their adaptive*
*value made for ultimate retention*
*within the pool of genes*

*Nevertheless*
*we face the startling prospect that the mind*
*being thus conscious will eventually*
*stumble on this simple lonely truth*
*after a history of monumental*
*efforts to use this consciousness to weave*
*the rich illusion of necessity*

# NOTE TO THE THEOLOGIAN

(as an afterthought to the foregoing reflections of the
philosopher of mind who somehow got in on this act)

If God is independent of our flesh
(not a by-product* but the primal cause)
God cannot help   Pure thought addressing thought
(perhaps consumed with curiosity
that matter could achieve the same result)
became incarnate in the Word made Flesh
and so experienced humanity
died at its hands   brooded three days   then fled
with vague assurances   (still unfulfilled)

It's not quite that Divinity is dead
it just abandoned the experiment
absconded to the safer sphere of thought
thinking about itself
                        But maybe God
is haunted by the sojourn in the flesh
The independent Word that gave us form
is tainted by its own creation
                        Once
fear simmered only in the hearts of men
But since the incarnation there is fear
at the very epicenter of all being

*as in the philosopher's argument (vide supra)

**64**

# Two

# The Trial of George Washington: Documents in the Case

# HOW WE CAME BY THEM

## LETTER TO THE PUBLISHER

Dear Irving,

Just before he died, Senator James Handler gave me the enclosed manuscripts. As you *do* know, I met him through Senator Fulbright; what you don't know is that we discovered, to our surprise, that his wife and I had an ancestor in common—my great-great grandfather—a Dublin lawyer and legal historian, Augustin Fox. I did not know the senator's son John very well. He was killed in Vietnam, as you also know. But before he left he gave his father the manuscript (his letter is enclosed). The senator did not think that he himself had long to live (he proved right) and given the odd family connection, (the relevance of which will become obvious on reading the stuff), and my contacts in the publishing world, he thought I would be the appropriate person to do something about it all.

I would suggest, in the first instance, just publishing it "raw" before letting the historians and other vultures get at it. It is so close now to the bicentennial of the notorious trial. Anyway, here are the photocopies, the rest is up to you.

As ever,

Robin

P.S. My otherwise rather pedantic ancestor refers to the "Duke of Wellington" making a speech "in the House of Lords" in 1811. At that time Wellesley was still only a Viscount and, I thought, in Portugal. So who's perfect?

## LETTER FROM LT. JOHN BRIDGES HANDLER
## TO HIS FATHER SENATOR
## JAMES WHITMORE HANDLER

Fort Dix, N.J.
Dec. 12, 1970

Dear Dad,

This will be the last letter before I leave. I am allowed to tell you that I am at Fort Dix (which is no news) but nothing else, of course. I had said what I had to say in the previous letter—at least about how I felt, and you must have thought me ridiculously sentimental, but I meant it. Since Mom died I've felt closer, and we are all that is left of the "clan" now. But one more thing cropped up—something very strange, and you should know about it.

Just before she died, Mom gave me one of her treasured "heirlooms" (you know how she hoarded all that stuff from England—some junk, some antiques, some curios—but all precious to her.) Well, this was a plain, heavy, wooden box of no distinction (except its age!) It had a rusty lock and key that had obviously not been often turned. She told me to keep it until after she was dead. (She never flinched about dying did she?) She knew I might go to Vietnam and she asked me to look at what was inside before I went. It came to her, she said, from *her* mother—Grandma Bridges (who I met when I was little—I think—on one of those trips to see the English relatives, but I don't really remember.) It had "come down to" Grandma Bridges from her mother, and even perhaps from hers—I'm not sure, but her name was "Anne," and it was "Anne's box." (Mom was the keeper of the family history, of course, but you may *just* know who she meant.) Anyway, I was to read what was in it if ever I "decided to go off and die for my country" as she put it (as she would put it.)

Dad, it's the strangest thing. "Anne's" husband was evidently a legal historian, a retired lawyer, who lived in Dublin although he'd practiced law in England and had been something called a "Parliamentary draftsman"—whatever that was. Anyway, he'd gotten hold of some fragments of *the actual record of Washington's trial!* Can you imagine? They seem genuine enough, and his covering note speaks for itself. He obviously meant it to be published, but for reasons I don't understand, "Anne" just locked it up and put it with his other stuff and never did anything about it. It was among the odds and ends that "came down" from mother to daughter I guess until it came to Mom. I think perhaps no one had even bothered to read it before her, and all she said to me was what I told you—except for that odd remark of hers about war and politics being "a comedy for male voices." To a son who was about to be a soldier and a husband who was a politician! Well. That was Mom.

Now I don't know what to do. I've read the whole thing and I see what she means. I don't want to rehash our arguments, but now *I* am going off to fight in someone else's civil war when I don't approve of going or fighting—and because "my country" demands it. Or is it just the politicians who demand it to save their faces? I'm sorry. Oh. I'll go. I'm on my way. Like those English (our ancestors in fact) who went when they didn't want to go. It was their Vietnam, Dad. They didn't learn, neither have we. Washington had. You'll see what I mean when you read it. So I'm sending it to you. It's a gem, historically I mean. You'll know what to do with it. But I guess if I'd had a sister it may never have seen the light of day! Will we ever understand women? I meant what I said in the other letter Dad. I'm glad our last talk was by the Charles with the crews out and the leaves turning. I'll do my best and pray to God that we see each other before long.

> Your loving son,
> John

## HANDWRITTEN MANUSCRIPT FROM THE BOX

Dublin 1861

"To hang George Washington was our worst mistake."

Every schoolboy knows these famous words of the Duke of Wellington in the House of Lords on the occasion of the granting of independence to the former American colonies in 1811 (to forestall another alliance with the French it seems.) That the government took the whole thing badly was expected, but it had decided to accept the inevitable. There was no way to retain the allegiance of the colonies without another costly and probably disastrous war like the one of 1775–81. It was true that technically Great Britain had "won" that particular struggle, but was there ever a victory so Pyrrhic, or damage done to crown and country so extensive? The Tories never recovered after North's fall from grace; the King's friends were pretty well discredited despite Charles James Fox's never-forgiven attempt to prop them up; the Whigs gained so rapid an ascendancy that only the prestige of the Iron Duke himself held the Tories together in a semblance of unity and narrow probability of occasional governance—and this largely due to the fractious nature of the Whigs and their passion for factions.

All this is well enough known, but we lack very much reliable evidence of the signal event by which the crown so sadly miscalculated: the trial and execution of George Washington himself. The details of his final defeat at Yorktown are also well enough known but should perhaps be summarized.

The battered "American" army had hoped to bluff Sir George Clinton in New York by leaving four thousand men with bogus camps and even bakeries in New Jersey to suggest a long stay. This would keep Clinton and his sizable force locked up in New York where they felt safe among the Loyalists. (The brave Irish volunteers of the King's Loyal American Regiments had already staged, on the day of their patron saint, a march down the Broad Way in the city of New York. It has become a annual event I gather, although its origins are not much spoken of.) Meanwhile, Washington was to march to Yorktown and catch Cornwallis napping, forcing him into a siege. The French navy was to blockade the coast thus preventing relief for "the British" from the sea, and the French army under de Rochambeau (*not* de Lafayette as so many school-boys insist with typical sloppiness) was to come through the Carolinas to Washington's support, thus bottling Cornwallis up at the end of the Yorktown peninsula. Faced with two armies in front and the French navy behind, he would be forced to surrender.

What exactly happened to wreck this admittedly brilliant plan is still confusing to historians, but some things are clear. Cornwallis received intelligence of the plan and warned Clinton, or Clinton perceived the bluff and warned Cornwallis, or spies of the American side got word to both. In any case, Cornwallis anticipated the joining of the two forces and moved his own, with a brilliant manoeuvre, between them. As far as we understand it, Washington (and his chief advisors Lee, Lincoln, von Steuben, and de Lafayette) saw this as a blunder in which Cornwallis would be trapped. But Clinton meanwhile had marched from New York, swept aside the four thousand surprised Americans with his own eighteen thousand men, and was marching on de Rochambeau's rear. There was still the French navy; but then disaster struck. Admiral de Grasse made the crucial miscalculation of the war, strung his ships out too far, and allowed the British fleet to cut his line in half, sink two of his ships and send the rest scuttling for the Indies.

Item: Washington was between the fleet and Cornwallis. Item: de Rochambeau was between Cornwallis and Clinton. Item: at that moment Cornwallis struck in the most brilliant stroke of a brilliant career: he attacked the French *centre* at exactly the time the fleet opened with a bombardment of the Americans from the sea. He cut the French in two and joined up with Clinton while the British bombardment kept the already exhausted and undersupplied Americans helpless.

The surrender was inevitable and was received by Brigadier (not General as most history books insist with typical lack of attention to scholarship) Charles O'Hara, since Cornwallis would not deal directly with rebels. However—and this became an important point in the trial it seems—he did allow them to surrender with full honours of war. One presumes that this was to avoid further foolish fighting on their part that, while ultimately futile, would have cost many British lives. Cornered rats fight the fiercest, as the popular saying has it. Cornwallis, in view of later events, had been naturally reticent about his motives in this matter, but he did proceed, properly, to arrest Washington and his officers and to round up as many of the rebel leaders as possible. (Franklin was safe in Paris, and a great number, led by the Rev. Mr. Witherspoon, rushed to renounce their former adherence and swear allegiance to the crown. This, again, Cornwallis wisely accepted and Lord Howe confirmed, although there were those who hurled unwarranted charges of "leniency" at them later as we know.)

Again, what happened back in London at the court is not as clear as it might be. Apart from some cautious letters between the King and Lord North—largely to do with the latter's health and the King's advice of "abstinence and water!"—we have little hard evidence and much of that is merely circumstantial or hearsay. (This has not prevented novelists, dramatists, journalists, and others from speculating wildly and with complete lack of respect for historicity of course.) What is certain from the outcome is that the King—on the advice of North and probably Thurlow (the violently anti-American attorney general)—decided not to hold the trial in America (for what are surely obvious reasons); decided to hold it in London (where it could be better controlled); decided to try Washington first (as an example); and decided to try him by special court martial rather than in a civil court (again for obvious reasons). The last move was on the surface a clever one, but almost, as we know, had the engineers hoist on their own petards (whatever they may be). Military men can be remarkably independent-minded, particularly when they have their peerages and are not looking for further promotion. But, despite the ravings of some Whig "experts," it was quite legal. The special act of Parliament was probably not even necessary. Washington was a commissioned Colonel of Militia (Virginia) and hence open to court martial for treason. But the act was easily passed in the aftermath of the collapse of the parliamentary opposition in the wake of the Yorktown debacle.

The question of the role of the aforementioned opposition is the subsequent events, and of Franklin's even stranger part in them—cloaked in his immunity as an accredited French diplomat—is the more tangled part of a most tangled tale. Their initial vociferous support for Washington; their equally precipitous withdrawal of same; their largely successful exploitation of public ambivalence over the execution—all suggest murky politicking of

a questionable nature by men more concerned with political advantage than the rights and wrongs of Washington's case. But
should we expect otherwise? Burke, of course, and the peers
(Amherst, Dartmouth, Conway, Effingham) stood firmly and
honourably by the beleaguered American as was consistent with
their opposition to the war throughout. (We have every reason
here in Dublin, and at Trinity especially, to be proud of Mr. Burke's
totally honourable—if at times a little verbose—part in an affair
where the English, and in particular my distant collateral relative
Fox, played such a dubious role.) Again, in the Commons, Mr.
Barré was perhaps without blemish. (It is curious to me that his
name should have been linked with that of the reprobate Wilkes
in naming a town in Pennsylvania; but those were early days.)
Wilkes in particular, and Fox with his talent for opposition and
great hunger for office, played a curious and suspect part, the
details of which will probably never be known. (Not that this prevents the wildest rumours being presented by so called popular
historians as undeniable facts. Macaulay has a lot to answer for. I
allude chiefly to the ridiculous rumour that through the offices of
Franklin, George Washington was actually conducted into the
presence of His Majesty King George the Third of England; that
the King offered him a "bargain": American independence—or
at least all that was promised in North's "conciliation bill"—in
return for a plea of guilty followed by a royal pardon; that Washington was persuaded by the radicals to refuse—with the terrible
consequences that ensued. It is impossible to apprehend what the
motives of the principals might have been in such a bizarre affair;
but many believe it took place. Unfortunately, the King's madness, Washington's death, and Franklin's disappearance have ob-
viated any possibility of ever knowing the truth. Tales of "hooded
figures being taken from the Tower by night" are the stuff of popular fantasy, nothing more.)

For us, however, as historians of the legal process, the saddest
lacuna of all is the almost complete absence of any record of the
trial itself. The burning of the Houses of Parliament left us nothing but the charred remains of the only court record that had
been allowed but had been locked away with a fifty-year secrecy
clause by yet another of those convenient acts of Parliament that
should not, but often do, bend if not actually break the constitutional process. The fact that there was, then, virtually no record

has not prevented the various protagonists from being variously loquacious on the subject; but with the three military judges having been sworn to silence and now dead, the prosecution and defense counsel having killed each other in a duel, and the other witnesses differing so much in what they remember, only the records themselves can give us the unvarnished truth.

The court's summing up (which we shall append) was published of course; but as for the rest we have only these fragments—bits and pieces of the actual court record that escaped the flames and have only now come to light (through circumstances I cannot detail but in which my position as a former parliamentary draftsman was not without consequence). Perhaps it is as well; we have been too close to the events until now to assess them with cool enough blood; but since, within the last year, the whole issue in another form has been revived with the unfortunate outbreak of hostilities between the "Union" and the newly described "Confederacy," it is perhaps timely to reconsider if we cannot learn from history.

Sympathy at the moment seems to be with the Confederacy; but we must ask ourselves, is their case at the bar of history any stronger than that of the colonies? Are we not in danger here of supporting so eagerly what we condemned so readily in 1782? Is armed rebellion against a duly constituted sovereign authority ever justified? And if so, for what reasons? Must we with the cynic agree that it is justified only if it prospers, for then "none dare call it treason"? And in what is essentially a civil war, what part should a foreign nation play? If we support the Confederacy are we not playing France to Mr. Davis's George Washington? These matters will continue to be debated. The trial of George Washington scarcely settles them. His remarkable closing speech—after, presumably on his attorney's advice, remaining silent throughout the trial—attests to a change of vision that his ordeal engendered. Perhaps there is time to learn from that?

But I stray from my task, and can only plead age and infirmity for these wanderings that are not relevant to our appreciation of the historical value and admitted veracity of the fragmentary records we have here. To straighten the record is our aim, and to this end a word must be said about the court and its principals.

The office of the Judge Advocate had appointed three military judges but had been careful not to pick any whose views were strong or controversial and who had been known to take any particular public stand on the issue of the rebellion. General the Earl of Thornton was Commander-in-Chief Northern Command, a sound officer, versed in military court procedure, known for his fair if severe conduct of trials. Major-General Lord Brooke was the most obscure of the three, and as one wag put it was only known to have strong opinions about recessing early for lunch. Sir George Campbell was the most interesting of the three. He had been knighted by King George II for his services against the Stuarts in '45, and presumably Thurlow at least assumed that all Campbells hated all rebels. Also, given the large contingent of Scots in the British forces, it was perhaps thought judicious to give them some representation in the court (or perhaps even to remind them of the awful consequences of rebellion for one last time). But Campbell was interesting. He was, as a result of his wounds, no longer on active service but was a very learned man, well read in philosophy and an admirer of Lord Kames. He had the very unmilitary habit of taking legal issues seriously, which must have caused the prosecution some bad moments even though they could have had no real qualms about the verdict.

I am forgetting, of course, the evidently spectacular appearance of Lord Cornwallis for the defense—on the plea that "the rules of war having been observed, a de facto state of war did exist" and that Washington should be treated as a prisoner of war. It was, naturally, disallowed; but evidently the army (that is, Cornwallis) was furious at being made to stage a military trial. They—and I think in particular Howe, who had clung throughout his generalship to his opposition to the war and insisted on his role as "peace commissioner"—wanted none of it, and had assumed the civil arm would "do the dirty work," as Cornwallis is reputed to have said. But again we are drifting into hearsay. (Why *is* it so tempting?) Oh yes! It very nearly misfired!

The choice of prosecutor was brilliant. Colonel the honourable John Hampshire was perhaps the best legal mind in the army, and certainly the *decanus* of cross-examiners. It is also rumoured that he had a passion for the conviction and death of Washington stemming from his friendship with Major André—the unfortunate young officer Washington felt obliged to hang for spying in the curious affair of Sir Benedict Arnold (of whom more later). Washington's motives were simple and even logical. He had to maintain that he was the commander of the army of a sovereign state, and André clearly was spying—he was in civilian dress for a start. Spies must be hanged if the war is a legal war. So André had to die. But not one of the Americans—Washington included—wanted to hang this charming young officer (who was said to have been engaged to the young lady from Philadelphia who subsequently married Arnold! More and more curious)! However, Hampshire never forgave Washington, and although no great issue was made of this at the trial, it seems, the undertones can be seen occasionally in Hampshire's questions.

(How strange these human passions are. How irrelevant to our task of dealing with the history of jurisprudence. Yet their fascination for us is surely something that the science of man—if, as Lord Melbourne said, it be a science—should explore. I find Mr. Mill remarkably unhelpful on this score; less so than Bishop Butler; and Mr. Darwin is, I confess, too new for me to assimilate the possible revolutionary consequences of his claims to truth.) But again I wander. Tiredness afflicts me easily these days; but since I am the only person with these records I must put them in some order, edit them, explain as best I can, which is so little.

Yes. Fenway. Got as a civil counsel for Washington (quite proper in a military trial) by Wilkes and Fox presumably, with Franklin in the background, as usual. Strange man Franklin: eloquent but untrustworthy, brilliant but dissolute. No wonder he was fond of the radicals. And Fox and Wilkes—always at each others throats and yet conniving together when they saw advantage, as in exploiting Washington. Can it be that there is a special "race" (Mr. Darwin?) of these radical politicians who seem to have so much more energy than the rest of us and so little scruple? Or is this just age speaking? But I wander. No. Fenway was picked because he was not one of the radicals. He was in fact a nephew of Amherst, which gave him some Whig credentials but on the other hand also put him close to the army (at least the Ordnance Department). He evidently, according to those who knew him before his untimely death (so young) used often to tell the story of the queer Granville Sharp, clerk at the Ordnance Office, who spent his life trying to free negro slaves at the ports. (If they spent one night—or was it two nights—on English soil they were legally free, I think. So he used to smuggle them off the boats, hide them, and rush them to court for a freedom order after two days.) Well, he had no fortune, no means, no patron, but he resigned from the Ordnance Office at the outbreak of the American hostilities because he wanted, as he said, "no part in this bad business." He was like so many—he was for Washington's acquittal but detested his keeping of slaves. "The yelps for liberty," said Dr. Johnson, "came loudest from the keepers of slaves." Hampshire says that somewhere in the trial as I recall. And now the proverbial chickens have come home to roost and the "free" keepers of slaves are fighting for "freedom" from the keepers of "free" America! Eheu! Eheu! But Fenway. Yes. Young. Yes. Brilliant. Less experienced, less cunning than Hampshire. My hand tires. The fragments are here. Ah yes, the prosecution.

It has been remarked, often with surprise, that it only produced two witnesses: The Massachusetts judge Jonathan Sewall, and, of course, General Sir Benedict Arnold, the hero. Why only two? There may have been other reasons, but one looms large: according to the treason act of King Henry VIII, only two were needed. That was all the law required: two witnesses that the accused had "made armed rebellion against the King in his realm; put himself at the head of rebellious forces; allied himself with the King's enemies; caused the King's justices to be slain…" and so on. (There is something in the act about "violating the King's consort and eldest unmarried daughter"—heaven knows why. Keen as they were to press the whole catalogue of charges, that one was, I believe, omitted, although "imagining the death of the King and the Royal Family" *was* left in. How on earth does one prove *that* for goodness sake?) Yes. Two witnesses.

The defense of course was out to prove that Washington's actions were *not* treason but self-defense against the crown (or Ministry) that had attacked lives and liberties, etc. A moot plea, one would have thought—Campbell thought so; but ultimately unpersuasive.

Still the fragments speak for themselves. Of the defense witnesses represented here one can only admit that while they spoke well enough for *themselves,* the courtroom was not their arena. True, John Adams was a lawyer, but on the witness stand this could only tell against him. He was too easily trapped into defending his own legalistic niceties. Jefferson was perhaps a great writer, certainly a great politician, perhaps a great philosopher (obviously influenced by Mr. Hutcheson), but he was not a good speaker. The defense, even so, probably saw these as preferable witnesses to Washington himself. It is well known that he mumbled and was embarrassed by his artificial, wooden teeth.

The fragments speak for themselves and so they must, for I must rest. I was scarcely born at the time and now am close to the end. I will put this and the fragments into the box. My dear, good Anne will know to open it should I not last until she returns from England. What a time for her aunt to sicken unto death! The world will know of it. Whether it will learn from it—but I philosophize again. A little madeira, then sleep. Why do I even write this, these tired words? A need to leave some mark of my own passing? For I feel I must pass very soon.

I neither fear it nor anticipate it with any great hope of a blessed life to come. I am simply tired. They shall go in the box now. My last task is done. It is not done well, but how often do we meet our own high standards? "Video meliora proboque: deteriora sequor." Then the wine. And sleep.

Augustin Fox M.A.
of Trinity College, Dublin;
and of the Inner Temple
Barrister-at-Law

# FRAGMENTS FROM THE BOX

## FRAGMENT 1. THE CHARGE AGAINST COLONEL WASHINGTON

George Washington, it is hereby charged against you that, not having the fear of Almighty God before your eyes, you did wilfully and knowingly engage in treasonous acts against your lawful sovereign His Majesty King George III. Namely, you did compass or imagine the death of the King and the Royal Family by vile plots and connivances; that you did levy war upon the King in his realm by placing yourself at the head of rebel armies; that you did adhere to the King's enemies within his realm, to whit the kings of France and Spain; that you did give aid and comfort to these enemies in his realm and elsewhere; that you have caused the King's justices to be slain; and that by these divers acts you have shown yourself to be a traitor against His Majesty deserving of no mercy but only of the full and terrible penalty of the law.

## FRAGMENT 2. THE EVIDENCE OF JUDGE JONATHAN SEWALL

(*Courtroom*)

THORNTON: State your name and place of residence.

SEWALL: Jonathan Sewall, formerly of the town of Cambridge, in the Massachusetts Bay Colony, now No. 1 Brompton Road, in the City of London.

THORNTON: Thank you. You may proceed, Colonel.

HAMPSHIRE: Mr. Sewall, before moving to London in 1775, you were in turn Solicitor General, Advocate General, and then

Attorney General of the Massachusetts Bay Colony, were you not?

SEWALL: I was, sir.

HAMPSHIRE: And now you hold the position of Chief Judge of the Admiralty of Lower Canada?

SEWALL: Of the Vice-Admiralty Bench, sir, of Halifax and Quebec, yes sir.

HAMPSHIRE: You were in Massachusetts during the years preceding the insurrection then, and in Boston during its state of siege?

SEWALL: I was, sir.

HAMPSHIRE: Do you recognize the accused?

SEWALL: I do. He is George Washington, self-styled General and commander of the rebel army.

(*Fenway rises.*)

FENWAY: My Lords, I object. The style of General was conferred on Colonel Washington by the Continental Congress; he was in no way self-styled.

THORNTON: I cannot entertain that objection. This court does not recognise any body calling itself a Continental Congress as having the right to bestow military titles in His Majesty's realms. That privilege belongs to His Majesty the King alone. The prisoner was a colonel of militia and since this is a court martial he can be accorded the courtesy of that title, duly and legally conferred, and none other. Proceed, Colonel Hampshire.

(*Defense sits.*)

HAMPSHIRE: (*Nods and smiles wryly at Fenway.*) On what occasions did you see *Colonel* Washington?

SEWALL: Oh, many, many. He was in and around with his troops the whole time. He was plainly visible.

HAMPSHIRE: And during this time attacks were made upon the King's troops?

SEWALL: Indeed, sir. Of course, sir. We all know that.

HAMPSHIRE: Indeed we do, Mr. Sewall, but we have to have it recorded and established here in court that it was so. How did you know that Colonel Washington styled himself "General"?

SEWALL: Why, Sir, we all knew. And when I was assistant to General Gage we received a letter from Washington signed

"General." Well, General Gage sent it back, sir, making the Court's point that he could not recognise such a title. And Washington answered that it had been bestowed on him by a higher authority than the King's.

(*Consternation in the courtroom*)

HAMPSHIRE: And whose, pray?

SEWALL: That of the people, he said.

(*More consternation*)

HAMPSHIRE: "The people" in this case did not include you and other loyal subjects starving to death in Boston as a result of Washington's designs, presumably?

SEWALL: Scarcely that, sir. There were many thousands trapped there who would rather have seen him with a rope around his neck than a ribbon. And many thousands outside the city who went silently in fear of their lives.

HAMPSHIRE: In other words, Washington was not a true representative of the people from whom he claimed to derive his authority for waging war against the King in his realm.

SEWALL: He represented a faction, sir, only. It was a noisy, brutal, and effective faction, but only a fool would claim it was "the people" of the Colonies.

HAMPSHIRE: How many were in this faction?

SEWALL: I can't say, sir. I can only say they had power and influence beyond their numbers. But I doubt a quarter of the population ever really followed them with conviction.

HAMPSHIRE: If Colonel Washington, then, did not derive his authority from a united people, presumably he would claim that he derived it from the so-called Continental Congress, which in turn derived it from the people?

SEWALL: That would be false. The Continental Congress was an illegal assembly, a contrivance of the Committees of Correspondence, who were also illegal. No one voted for them.

HAMPSHIRE: Did you know the members of the Massachusetts committee?

SEWALL: I did. James Otis, John Hancock, and Sam Adams were the ringleaders.

HAMPSHIRE: What of John Adams?

SEWALL: May I ask a question of the Court?

THORNTON: Certainly, Mr. Sewall.

SEWALL: Must I say anything that might incriminate John Adams?

You see, my lord, I know he is in this country and may soon
be on trial for his life. And much as I despise his politics, he
was and is my friend. Unless the Court finds it absolutely
necessary I would be obliged if…

THORNTON: Does Counsel wish to press this point?

HAMPSHIRE: No, my lord. We shall proceed, if you will, Mr.
Sewall, to the activities of the rebels prior to the insurrection.

SEWALL: Yes, sir. Of course. James Otis and his cabal, the "Caucus
Club" were the centre of it. Years before the Declaration of
Independence they set up what was virtually an opposition
government and took the law into their own hands, exploiting both legitimate and illegitimate grievances to rouse the
populace.

HAMPSHIRE: Legitimate grievances, Mr. Sewall? Like what, pray?

SEWALL: The Stamp Act, sir—an act about which we all felt
aggrieved. Governors Hutchinson and Bernard worked as
hard for its repeal, as did Otis and Sam Adams.

HAMPSHIRE: Their methods, however, were different, I imagine.

SEWALL: Indeed. Governor Hutchinson sent a humble petition to
Parliament; Adams intimidated the collectors. Governor
Hutchinson would have submitted regretfully had Parliament
insisted. Otis and Adams were determined to resist.

HAMPSHIRE: Why?

SEWALL: Because they were hell-bent on independency from the
start! They had no high principles—John Adams excepted—
but they had high ambition and thirst for power. They roused
the mob to intimidate the King's officers and to attack their
property, family, and lives. They tarred and feathered poor
John Malcolm twice! I escaped only by good fortune.

HAMPSHIRE: Escaped? Did you personally experience the results
of this activation of the mob?

SEWALL: I did. One day when I was in Boston, some fifty men and
boys—"Sons of Liberty," they called themselves, (and Mr.
Barré of the House of Commons has much to answer for in
coining that wretched phrase). Anyway, these noble defenders of liberty and free speech and the like surrounded my
house in Brattle Street in Cambridge, broke all of the windows, threatened the lives of my family, and only made off
when my poor terrified wife submitted to their demands for
the whole of my wine cellar.

(*Court is horrified.*)

BROOKE: Good God!

HAMPSHIRE: And what brutal and tyrannical things in the name of King and Parliament had you inflicted on these "Sons of Liberty," Mr. Sewall, to arouse their wrath so?

SEWALL: Nothing, of which I am aware, sir, except that, under various names, I wrote for the local papers articles on good government and vindications of the Governor's character.

HAMPSHIRE: And had the King's officers ever harassed them or attacked their persons or property?

SEWALL: Never.

HAMPSHIRE: Was Mr. Hancock among those who supported the Sons of Liberty?

SEWALL: Fervently, sir.

HAMPSHIRE: What dealings had you with him in legal matters?

SEWALL: As Advocate General, sir, I was asked to prosecute him on the grounds of information laid against him in the matter of smuggling.

HAMPSHIRE: Was he a well-known smuggler?

SEWALL: Indeed, yes, sir. Confessed and boastful of it.

HAMPSHIRE: How did you proceed?

SEWALL: I refused to proceed.

(*Murmurs in the court*)

SEWALL: There was not sufficient evidence; and the procedure of laying information, which bypassed a grand jury, was not sound.

HAMPSHIRE: Hardly the act of a dupe of the Customs Board.

SEWALL: No, sir. In fact, the Board of Customs complained to the Lords of the Treasury, but they upheld my decision.

HAMPSHIRE: But you did finally prosecute Hancock, did you not?

SEWALL: I was obliged to, Sir, by definite evidence being laid against him in regard to his ship, the *Liberty*.

HAMPSHIRE: And did Mr. Hancock, apprised by now of your just dealing, submit himself honestly to the process of law?

SEWALL: No, sir. He and Otis raised the mob again. The Commissioners and myself were endangered and threatened.

HAMPSHIRE: How did you proceed?

SEWALL: Well, sir, I proceeded as I had to. I allowed that we should proceed on the case *in rem* concerning the ship and the cargo aboard under Clause 29 of the Sugar Act, but on the libel *in personam* concerning the smuggling of wine, I refused to proceed on the grounds of insufficient evidence. It was...

HAMPSHIRE: Mr. Sewall, there are those here to whom these particular legal matters are a mystery; not least myself. (*Laughter in the court*) Can we say, however, that while allowing a lesser charge you refused to proceed on the graver charge for lack of evidence?

SEWALL: Exactly. The Attorney General of England then ordered me to proceed on the graver charge.

HAMPSHIRE: And you did so.

SEWALL: No, sir. I tendered my resignation to the Governor rather than do so. (*Murmurs in the court*) Eventually, however, the *in personam* libel—the graver charge—was dropped, and I withdrew my resignation.

HAMPSHIRE: Now, Mr. Sewall. You have been painted by the Sons of Liberty as one of the tyrants and villains against whom legitimate rebellion could be waged because of your brutal infringement of their liberties. Hancock and Otis and Adams inveigh against you, vilify and attack and intimidate you. Yet here we see you scrupulously attending to your office to the extent of refusing to prosecute Hancock on the grounds of insufficient evidence—even when it was in your power to do so and when higher authority ordered you to do so. Do you consider Hancock's response a fair response, Mr. Sewall?

SEWALL: Hardly that, sir.

HAMPSHIRE: What was the outcome for yourself, Mr. Sewall, of this sad business?

SEWALL: I had to flee Cambridge, sir, for the protection of Boston and General Gage.

HAMPSHIRE: Who was sent to Boston in response to persistent outrages of the kind you have described?

SEWALL: Indeed, yes, sir. I was one of those who pressed for his presence.

HAMPSHIRE: And your property?

SEWALL: My houses, my farm, my land were all taken and reassigned to others—illegally and without warrant—as were those of other loyal subjects of His Majesty who fled likewise.

HAMPSHIRE: Now, Mr. Sewall. This point is crucial. The defense intends to say that Washington placed himself at the head of an army composed of otherwise loyal Englishmen forced by a tyrannical government to defend themselves against abusive authority. You are a representative of that authority and well qualified to tell this court, in summary, what you make of that defense.

SEWALL: It is sheer hypocrisy, Sir. This was a calculated rebellion, led by men who wished to exercise ultimate power. To this end they seized on any excuse presented by legislation that was either precedented and unchallenged, or necessary, or even benign, to assert rights that never existed. They invented tyrannies that never were. They made of men like myself and the Governors scapegoats—men who had dealt them only justice and kindness, despite their open and confessed illegal acts. They roused the populace and formed illegal assemblies; they terrorised and intimidated loyal citizens; they molested the King's troops, and when these defended themselves, they dubbed them murderers.

HAMPSHIRE: Who provoked the first shots in this affair?

SEWALL: The rebels at Lexington, sir. The King's troops were on legitimate business seeking to destroy illegal powder supplies. They were resisted. The rebels will say they were defending liberties, but what liberty is it, sir, to hoard arms in order to fight your legal Sovereign? (*to the judges*) They were not concerned with defense, my lords. Against whom were they defending themselves when they terrorized my wife and children and robbed me of my wine? What tyranny had I, or thousands like me who were forced to flee, exercised over them? No, my lords; they were hell-bent, my lords, hell-bent on power that could only be achieved through independency—through armed rebellion and the murder and intimidation of loyal subjects, forcing us to flee to strange places—to Canada, to England, to New York even! No, my lords, defenders they were not, but tyrants of their own kind ever ready to cry "Liberty" when their designs for power were thwarted.

HAMPSHIRE: Mr. Sewall, if the action of Colonel Washington and his associates was not a justified defense of liberties against tyranny, but a true premeditated rebellion, then from when do you date the commencement of this rebellion?

SEWALL: From the day, sir, that the *Mayflower* set sail from Plymouth!

HAMPSHIRE: Thank you, Mr. Sewall. I have no further questions.

THORNTON: Mr. Fenway. Do you wish to cross-examine?

FENWAY: Yes, indeed, my Lord.

(*Fenway rises.*)

FENWAY: Mr. Sewall, you must understand that it is George Washington on trial here, not the Massachusetts Cabal. I did not intervene during your testimony because it seemed to me that their lordships would see it to be self-evidently irrelevant. I will accept that a faction in Massachusetts comported itself as you describe, but would you tell the court what evidence you have that George Washington was, to quote your words, "hell-bent on independency from the start."

SEWALL: Why, sir, the whole Virginia clique was as bad as the Massachusetts Cabal. Lee, Jefferson, Washington—it was the two cliques between them that led the rest by the nose. There is no distinguishing between them.

FENWAY: I repeat, Mr. Sewall, what *evidence* have you of Washington's rebellious intentions?

SEWALL: His intentions were clear enough. Why—when the Congress was in suspense and a vote for independence was in the balance—what did Washington do? He arrived, sir, in full blue regimentals of the Virginia militia, sir. To impress the recalcitrants.

FENWAY: But that was late in the day, Mr. Sewall. That was after the King's troops had arrived, battles had been fought, and a de facto state of belligerency had come into existence. What evidence is there of long-standing rebellious intent on the part of the prisoner?

SEWALL: Well, sir, how do I know, sir? What goes on in a man's head is his business, sir. I am not privy to that. His intention can be judged by his actions, sir, and they were plain enough.

FENWAY: Not plain enough to establish premeditation, Mr. Sewall. I must insist...

HAMPSHIRE: And so must I, my lords. This course of questioning is irrelevant. The witness cannot know what the prisoner secretly intended. He can only report his actions, which he has done.

THORNTON: Really, Mr. Fenway. This line of questioning seems to be going nowhere. Could we not press on?

CAMPBELL: My lord, I feel the Defense may have a point. (*To Fenway*) As I understand it, Mr. Fenway, you are saying that there is no evidence that Colonel Washington intended rebellion before the advent of the troops, and that after that he merely intended to act defensively? I am not agreeing that this is so, but am asking if this is your point.

FENWAY: It is indeed, Sir George.

CAMPBELL: Aye, well. A fine point.

THORNTON: Too fine, perhaps. Mr. Fenway, please press on.

FENWAY: Yes, my lord. Mr. Sewall, you have made much of how you, an impartial administrator of justice, were abused by the radicals in Boston.

SEWALL: Quite so.

FENWAY: And it was only as an impartial servant of justice that you refused to prosecute John Hancock?

SEWALL: Of course.

FENWAY: Would you tell the court your relationship of kinship to John Hancock.

SEWALL: Well—he—he is the husband of my wife's sister. My brother-in-law. But…

(*Hampshire rises.*)

HAMPSHIRE: My lords, I object!

(*Thornton uses the gavel.*)

THORNTON: Order, gentlemen! Mr. Fenway, that question is irrelevant, surely?

FENWAY: Well, my lord…

CAMPBELL: Oh, I think not, my lord. Credibility of witness is an issue.

HAMPSHIRE: Sir George! The witness is, like yourself, a judge!

CAMPBELL: A guarantee of very little as concerns rectitude, Colonel. Some of the biggest rogues in history have been judges. I am but a judge *pro tempore*, Colonel. No. Credibility is an issue.

SEWALL: But, my lords, he has done nothing but show I was related to Hancock. Good God, sirs, in Massachusetts everyone is related to everyone else!

THORNTON: For pity's sake, gentlemen, let us proceed. Mr. Fenway.

FENWAY: Yes, my lord. Mr. Sewall. Again you have painted yourself as a defender of truth in writing pamphlets and articles in defense of the Governors and the Crown.

SEWALL: Indeed. Yes. I did my best.

FENWAY: And were you not well rewarded by offices and remuneration for your pains?

SEWALL: I rose—achieved advancement—by merit, sir.

FENWAY: Yes. But once advanced you devoted much time and ink to the defense of your employers.

(*Hampshire rises.*)

HAMPSHIRE: My lords…

THORNTON: Yes, Colonel, you object to this attempt to paint Judge Sewall as a paid lackey of the government, and so do I.

CAMPBELL: Credibility, my lord. Credibility.

THORNTON: Mr. Fenway. You have made your point. May we proceed to matters of substance?

FENWAY: My lord, I would if there were any. We have heard much of the activity of the Massachusetts rebels—so-called—but nothing of the prisoner's involvement with them until he took command of the troops outside Boston.

THORNTON: And is that not enough?

FENWAY: No, my lords. No. Not if premeditation is the issue. This witness has proven nothing except that he is a loyal, paid servant of the Crown. He has produced no evidence that Colonel Washington "imagined the death of the King," contrived rebellion, or anything such, merely that he commanded the American armies, which no one is disputing.

HAMPSHIRE: My lords, is there anything else to establish? A man's intentions are not at issue here. His actions are.

CAMPBELL: Well, now, Colonel. If in a case of murder, for example, one is pleading self-defense, then intentions do enter into consideration…

THORNTON: Yes, yes, Sir George. But we cannot digress on the law of murder just now. Mr. Fenway, please come to the point.

FENWAY: I have one more point, my lord. Mr. Sewall, you have agreed that Washington took his commission from the Continental Congress. (*Sewall nods.*) Now, you have pictured this body as a cabal of cabals. If it was indeed, sir, a contrivance of the radicals, is it not strange that it was so divided? That it took so long to reach a decision? That it petitioned the King so often?

SEWALL: Yes, yes. There were others than radicals, of course. I said they were a minority. But the congress was illegal, sir. What it argued about was not rebellion—it encouraged that openly. What it argued about, what it was divided about, was independence. And Virginia and Massachusetts pressed and bullied the others to accept *that*.

FENWAY: This was then not just a rebel cabal, but a representative deliberative assembly that argued its way to decisions— including the decision to have George Washington as its Commander- in-Chief ?

SEWALL: It was an illegal assembly, sir. It countenanced armed rebellion without debate. Its petitions were sops to the loyalists, devices to gain time. And Washington was deep into this, sir, deep into it! He will surely hang for his treachery!

( *Thornton gavels for order.*)

THORNTON: Mr. Sewall. If you please, sir, no more speeches. Your opinion of the prisoner is not at issue; only the facts.

FENWAY: My lord, I submit there *are* no facts of any substance. I will, therefore, not weary the court further with empty accusations. I have no more questions.

THORNTON: Thank you Mr. Fenway. Mr. Sewall, you may step down. Gentlemen, should we proceed to the next witness?

BROOKE: Oh surely not, my lord. It is close to lunchtime already.

THORNTON: In deference to your lordship, court is adjourned until two o'clock.

BROOKE: Perhaps two-thirty…?

THORNTON: Two-thirty… ( *Gavels*)


## FRAGMENT 3. THE EVIDENCE OF GENERAL

## SIR BENEDICT ARNOLD

( *Courtroom*)

USHER: Call General Sir Benedict Arnold!

SOLDIER: General Sir Benedict Arnold!

( *Arnold enters in full regalia.*)

USHER: Do you swear by Almighty God that the evidence you shall give before this court will be the truth, the whole truth, and nothing but the truth?

ARNOLD: I do.

THORNTON: Please state your name and rank.

ARNOLD: Benedict Arnold, Knight Commander of the Order of St. Michael and St. George, General of his Majesty's forces.

THORNTON: Thank you, Sir Benedict. Proceed, Colonel.

HAMPSHIRE: Sir Benedict. Painful as it may be for you, we must recapitulate something of your involvement with the rebel armies and their commander.

(*Arnold nods assent.*)

HAMPSHIRE: You were, before returning to your allegiance to the Crown, an officer in the rebel army. What rank did you hold?

ARNOLD: That of Brigadier General, sir.

HAMPSHIRE: And in that capacity—with that high rank—you were much involved with the prisoner?

ARNOLD: Yes, sir. He was my Commander-in-Chief.

HAMPSHIRE: For the record, then, could you name some of the occasions on which you saw him in command of rebel troops?

ARNOLD: Oh, many, sir. Outside Boston during the siege. At Valley Forge in Pennsylvania where he held the American army together before his brilliant attack on Trenton.

HAMPSHIRE: That will suffice, Sir Benedict. In particular, sir, we would like you to specify for the court whether he, to quote the words of the charge, "conspired with the King's enemies within his realm." That is, allied with the French.

ARNOLD: That he did. Why, when he almost surprised me and I had to flee to the *Vulture* there on Hudson's River, he was on his way to treat with the French. And all the while I was Military Governor of Philadelphia, he was deep into negotiations with them. It was this, sir, in fact, that made me disgusted with the American cause.

HAMPSHIRE: Before we get to that, Sir Benedict, perhaps you would outline the history of your involvement.

ARNOLD: Certainly. Well, sir, before the war started I had been an apothecary. Not much profit in that, y'know, so I turned to one of the most profitable and respectable trades open in America.

HAMPSHIRE: What was that, pray?

ARNOLD: Smuggling, Colonel, smuggling.

(*Murmurs in the court*)

HAMPSHIRE: A respectable trade, Sir Benedict?

ARNOLD: Why, yes. Every other man was a smuggler, and those

who weren't profited by it anyway. I made a good living until the British Parliament began to tighten its laws and send out all those revenue cutters and customs officers. That hit us all hard, sir, very hard, and we didn't like it. We didn't like it a bit. And the local Sons of Liberty seized on our dissatisfaction and persuaded us to resist the tyranny of those who wished to invoke the law to our disadvantage.

HAMPSHIRE: You were not, then, much concerned with the arguments about rights and liberty and taxation and sovereignty?

ARNOLD: No, Colonel. If you're an ordinary American, not educated, not of high society, you don't have the time to argue about those things. You're busy making a living. We didn't say, "What are our rights according to the laws of nature?" We said, "My friends have been abused; my pocket's been hurt; I won't stand for it."

HAMPSHIRE: But surely there must have been some qualms about the legality of rebellion? About allegiance to the King?

ARNOLD: Well, Colonel, not much y'know. Ordinary Americans like myself didn't have much to do with England. Not like the gentry with their books and fashions. It was far away. We had no dealings with it. We were Americans. Anyway, we never reckoned we were disloyal to the King. I would never have signed the Declaration of Independence, sir; but like John Dickinson who refused to sign yet joined the continental armies, I decided to fight back when the ministry sent troops over to attack us. We resented that, bitterly, but we didn't so much blame the King for it.

HAMPSHIRE: Then independence was not one of your motives, Sir Benedict?

ARNOLD: No, sir. Not mine. It could well have been others, though. You see, they saw—Ben Franklin and the rest—they saw that America would grow—become a big rich nation. And they wanted to run it themselves—not have it run from Britain. So all these regulations irked them. No expansion westward, all trade to be with Britain, and the like. They wanted rid of these restrictions. But that wasn't in my head, sir. No. Like the prince of smugglers himself, John Hancock, I wanted the cutters off my back and not much else. I was only an apothecary turned smuggler then—nothing to expect from England and much to expect from my clients, my fellow Americans.

HAMPSHIRE: But you nevertheless served with great distinction in the rebel army, moving rapidly to high command, leading attacks in Canada, and defeating Burgoyne at Saratoga. So much we know, Sir Benedict. Now, tell the court about your reasons for deserting the rebel cause.

ARNOLD: Well, Colonel. As I said, I wasn't ever much concerned with the higher issues. I thought the war'd be short, the British army'd go home, and we'd all get back to smuggling again. (Laughter) But no. It dragged on. And then independence became the big issue and I'd never liked that much. Then on top of that came the French alliance. Now, sir, to fight amongst ourselves—among Englishmen—was one thing. That was a family quarrel, you might say. But to ally with the Frenchies, sir, the very enemies that English and Americans had stood together to defeat not twenty years before! That was not fighting fair, I thought. I couldn't take that.

HAMPSHIRE: Were you alone?

ARNOLD: Good God, no. Robert Morris, who signed the Declaration, was against it, and Charles Lee, too, but we were drowned out. By this time the fanatics had hold, and when we wanted to treat with the peace commissioners, we were shouted down.

HAMPSHIRE: Was this when you began negotiations with Major André later murdered at George Washington's order—to return to your true allegiance?

ARNOLD: Yes, sir.

CAMPBELL: Sir Benedict, I wonder if you would indulge my curiosity a moment. You signed your letters to André "Monk," I understand. Why was that?

ARNOLD: Why? Well, Sir George, because I admired General Monk of Cromwell's army who returned to his true allegiance—to Charles II—for the same reasons.

CAMPBELL: What reasons, Sir Benedict?

ARNOLD: Well, Monk saw that the "model army" that arose to defend English liberties against the King had become a worse tyrant than the King himself. The same was true of the American Congress. They were no better than the worst of the

Royal Governors. Dishonest, corrupt, riddled with faction, and out for their own privileges—while my men and I suffered at the front. They were not what they appeared to be in their solemn declarations. They were but a bunch of mean, petty-minded speculators. Why, even Washington wrote to me to say that he would do well out of the war since land prices would rise. But Washington was honester than most of 'em. Behaved well enough to me, which is more than I can say about the rest.

CAMPBELL: I see. Thank you, Sir Benedict.

HAMPSHIRE: Nevertheless, Washington did conspire with the French?

ARNOLD: Yes. And for me that was the last straw.

HAMPSHIRE: Was it not also treason?

ARNOLD: The court must decide that.

HAMPSHIRE: But surely, General, you must have thought that it was when you contemplated and rejected the French alliance?

ARNOLD: I suppose so. But it wasn't the treason so much—it was just that it stuck in my throat to join the Frenchies in killing Englishmen.

HAMPSHIRE: Be that as it may, Sir Benedict, others had opinions about treason. What might the Americans have done to you if, after you returned to our side, they had won the war and taken you prisoner?

ARNOLD: Hanged me for a traitor, I suppose. But they didn't win, sir. We did.

HAMPSHIRE: Quite so, Sir Benedict. Quite so. No more questions, my lords. (*Hampshire sits.*)

THORNTON: Mr. Fenway?

FENWAY: Sir Benedict: Were you not originally a zealous supporter of the American cause?

ARNOLD: At first, sir, yes, I was.

FENWAY: Did you not take the initiative in forcing the Massachusetts assembly to let you attack Fort Ticonderoga—even when it was clear Congress would not approve the attack?

ARNOLD: I did. I don't deny it.

FENWAY: Did you not finance this expedition yourself?

ARNOLD: I did. I expected reimbursement.

FENWAY: Were you not commonly regarded as the best general

the Americans had—even by the British?

ARNOLD: I suppose I was. It was not an incorrect judgment, though I'd put Washington a close second.

FENWAY: And despite your zeal, your initiative, your investment and your reputation, were you not repeatedly disappointed by Congress and your colleagues?

ARNOLD: I was disappointed, yes, by the whole bunch except for Washington.

FENWAY: Did they not pass you over for promotion, fail to pay your expenses, deprive you of your seniority?

ARNOLD: Yes, they did...

FENWAY: Were you not court-martialed for your conduct as Military Governor of Philadelphia?

ARNOLD: At my own request. To clear my name.

FENWAY: And what was the verdict?

ARNOLD: I was found guilty of two trivial charges, and sentenced to a reprimand.

FENWAY: A reprimand? From whom?

ARNOLD: The Commander-in-Chief. General Washington.

FENWAY: The prisoner.

ARNOLD: Yes.

FENWAY: Thank you. Now, then. Was it not indeed from that date that you decided to plan revenge on them all and change sides?

ARNOLD: Is that what you're getting at? No! Damn it, sir. From before that, sir.

FENWAY: Can you prove that?

ARNOLD: Well. How can I prove it? My wife destroyed my letters when I fled. André burned my notes. But what you're getting at is wrong. My reason was the French Alliance.

FENWAY: The French Alliance? Not bitterness, thwarted ambition, disappointed hopes?

ARNOLD: No. None of these.

FENWAY: If you were against the alliance, Sir Benedict, why did you request a loan from the French Ambassador?

ARNOLD: That? That was a private matter. Congress withheld my money. I had to pay my debts. I didn't care where the money came from. I would've borrowed from the Devil himself.

FENWAY: Of course, one way to avoid debts was to flee to the other side.

ARNOLD: I resent that, sir. That's not why I went. It was the alliance. You're insinuating it was thwarted ambition, but look at the facts: After I had begun negotiations with André my seniority was restored and Washington offered me command of the left wing of the army—the cavalry and light foot. I declined, sir, because of my promise to André and Sir Henry Clinton to take command at West Point.

FENWAY: But only after Clinton had offered you money, a title, and high rank, no?

HAMPSHIRE: My lords, I must object. The witness is not on trial.

THORNTON: Yes, yes, Colonel Hampshire. I think, Mr. Fenway, that your cross-examination does indeed border on harassment.

CAMPBELL: Well, my lord, he has a point, and should perhaps be allowed to make it.

THORNTON: Yes, yes, Sir George, but in a civil fashion.

CAMPBELL: Well, we could scarcely expect a barrister to do it in a military fashion, my lord.

(*Laughter*)

(*Thornton gavels.*)

THORNTON: Gentlemen, please. Mr. Fenway, do you wish to question the witness further?

FENWAY: One more question, my lord. Sir Benedict, were you subpoenaed to appear at this trial?

ARNOLD: No.

FENWAY: In other words, you appeared voluntarily to give evidence against a man who had defended you and treated you honourably always, and who is now fighting for his life.

(*Hampshire starts to interrupt.*)

FENWAY: Thank you, Sir Benedict, that is all.


## FRAGMENT 4: THE EVIDENCE OF MR. JOHN ADAMS

(*Courtroom. John Adams is in the witness box.*)

FENWAY: Mr. Adams, you are by profession a lawyer?

ADAMS: And a farmer, sir, like my father before me.

FENWAY: Lawyer and farmer, then. You are a graduate of Harvard College, and you have been prominent in legal circles in Boston and Massachusetts. You were a delegate to the Continental Congress, and under the brief independent regime of the American States, you were appointed Chief Justice of Massachusetts?

ADAMS: Yes, sir. I was. It was probably the greatest honour of my life.

(*Murmurs in court*)

FENWAY: You had previously been offered the post of Advocate General of Massachusetts Bay Colony, I believe, by Governor Hutchinson and Attorney General Sewall.

ADAMS: I had, sir, but I declined.

FENWAY: Why was that, Mr. Adams?

ADAMS: By that time, sir, matters had come to a head between those of us who felt the Royal officers were acting oppressively and those who, like Jonathan Sewall, believed them to be acting legitimately. It would have been hypocritical of me to accept a position from those I was bound to oppose on principle.

FENWAY: We shall return to the question of your opposition, Mr. Adams. But first I would like to ask you why, if you were so opposed to the actions of the Crown, you undertook to defend the British soldiers involved in what has become known as the Boston Massacre?

ADAMS: Because, Mr. Fenway, I love justice. The mob and the fanatics would have sacrificed those innocent men for sheer revenge. I could not stand by and see that happen in my beloved commonwealth, which had always cherished the principle of justice and the rule of law.

FENWAY: And would you remind the court of the outcome of that by now notorious trial?

ADAMS: A jury of twelve of my fellow countrymen acquitted the soldiers on the grounds of self-defense. Two were found guilty of manslaughter and subjected to a minor penalty.

(*Murmurs in the court*)

FENWAY: Thank you, Mr. Adams. Now let us proceed to your knowledge of the prisoner. You had, I believe, a direct hand in his elevation to Commander-in-Chief?

ADAMS: Yes, indeed. I proposed him for that position. My cousin, Samuel Adams, was the seconder.

FENWAY: It is charged, Mr. Adams, that his acceptance of that post makes him guilty of the crime of treason—of which, by implication, you must be an accomplice. What do you say to this charge?

THORNTON: I must remind the witness that he need not say anything that might incriminate him. Do you understand that, Mr. Adams?

ADAMS: Yes, my lord. But since I am no more guilty of treason than George Washington, I am not afraid to speak my mind.

THORNTON: Very well. Proceed, Mr. Fenway.

FENWAY: Thank you, my lord. Mr. Adams?

ADAMS: No, sir, it was not treason. George Washington's appointment and his acceptance of command were among many actions taken out of dire and desperate necessity, and in great sorrow. You must understand how we stood at that time. We were proud of our liberties, our rights as enshrined in our charters, our common law, and our traditions of responsible self-government. We were proud also of our ties of loyalty and kinship with Britain, but these ties had been strained. Over the years attack after attack had been made by the ministers upon our liberties, which we had resisted, as was our right through all legal and constitutional means open to us. Since we had no representation in Parliament, we resisted by resolutions, by petitions to the King and Parliament, and by actions in the courts. We were rebuffed at every turn. In moments of anger, sir, some of our people responded with excesses of which none of us wholly approved, although we sympathized with their frustrations. As a result, our port was closed, our manufactures ruined, troops were sent against us. In short, we were treated like naughty children rather than responsible adults who had for generations governed their own affairs. We are a proud people, Mr. Fenway, and we would not submit. In the end, unhappily, as you know, fighting broke out, our people were killed, and we rose in arms to defend ourselves. Not to sever ourselves from Britain, but simply to say to the ministers: We will not be enslaved without a struggle. By the time we met in Philadelphia for the second time, the ministry was sending a fleet and an army of foreign mercenaries against us. We were at war. We had no choice but to appoint a commander, and I proposed George Washington. It is not treason, sir, to save one's life and liberty from attack. If I am attacked by the law, I defend myself in the courts, and none call it treason. If I am attacked with a gun, I can only defend myself with a gun, and what, sir, makes that into treason?

(*Murmurs in the court*)

FENWAY: Thank you, Mr. Adams. Mr. Sewall has said, however, that there was a faction "hell-bent on independency from the start." Were you of that faction? Or is Mr. Sewall not telling the truth?

ADAMS: Jonathan Sewall never told a lie in his life, sir! He has a different view of things from mine—but that is to be expected. In answer to your question: there was a faction, very small, to whom the idea of independency was sweet. I was not one of them, until it was too late to contemplate anything else. But you must remember, Sir, that we were a very political people. We had our conservatives, our moderates, our radicals, our zealots, and of course our mob. No Londoner needs to be lectured on the nature of mobs. But one cannot characterize the whole of a people by its extremes. I would certainly not represent all the English as raving radicals or mobsters because there are some radicals and there is a mob.

(*Murmurs of assent in court*)

FENWAY: But in the end, Mr. Adams, the break did come. You did declare for independence—and you and Washington were firm for it. It has been argued here that this was your aim all along. Is this so?

ADAMS: No, Sir. Again we were forced into that position. Our petitions had been ignored. And Parliament and the King declared us to be "in open rebellion." We were to be treated as enemies, our ships as enemy prizes. Armies were to be sent to subdue us. What choice had we, Sir? It was they who declared us independent long before we so declared ourselves.

(*Murmurs*)

FENWAY: Is not a long history of disobedience of the King's laws—particularly on taxation—evidence of premeditation and intent to rebel?

ADAMS: No, Sir. The issue is not one of obedience by one party to another, but the obedience of both to the Constitution, and the established practices, written and unwritten, by which the colonies and the mother country had lived in harmony. I would say, Sir, that it is fairer to say that the King and Parliament disobeyed the Constitution, than that we disobeyed the King and Parliament. They, Sir, were the rebels—not we.

(*Murmurs*)

ADAMS: No one considers the Glorious Revolution of 1688 treasonable, and then the British threw out a Monarch who abused their rights. The Americans today did no more than their English cousins had done. They defended the Constitution against attack.

FENWAY: But the issue will be raised, Mr. Adams: are subjects ever justified in making such judgments for themselves—albeit they sometimes succeed by force in doing so?

ADAMS: I would say they are not so justified if they act lightly, without just cause, or for personal gain. This was not true of the Americans. Only after great deliberation, many petitions, and much suffering did they take the irrevocable step; and when they did so, it was solely to protect the principles of liberty and self-government at the heart of the Constitution— principles that are the birthright of all Englishmen.

(*Applause*)

(*Thornton gavels.*)

FENWAY: Thank you, Mr. Adams. I have no more questions.

(*Hampshire rises.*)

HAMPSHIRE: Mr. Adams. Might I say, however much I might disagree with your arguments, I admire greatly the clarity and skill with which they were presented. I think we are all grateful that the defense has been so ably served.

ADAMS: Thank you, Sir.

HAMPSHIRE: I have listened, not unmoved, to your statements of the high principles on which the rebels acted. If indeed this were the case, then I think there is not a man here who would not accord some measure of sympathy to you and your fellow Americans in your distress and your struggle for the preservation of your liberties. Your convincing precision in these matters has laid the issue squarely before us, to wit: When the King or his ministers make vicious and tyrannical incursions into the liberties of the people—liberties guaranteed by the Constitution—then the people can, nay, must resist. Is that not so?

ADAMS: Yes, Sir. That is what I argued.

HAMPSHIRE: And argued brilliantly, Mr. Adams. So let us examine some of these unconstitutional incursions into your liberties, shall we? Perhaps, Mr. Adams, you could, with your precise, legal mind, enlighten the court on that burning issue that sent your countrymen flying for their muskets—the issue of internal versus external taxation. For was that not one of the most tyrannical and most resisted of the evil measures? Tell us, Sir, why was internal taxation so much worse than external, and what, pray, was the difference? Remember, Sir, we are not all lawyers, just plain men of common sense.

ADAMS: The distinction was an important one, Sir. We had always accepted the right of Parliament to tax us *externally,* that is to lay taxes on goods coming from abroad and the like; but this had to be distinguished from their right to tax us *internally,* that is, to raise revenue directly from us by taxes on, for example, our legal documents. We had always understood it to be our right, not Parliament's, to decide on direct, internal taxation.

HAMPSHIRE: Now, Mr. Adams. Forgive me if I am confused. To me, Sir, a tax is a tax. It takes money from my pocket. Now, Sir, on your principle, if the Government had put huge taxes on imported goods, that would have been very well, but even a *minuscule* tax on documents would be an occasion for rebellion? Forgive me if I find this odd.

ADAMS: You may find it odd, sir, we did not. It was a matter *of* principle…

HAMPSHIRE: Ah, yes, Mr. Adams, principle, Mr. Adams. I have yet to see, though, quite what the principle is.

ADAMS: Sir: If you put a tax on goods, I may or may not buy them, thus avoiding the tax if I choose. If you tax me directly I cannot avoid paying.

HAMPSHIRE: But if the external tax is on necessities, Mr. Adams, am I not equally forced to pay it? And what of the post office that you accepted? Are not charges for postal stamps a tax?

ADAMS: No, sir, they are a *quantum meruit;* a payment for service rendered.

HAMPSHIRE: But in effect, Mr. Adams, the distinction is a fine one, and the external taxes could be more burdensome, in fact, than the rather trivial internal ones?

ADAMS: They could be, yes…

HAMPSHIRE: So it was, at its extremities, something of a legal quibble, eh, Mr. Adams?

ADAMS: Well, sir, it was much argued and the fine points...

HAMPSHIRE: Quibbled over, Mr. Adams. Tell me, sir, how many of the King's subjects died in this war?

ADAMS: I think between twenty and thirty thousand, Colonel.

HAMPSHIRE: And for a quibble, Mr. Adams—for a quibble? Let us go on. When Lord Townshend accepted the quibble, sir, when he proposed only external taxes, then, sir, the patient defenders of liberty switched horses, did they not? Could you explain to us, again, Mr. Adams, why you did not accept Lord Townshend's capitulation on this great issue of principle?

ADAMS: Because, sir, Lord Townshend made the external taxes answer to all the purposes of internal taxes.

HAMPSHIRE: Ah, the cunning of the man! Caught you out, did he? Well, well, well.

(*Laughter*)

HAMPSHIRE: And how did he do this, pray, Mr. Adams?

ADAMS: By making taxes that appeared to be in regulation of trade in fact answer to the purpose of taxes for raising revenue. I had always...

HAMPSHIRE: Hold a moment, sir! Did I not detect yet another high principle? What was it—regulation of trade versus raising of revenue? The former just and the latter vicious and tyrannical? Is that right, Mr. Adams? And how does it relate to the previous quibble—I mean distinction, sir?

ADAMS: The distinction is common enough in English law, sir. It is not an American invention.

HAMPSHIRE: But it was seized upon, was it not? When Townshend's acts were repealed and you were satisfied on that count, you had to turn to this other quibble lest the momentum of your movement for independence—your attempts to work up the indignation of the colonies—was lost, eh, Mr. Adams?

ADAMS: No, sir. It was a genuine issue of principle.

HAMPSHIRE: Of principle, Mr. Adams! Yes, of principle! A principle so obscure that even your precise legal mind cannot make it clear to us. How many deaths, Mr. Adams, in this conflict?

ADAMS: I said, sir, about 30,000, 1 think.

HAMPSHIRE: All went to their deaths, Mr. Adams, because of principles so obscure we cannot make sense of them? When His Majesty's Government generously allows you the first point you scuttle to a second in desperation. Is this not evidence that you had decided to rebel and were deliberately searching for excuses?

ADAMS: There were other causes, sir, many other causes.

HAMPSHIRE: Mr. Adams, there had better have been. Was one of these great causes the wicked, tyrannical, and vicious tax on legal documents known as the Stamp Act?

ADAMS: It was.

HAMPSHIRE: What was the purpose of the Stamp Act?

ADAMS: To raise revenue.

HAMPSHIRE: Ah, yes, and therefore iniquitous under Quibble Number Two. What was this revenue for?

ADAMS: Ostensibly to pay for the expenses of the French War.

HAMPSHIRE: Ostensibly? Were there not such expenses?

ADAMS: Yes, but we had contributed, and if more was needed it should have been left to our assemblies to vote it.

HAMPSHIRE: And it was iniquitous of Parliament to try to raise some trivial sum through stamps?

ADAMS: We judged it so.

HAMPSHIRE: All of you, Mr. Adams?

ADAMS: What do you mean, sir?

HAMPSHIRE: Did not Dr. Franklin attempt to obtain a position as distributor of stamps for his friend Mr. Hughes? Was this testimony to the act's iniquity? And did not "General" Lee, now awaiting his own trial, try to obtain such a post?

ADAMS: I cannot be responsible for the misjudgment of my friends. These things were not always clearly appreciated.

HAMPSHIRE: Not clearly appreciated by the great defenders of constitutional liberty, Mr. Adams? Not clearly appreciated? And on the basis of this lack of clarity, 30,000 men went to their miserable deaths?

ADAMS: There were other causes.

HAMPSHIRE: Indeed there would have to have been, Mr. Adams. The great cause of the tax on tea, perhaps. Was that an internal versus external trade problem or a revenue versus regulation quibble, Mr. Adams?

ADAMS: It was the general principle of taxation...

HAMPSHIRE: Ah, the general principle…But, Mr. Adams, was it not the case that this wicked and tyrannical parliament and this unconstitutional monarch decided on a plan to produce for their tea—loving subjects cheaper tea?

ADAMS: The tea was cheaper, yes.

HAMPSHIRE: And did not the people in the colonies cheerfully pay the tax?

ADAMS: Most paid.

HAMPSHIRE: Until the famous Boston Tea Party when several of your fellow defenders of liberty and rights dumped this providentially cheap beverage into the sea. Did not your representative here in London, Dr. Franklin, express horror at the extremity of the act? Did he not offer to pay for the tea from his own fortune?

ADAMS: I cannot say.

HAMPSHIRE: Well, I can, Sir. And this tyrant, sir, this wicked usurper of rights, this infamous King, asked only one question of his minister when he heard of Boston's rebellious act—"Will my people in Boston," he asked, "be able to get their tea?"

(*Murmurs*)

ADAMS: His response then was strange, for he occupied the town and took away our liberties.

HAMPSHIRE: And what else was any chief magistrate—as you would say—of any commonwealth to do when his authority was flouted on such flimsy grounds by those who clearly intended, given cause or no, to defy his laws and destroy the property of his subjects? Perhaps your friend Mr. Hancock was afraid that his profitable smuggling might be undermined by such generosity from the King and Parliament.

ADAMS: That was never an issue with me, or, more to the point, with General Washington.

HAMPSHIRE: Then what was, Mr. Adams? What was? So far we have isolated no issues that do not, on examination, slip from our grasp like wet soap. What issues? Taxes? Tea? These are mere excuses, sir, and when robbed of one you seize another. What issues? Liberty? Rights? These are empty words, sir, empty words used to rouse passion in simple minds by men unscrupulous in their lust for power. If these are the best you can produce in the way of causes and justifications for rebellion against the Crown, Mr. Adams, then your sanctimonious claims to be a defender of constitutional liberties are patently false. I have no more to ask.

THORNTON: In that case . . .

BROOKE: My lord. . .?

THORNTON: Yes of course, my lord. We shall reconvene after lunch. (*Gavels*)

## FRAGMENT 5. THE EVIDENCE OF MR. THOMAS JEFFERSON

(*Courtroom. Jefferson is on the stand.*)

FENWAY: Would you state your name and place of residence?

JEFFERSON: Thomas Jefferson of Monticello in the Commonwealth of Virginia.

FENWAY: Mr. Jefferson, you of all people are familiar with the exact events that led up to the signing of the Declaration of Independence, and the painful decision to take up arms against the King's troops. It has been mentioned here that these constituted premeditated acts of treason, and that the prisoner, in placing himself at the head of the American forces, is guilty of treason. Can you answer that charge?

JEFFERSON: Treason was never our intention, sir.

FENWAY: It is however argued that it *was* your intention, that you were "hell-bent on independency." Can you elaborate on your denial?

JEFFERSON: Well, sir. There was no question of premeditated rebellion. It was a cumulation of events. Nothing had been further from our minds than independence. Dr. Franklin testified as much before the House of Commons in 1766, when he said he had never heard a word for independence from any person drunk or sober. There were grievances sir. There was opposition to acts of Parliament, yes; and there were some foolish actions by the mob. But independence, never. Redress of grievances was all that was sought and that by nonviolent acts like boycotts—and no law compelled us to buy British goods—and by petitions—always loyal, always conciliatory.

FENWAY: Could you give examples of the latter?

JEFFERSON: Certainly. The Congress of 1765 declared its sentiments for the perpetual continuance of the tie; the most radical Whigs endorsed this. Even James Otis, protesting against the taxation policy of 1768, deemed independence the greatest misfortune. Massachusetts is painted as the most radical, but in 1774 its House of Representatives, led by Sam Adams, instructed its members to work for unity and harmony. The first Continental Congress of that year sent a loyal address and petition for redress of grievances fully accepting Royal authority and questioning only acts of Parliament.

FENWAY: But fighting started in '75, and it has been held that you were plotting independence and training troops to this end.

JEFFERSON: No, sir. These troops were only the regular militia. Others, like the Minutemen, were merely citizens alarmed at the arrival of 2,000 troops in Boston in '68. They only armed in anticipation of attacks upon themselves.

FENWAY: Was George Washington ever for independence at this time?

JEFFERSON: Never. I remember talking to a friend of Washington's who met him as he was on his way to Congress in '75. This friend said to him: "You are leading the people to civil war and independence." Washington replied that if ever he was known to have joined himself to such an effort, he could be set down for everything wicked. Now this was in May. Lexington had been in April. And he would never let his troops refer to the British as the "King's troops", always "the Ministry's troops"—at first, I mean.

HAMPSHIRE: My lords, this evidence of the prisoner's motives is mere hearsay.

THORNTON: I must agree, Colonel Hampshire.

CAMPBELL: Well, now, milord. It is consistent with other things we have heard about the accused. We should perhaps note it.

THORNTON: Yes, yes—note it and pass on, I think, without hearsay.

FENWAY: Yes, milord. Mr. Jefferson: It will be maintained that even while you were proffering olive branches you were arming and attacking the King's troops.

JEFFERSON: We had no recourse but to arm in self-defense, and we never attacked but were attacked ourselves. Even as we were forced to arm, we expressed an abhorrence of separation. New York, New Hampshire, New Jersey, Delaware, and Maryland all instructed their delegates to have nothing to do with independence. As to arms, we had to convince Parliament of our firmness of purpose. That was all.

FENWAY: What further attempts were made at reconciliation?

JEFFERSON: Several, but chiefly Mr. Dickinson's "Olive Branch" petition. "Right our wrongs, withdraw your armies, remove your tyrannical officials," it said, "and you will have no more loyal subjects than ourselves. But if these things are not done, we must fight rather than be enslaved."

(*Murmurs in the court*)

FENWAY: And what was the King and Parliament's response to this olive branch?

JEFFERSON: The petition was disregarded. On the day he was to have received it—and he refused—His Majesty denounced us as traitors in Parliament and declared us rebels who wanted, in his words, "to establish an independent empire."

FENWAY: What was the reaction of Congress?

JEFFERSON: Shock and horror. Even those most violently opposed to independence, sir, came to see that their hands were being forced. King and Parliament had declared them rebels even as they pronounced their loyalty. The King, with 12,000 Germans, meant to punish them: they had no means of redress; they had to fight.

FENWAY: Was the decision on independence immediate and unanimous?

JEFFERSON: No. It was still much debated. But finally it was unanimous.

FENWAY: As was the decision to appoint George Washington Commander-in-Chief.

JEFFERSON: Yes, sir.

FENWAY: In summary, then, Mr. Jefferson, there was no treasonable intent on the part of the prisoner, or yourself, or any other Americans, until you were forced to arms in self-defense against punitive measures by King and Parliament.

JEFFERSON: That is exactly the case, sir.

FENWAY: My Lords, I have no more questions to ask Mr. Jefferson.

(*Hampshire rises.*)

HAMPSHIRE: My Lords, I am not going to concern myself with the question of the honesty of these petitions, protestations of loyalty and the like. I will let that pass. Whatever hesitancy it might, and should have, shown, the rebel congress finally declared for independence and produced this remarkable paper (*He waves a document*) this so-called "Declaration of Independence" to justify its action to the world. I understand, Mr. Jefferson, that this is largely your handiwork?

JEFFERSON: I drafted it, sir. It was amended by Congress.

HAMPSHIRE: Then I shall concentrate on this, for here is the distilled essence of the American case, the basis for insisting that Washington is not a traitor but a loyal subject forced by a wicked King to defend his liberty. I will not bother, milords, with the rather wordy Preamble. I find it largely unintelligible, the opinions of modern Americans on government being as bizarre as those of their ancestors on witchcraft...

CAMPBELL: No more bizarre than the opinions of his late Majesty King James, Colonel. If, Colonel Hampshire, you do not wish to deal with this Preamble, then you will allow me to ask the witness a question or two regarding it.

HAMPSHIRE: Certainly, milord.

(*Thornton nods assent.*)

CAMPBELL: Mr. Jefferson, in your eloquently written preamble you have advanced a theory of government that I find decidedly odd. You say that men have inalienable rights to life, liberty, and the pursuit of happiness; that governments are instituted to this end; and that if governments fail to preserve these rights they can be abolished. Now, sir, is that your intent?

JEFFERSON: It is, Sir George.

CAMPBELL: Surely what you mean is that men have the right to *enjoy* liberty, *enjoy* life, and *enjoy* happiness. Now, any one man's enjoyment of these ends is likely to interfere with the liberty of another, is it not?

JEFFERSON: It could, sir.

CAMPBELL: Then governments exist, Mr. Jefferson, precisely to abridge one man's rights so that they may not so interfere. The essence of government, Mr. Jefferson, is then the abridgment of liberty, and it cannot be faulted for abridgment of liberty per se. I do not wish to make a big issue of it. Lord

Kames would have held . . .

THORNTON: Yes, yes, Sir George, but perhaps we should let prosecution continue?

(*Hampshire rises.*)

HAMPSHIRE: Thank you. My Lords, I will concentrate on the so-called complaints against His Majesty. And let the court take careful note; for here is the solemn and declared case for the awful decision, here is the overwhelming evidence for the right of the rebel armies under George Washington to wage war on the King's troops and ally with the King's enemies.

CAMPBELL: And on this issue, too, milords, I have a question for Mr. Jefferson. With your Lordships' permission...

THORNTON: Yes, of course, Sir George.

CAMPBELL: I find it remarkable, Mr. Jefferson, that while the arguments of your Congress had been all against Parliament with protestations of loyalty to the King, in your Declaration here, Parliament is never mentioned and the King is sorely abused. If the grievances were indeed against Parliament, then why was it not here indicted?

JEFFERSON: Congress did not agree that Parliament had any authority over it, so only the matter of dissolving allegiance to the King was involved.

CAMPBELL: Then it seems to me, Mr. Jefferson, that you were more interested in making history than in writing it. Please proceed, Colonel Hampshire.

HAMPSHIRE: Let us turn to the complaint that the King: (*He reads from the Declaration.*) "called together legislative bodies at places unusual, uncomfortable, and distant from the repository of their public records, for the sole purpose of fatiguing them into complaisance with his measures." This was a Massachusetts complaint, was it not?

JEFFERSON: Primarily, yes.

HAMPSHIRE: Massachusetts had the most complaints, did it not?

JEFFERSON: At least it complained the most, yes.

(*Laughter*)

HAMPSHIRE: Where was the unusual place in question?

JEFFERSON: In 1768 the Assembly was moved from Boston to Cambridge.

HAMPSHIRE: And was this not because the Assembly itself objected to meeting in Boston with General Gage's troops there, Mr. Jefferson?

JEFFERSON: They had objected to the presence of the troops, yes.

HAMPSHIRE: And the move to Cambridge involved what distance?

JEFFERSON: About four miles.

HAMPSHIRE: Four miles, yes. And was, of course, utterly without precedent.

JEFFERSON: It had happened once before when there was small-pox in Boston.

HAMPSHIRE: Quite so. And what was the uncomfortable place where they were forced to meet, Mr. Jefferson?

JEFFERSON: The meeting hall of Harvard College.

HAMPSHIRE: Really? Most uncomfortable....On the matter of fatigue, Mr. Jefferson, how often was the Assembly called?

JEFFERSON: I believe it was every day.

HAMPSHIRE: Then the Governor had to drive out from Boston every day.

JEFFERSON: I suppose so.

HAMPSHIRE: Mr. Jefferson, are you aware that once the Governor arrived the Assembly promptly adjourned, forcing him to drive back again?

(*Laughter*)

HAMPSHIRE: The only person, Mr. Jefferson, who would seem to have been unduly fatigued by this arrangement was the unfortunate Governor.

(*More laughter*)

HAMPSHIRE: Do you not consider rebellious claims to independence, war, ravage, destruction, and the deaths of thousands of Englishmen to be a serious and terrible thing, Mr. Jefferson?

(*Laughter dies.*)

JEFFERSON: Naturally. Of course.

HAMPSHIRE: And yet you produce this farce, this piece of tom-foolery, as justification for so terrible an action?

JEFFERSON: It was but a part, and in any case the complaints were not in themselves a justification for rebellion.

HAMPSHIRE: Then what were they, pray?

JEFFERSON: They were a proof that the King was deliberately trying to subjugate and enslave us. No one denied his right to legislate, to refuse his assent to legislation, or anything else; he had all these rights, but he had not the right to establish over us an absolute tyranny, to place us under absolute despotism.

HAMPSHIRE: Then let us examine this despotism, this absolute tyranny, against which, should it exist, you would rightfully complain...Let us take...(*He scans the document*) these charges: "That the King has refused his assent to laws. That he has refused to pass laws and refused to attend to them." Now, Mr. Jefferson, you have said that you did not question the King's rights in these matters. And in what sense can you blame this King for policies that had been enacted towards the Colonies by all previous Kings and were enshrined in their charters?

JEFFERSON: It was not the rights as such, it was the abuse of those rights. This King struck down more laws of more kinds than his predecessors.

HAMPSHIRE: And what subtle mathematics of morality decided the number of such acts that was tyrannical and justification for rebellion? Ten acts a year perhaps was tolerable, Mr. Jefferson, but twenty justified taking up arms? What number?

JEFFERSON: It was not simply the number, it was the intent.

HAMPSHIRE: Interesting. When we cannot fix on quantity we rush to a quality. I admire the American legal mind. It was the intent, Mr. Jefferson. And who judged the King's intentions?

JEFFERSON: His intention was clear from his repeated refusals of assent and suspensions. His intent was despotism.

HAMPSHIRE: And as a result of the King's despotism and before armed hostilities began, how many Americans were hanged at the King's orders?

JEFFERSON: None that I know of, but...

HAMPSHIRE: And how many languished in prison as a result of the King's arbitrary acts?

JEFFERSON: None, but...

HAMPSHIRE: And how many lost their property without due cause and fair trial?

JEFFERSON: Again none, but...

HAMPSHIRE: And how many newspapers were closed, books burned, authors tortured?

JEFFERSON: None, but...

HAMPSHIRE: But what, Mr. Jefferson? Where is your tyranny, your despotism, except in your own obscure reckonings, sir—your

metaphysical mathematics, sir, which tell you and your con-
spiratorial friends in some mysterious way best known to
yourselves that the King has refused his assent to one act too
many this year so that bloody rebellion against him is justified?

JEFFERSON: There was a cumulation of acts of tyranny that—

HAMPSHIRE: Indeed there was, Mr. Jefferson. Indeed. A cumulation. Let us look at some other examples of this vicious
tyrant's deeds. Let us examine the charge that he has "af-
fected to render the military independent of and superior to
the civil power," referring to General Gage's appointment as
Governor of Massachusetts, no doubt?

JEFFERSON: Yes.

HAMPSHIRE: Mr. Jefferson, when during the course of hostilities,
you withdrew as civil Governor of Virginia, in favour of whom
did you withdraw?

JEFFERSON: General Nelson.

HAMPSHIRE: Indeed. Then by what hypocrisy do you condemn in
the King an action that you yourself took on another occasion?

JEFFERSON: It was a different case.

HAMPSHIRE: Indeed, yes. In the King's case tyranny, in yours,
expediency. Now let us examine the charge that the King
"imposed taxes without our consent." The slogan your com-
patriot Patrick Henry made so popular was "No taxation
without representation," I believe. Would you tell the court,
Mr. Jefferson, whether all Americans were represented in the
colonial assemblies that taxed them?

JEFFERSON: Not all—directly.

HAMPSHIRE: Not directly?

JEFFERSON: No. But those who were not qualified to be were
virtually represented by the others; their landlords, for
example, their creditors, merchants.

HAMPSHIRE: *Virtually* represented. *Virtually* represented? And
how many Englishmen are *directly* represented in their own
Parliament?

JEFFERSON: Not all, again.

HAMPSHIRE: But perhaps, here, too, those who are not are *virtually* represented?

JEFFERSON: It could be argued, has indeed often been so argued.

I did not invent the distinction, sir. It is common in English political thinking.

HAMPSHIRE: Be that as it may, Mr. Jefferson, we are concerned here with your use of it. So, tell me: Were not the Americans, in that case, *virtually* represented in Parliament through their landlords, creditors, merchants in England?

JEFFERSON: There was a difference. America is 3,000 miles away. For a man to be in touch with his landlord in his own town and have him as a representative in an assembly is one thing. To have a creditor 3,000 miles away is another.

HAMPSHIRE: A fine point, Mr. Jefferson. Nicely argued. On such fine points, on such delicate quibbles as "virtual" representations and the number of acts to which His Majesty can refuse assent without being a tyrant, does the justification for bloody rebellion turn, it seems. Let us look then further at the iniquitous tyrannies of the King. "For transporting us beyond the seas to be tried for pretended offenses." Mr. Jefferson, how many people did the King so transport?

JEFFERSON: None, I think.

HAMPSHIRE: I think so too, Mr. Jefferson. Such tyranny! And an act passed, not by His Majesty, but by King Henry VIII! And, milords, need I detain the court on the most specious section of a specious document: the complaint that the King sent troops to suppress rebellion? Is it an argument *for* rebellion that the King sent troops to suppress one that undeniably already existed? And finally, Mr. Jefferson, your complaint about the Quebec Act—you objected to the establishment of the Catholic Church there? As a result of a petition from the people of Quebec to His Majesty?

JEFFERSON: We did. And the extension of Quebec's boundaries at the expense of our own.

HAMPSHIRE: Really, Mr. Jefferson. You complain that His Majesty won't listen to your petitions, but complain also that he does listen to Quebec's. You cannot have it both ways, Sir. But presumably you believe Catholics should have as few rights as Negroes.

JEFFERSON: The analogy is false.

HAMPSHIRE: But the hypocrisy is real, sir. May I remind you of Dr. Johnson's words that the yelps for liberty seem to come loudest from the drivers of slaves?

FENWAY: Milords, that is irrelevant.

THORNTON: Yes, yes. Proceed, Colonel Hampshire.

HAMPSHIRE: I am forced to conclude, my lords, that there is no substance or honesty in this specious document. Mr. Jefferson talks much of liberty and rights, but when asked to defend his specific so-called charges against the King, he shows them to be fallacious and hypocritical and even ludicrous....They relate either to things that the King did that were in his power to do, that his predecessors had done, or that the colonists themselves acknowledged his right to do. That some colonists—and nowhere near the majority—did not like what the King did is neither here nor there. A child may not like what its parent does, but this is not justification for murdering the parent. Even if the list of charges could in any way be sustained, it would still not constitute cause for rebellion. The only possible conclusion is that the rebellion the prisoner led was premeditated and intended, as witnesses have shown, and that this treacherous document is no more than a string of post facto justifications not worth the paper it is written on. (*He sits.*)

THORNTON: Mr. Jefferson, you may step down. Court is adjourned until tomorrow morning.

## FRAGMENT 6. THE VERDICT OF THE COURT

(*Thornton gavels for order.*)

THORNTON: The court has reached its verdict. It has listened to much argument and has been impressed by both sides. It has been concerned that the Defense should make as elaborate a case as it wished, since it does not regard a man's life— particularly the life of such a man as Colonel Washington—as a thing lightly to be disposed of. It has heard the undeniable facts of his command of rebel armies, his attacks on the King's troops, and his alliance with the King's enemies. These are not in dispute. It has heard the Defense plea that, nevertheless, these actions did not constitute treason since they were essentially defensive and unpremeditated and resulted from the wickedness of the King and his ministers rather than the rebellious intentions of the colonists. However, whatever merit they may have as political or philosophical arguments, after much deliberation, the Court is forced to conclude that there is little merit in these pleadings as they affect the issue of Washington's treason. For essentially they say that his objective treason should be forgiven because his reasons were noble and his grievances sore. Such a doctrine would lead to absolute anarchy, which no state could countenance. It is all too easy, having committed treason, then to plead that it was for noble reasons. Indeed, there can scarcely have been a rebel who did not think he had just and honest cause for his rebellion. It must be obvious to Defense that such a doctrine is untenable. The law of treason takes no account of the reasons for action. It says only that the accused should have understood the consequences of his action. There is no question that Washington committed open treason. The facts are not in dispute, and he cannot, having lost his rebellion, plead that he meant well and was justified. The Court therefore has no choice but to find him guilty of that offense and to pass sentence upon him. Prisoner will rise.

(*Washington stands.*)

THORNTON: Have you anything to say before the sentence of this court is passed upon you?

## FRAGMENT 7: STATEMENT OF COLONEL WASHINGTON

My Lords, I thank you for the opportunity to speak. I must first state again what I believe to be the true legal and moral position: That I cannot be guilty of treason because I am a prisoner of war, having been the commander of the army of an independent state at war with Great Britain. On the first day of this trial, the United States of America were deemed not to exist because the Americans had lost the war. But, my Lords, that cannot be true. Had England lost the war she would not therefore have ceased to exist; even if she had been conquered, she would have been a conquered nation. The United States of America exist because their people solemnly declared them to exist; they cannot be obliterated simply because they lost a war. America is now a conquered nation, but it will not always remain so; and when it regains—not its nationhood, but its independence, then the charter for its existence will be that very Declaration that the court here dismissed. This being so, my Lords, I state again that I am the Commander-in-Chief of the armies of an independent state and therefore not guilty of treason against His Majesty, but only of opposing his troops honourably in the field of battle.

But, my Lords, even the founding of new nations is not the real issue here. While I am not surprised by this verdict, nevertheless you see before you a man who is surprised. I, too, have listened carefully to the arguments of both sides here, and I have come to the conclusion that the law is a fickle thing. I have been raised to revere the law. Yet, as we all know, the judgment of treason would not have been passed upon me and my compatriots had we won. So it seems, astoundingly, that under the law, might is indeed right. Because we lost, we are wrong, we are traitors. Had we won, we would have been right, we would have been saviours. In the face of this logic, it is impossible not to ask whether there is not a higher law than that of the land, a law that does not change, a law to which all men of reason must listen. I accept the judgment of this court, but I accept also that I was led, with my countrymen, by a law that is superior to that of this court, and I cannot escape the conclusion that that law is the one that those who follow after me must listen to. Yesterday, we had the honour of hearing three gentlemen of high conscience who had searched their minds and decided they could not participate in the war against America. Had they not been men of position and influence, had they been simple soldiers, they would not have had the luxury of exercising that conscience. They would have been told that His Majesty's government knew what was right, that the law is clear that a man shall serve his king, and that the law must be right. That is a grave danger for them, for as we have seen, had the British forces failed to win, they would have been judged wrong. This may seem to you, gentlemen, very simpleminded, but to me it is a revelation. If the law is dependent on victory and defeat, then there must be a higher law, a law of humanity, that is not so changeable and to which even victorious nations must bow. For I fear, gentlemen, that even if we had won this war and established yet another new nation, we would certainly have repeated all the mistakes of the old ones: we would have persecuted our own dissenters; tyrannized our own colonies; conducted our own wars of arrogant domination. To this end we would have achieved no step forward. What we must—all of us—look forward to, is a time when it is held that a man cannot rebel against mankind: against human rights and human dignity.

How this can be achieved, I do not know. Men within nations achieve it by meeting in conclave and mutually agreeing to abide by laws they themselves make. Perhaps the time will come when nations themselves will assemble and agree similarly. I do not know. But unless that can be achieved, then all our struggle, and the struggle of those brave Englishmen who supported us, will have been for nothing.

My Lords, I was always told that travelling to London would "broaden my outlook." It is true. It did not quite happen the way I intended, but I am a man with a vision far more exciting now than when I left Yorktown. I thank you for that; the vision is worth dying for, but I hope with all my heart that it does not die with me.

## FRAGMENT 8. THE SENTENCE OF THE COURT

George Washington, you have been found guilty of the heinous crime of treason against His Majesty the King. The sentence of this court is that you be taken from here to a place of lawful imprisonment from where at an appointed time you are to be drawn on a hurdle to a place of execution where you are to be hanged by the neck but not until you are dead; for while you are still living your body is to be taken down, your bowels torn out and burned before your face, your head then cut off, and your body divided into four quarters, and your head and quarters to be then at the King's disposal. And may the Almighty God have mercy on your soul.

# Three

# Children of the Revolution

# HUMBERT REFLECTS

(more than twenty years on)


O my America   my new found land
once you were Lolita in her prime
(about eleven years) all innocent
and making love in mad motels with old
decrepit Europe   He with shaking hand
squeezed on your tiny breasts while all the time
you popped your gum   indifferent   intent
on making bubbles   rhythmically controlled
as were your pelvic movements   And the arse
of Humbert Europe flayed in desperation

O my America   where is your cool
your innocence   your gum   after the farce
of Vietnam has turned to hesitation
all the rude confidence only a fool
would underestimate
                                    But now you are
snappy   defensive   almost middle-aged
a sad declining whore mourning her past
with petulant assertiveness
                                    Your car is
Japanese   You drive but are enraged
Pearl Harbor was avenged   but now at last
they've hit you in the sagging underbelly
no credit cards can cure

You feel the strain
but   my once brash tart   are not prepared
(my glum Lolita sadly run to fat)
like an Imperial courtesan to maintain
a dignified indifference of the herd—
that jeering mob of nouveau powerful
who long to see you totter and fall flat
but haven't quite the courage yet to push

Well   somehow faded lady I shall pull
my own stiff joints erect and tip my hat
and gently help you through the vulgar crush—
stave off disaster for another hour—
and through your pouts and tempers try to see
nostalgic flashes of that innocence
that drove old Humbert crazy with desire
and then itself with pot and LSD
and indignation half devoid of sense

I'll stick around Lolita and I'll fill
the glasses for you for a little while
There's no where else to go   I had to come
and now I want to stay   But I'll not kill
to save your pride   or for your faded smile
Napalm tastes bad kid   should have stuck with gum

# THE MARINE ROOM RESTAURANT
(of the Olympic Hotel, Seattle, Washington)

That genius for the oil-and-water mix
of careful taste and gross vulgarity
erupts in walls of living timelessness—
glass-prisoned   nervous fish   that stare at us
across a million centuries
                       The roof
is blue   the light subdued   the tables ranged
in tiers down to a pit   where girls on legs
serve passive actors of this aqueous scene
with whisky (sour)   and with martini (dry)
with maraschino (red)   and olive (green)

Some middle-income lumpen bourgeosie
celebrate the anniversarie
of legal coupling   while the silent fish
look on unmoved   but are not looked upon
Who needs the colored flame that burns in tanks
of violent green   pale coral   amber rock
for   with a painful suddenness   the band
strikes   and we are drowned with cool trombones

Light   noise   hysteria   and then—oh God—
straight from Las Vegas—can you bear to wait?
"The Happy Jesters!"
                    Three sad   ancient men
in powder blue and cloying harmony
pull faces   put on hats   rotate their hips
do imitations of old movie stars

Meanwhile ten thousand quiet   brilliant forms
swim round our heads   as we consume huge steaks
of local salmon (broiled)   with spinach (creamed)
freezing our faces tight against the din
But in the pit the celebrants are pleased
They shriek applause and touch each others hands

Did you   comrade   turn to me and say
(struggling through your pain to rationalize)
"It's good that we should be exposed to this
for this is real   and intellectuals
should know how people live and what they like"
You did
                    But I had left you with the thought
that poor sweet Ludwig would have loved this room
and reproduced it on a mountain top
in warm Bavaria   There he and I
would flood the pit and all its ruminants
til they were happy   chomping   protean mud
churning to the sub-aquatic tones
of happy jesters and of sad trombones

Then in the swan boat on the lake we'd sit
and call up Parsifal from hidden choirs
eat cherries from a shallow   silver dish
and olives from a bowl of ivory
We'd scatter lilies to the mountain folk
who came to us for bread—yet loved us more
for flowers—and would die for us because
they know we are not mad   but half-divine
princes   who ripen olives with our gaze
who feed wild cherries to our hunting dogs
who feel the colored fish swim through our blood

# WORDS FOR A BOSTON BLUES

(tune: St James' Infirmary)

(from a true incident, 1957)


I went down to Boston harbor
to see what I could see there
and down on the sidewalk was a black man   dead
and blood ran from his throat   and blood was in his hair

A white woman bending over him
her eyes were wet and she bowed her head
then she turned her face toward me
these were the words she said

"He loved me like a proper man
I loved him back like a woman should
now he lies on the sidewalk dead
but his blood is as red as a white man's blood"

These truths we hold self-evident
from them no turning back
that man is equal born to man
unless that man be black

I knew as I left the harbor
with the blood wet under my feet
that only cold black violence
could clean that bloody street

I came back from Boston harbor
was the hottest time of the year
a nation lay on the sidewalk there
it smelled of blood   and it smelled of fear

# BORING CONFESSION

(written on napkins with a pencil borrowed from the
waitress in the Sandalwood Bar of the Sheraton Route 18
New Jersey)

When thick with hatred   usually I find
room for compassion   since I have been on
the receiving end of hatred   So when faced
with wall-to-wall vulgarity like this
         (must I describe it   you all know the scene)
I know that I would open up the cocks
and filled with mercy   flood the frantic mess
until its noisy pointlessness was drowned
in vodka clean with ice
                         (Somewhere before
         I had the same clear flash of cruelty
         Was it again because the band was bad
         and no one seemed to care   or even know?)
And furthermore   choked with distaste I'd feel
not even hatred but indifference
         (I never feel it in a truckers' bar
         when watching football   but I must confess
         I've felt it in Elaine's a time or two)
Somehow their earnest striving to be more
than nothing   leaves me robbed   exhausted
of understanding   I'm afraid to know
that Dachau   was no accident   no work
of lunatics   (too easy an excuse)
I am not mad or blood-crazed   but I am
an Eichmann of the disco bars   a fool
appointed Gauleiter of Route 18

Which tells me something about evil   but
an intuition I cannot explore
without a terror of the truth   a truth
undoubtedly banal   (which doesn't help)
I stop   accept   I drink   I dance   I laugh
and contemplate the soft alternatives
of passive curiosity   the escape
into the luxury of explanation

I should avoid all petty pick-up bars
all disco bands   all orders of tequila
sunrise   dropped into the polyester
laps of nervous blacks and orientals
that hint of pogroms and the smoky end
of things that have no purpose but to live

(Distracted by the waitress   the boring confession
takes a conventionally romantic turn—which is
a bit of a relief but not much)

But somehow when she wanders through the bar
her hair falls like a mermaid's   and the tinsel
floats behind like seaweed   and her skin
is pure as pearls   She converts the noise
into the thunder of a distant wave
that only adds to intimacy in
the liquefying chamber that envelopes
bodies and minds in vodka teased with lime
and sharp with ice   Swirling into depths
of hair-blown   sea-borne fantasy   she calls
me to the whirlpool of the drowning mass
into the peace that lies beyond all bands
all turnpikes   surf-and-turf   all Paul Masson
all lobsters Newburg   broiled or thermidor
and in some corner of polluted earth
gives promise of a sea-floor walk beside
the living scarlet claws   the silver smelts
the shining sea-bass and the patient clams—
and quiet death amid the tangled hair

(This boring reverie breaks off   another napkin
is requested   and the confession continues its dreary
and self-indulgent examination of the obvious)

Somewhere in the pointless certainty
of knowing one's distaste lies the unease
that by some gross political mischance
an idiot democracy will   out of fear
elect one to effective execution
of just those gruesome prejudices   which
are best when least explored   and worst
when given self-expression in the name
of higher values   which one will accept
knowing that such acceptance must embrace
a sickness only violence can cure

God save us sinners from such expurgation
Leave the world's banal impurity
free from our outrage   noisily content

(Here   mercifully   we run out of napkins and the
waitress demands her pencil back)

# FOR MY DAUGHTERS

(on the anniversary of the killings at Kent State, May 4, 1970)

I have dreams for you
cliché dreams little girls
dreams that father-everyman
has for daughter-everygirl
silly   romantic dreams

I would have you all
growing up in Georgian
houses in the summer
with beaches where your limbs
could test their firmness     crabs
in the pools and starfish and
colored rocks to puzzle
and intrigue   provoking
question after question

Careless hours stretching
through a carefree youth
with you all   all three
mad with the love of wind
of mountains and of donkeys
and of wolfhounds obedient
to your imperious little whims

Careless youth stretching
into grave   humorous   awkwardly
graceful ladyhood   My three
young ladies serious at the
table among the candles
and the silver and the
darting conversation
with question after question
with laughter   music   songs
with witty teasing words
for desperate young men
whom I would hate
                This I
would have for you
                But I
know where you would be
dressed in faded jeans
clinging to your friends
out on the grass unarmed
in tears of mad frustration
in bitter helplessness
in angry incoherence
screaming motherfucker
at the khaki   booted
untidy boys with rifles
itching for the chance
to pay you back the scorn
and fury you were spitting
not at them but at
the things their shaking rifles
stood for
                When they fired
and you turned and screamed
who would have died? My mind
is numb   One cannot bear
to contemplate the wretched
sick sad truth   and yet
some man's daughter died there
and were his dreams less precious
than my little dreams?

You would have been out there
in that sun before those
bayonets facing death
I would have died my own
cold death knowing that
nothing I had dreamed
for you could possibly
have equalled all your courage
knowing that I would be
passionately proud
and wide awake with no
dreams left   only a dead
reality and question
after question
                    You
cannot control the hounds
with all your innocence
and we wise dreamers fail
to curb the wolf with dreams
All I can give you now
serious   funny   girls
is question after question

# LIBERATED WOMAN:
# HAPPINESS PURSUED

*Poland's leaders still pinned their trust to the*
*value of a large mass of horsed cavalry, and*
*cherished a pathetic belief in the possibility of*
*carrying out cavalry charges. In that respect, it*
*might truly be said that their ideas were eighty*
*years out of date, since the futility of cavalry*
*charges had been shown as far back as the*
*American Civil War.*
B. H. Liddell Hart, *History of the Second*
*World War*

She has no history   yet she claims a name
that   though distorted   conjures slavic woods
goose herders
        vampires
            trolls
                but does it mean
anything to her?
        Nothing
            Well   perhaps
the echoes of a grandparental song—
of half-lost recipes
        She has no sense
of time
      Nothing connects
          Eternally
she recreates time for herself
          creates
her own
      is never moved by things that loom
through eastern European mists like fears
from childhood
        "But" I say "the Poles were brave
creative   brilliant   stubborn"
          "Yes" she says
But nothing registers
      not even echoes

She is eternal in her innocence
free from the grubby thrill of wickedness
lacking a twitch of mild perversity
The only sin she'll recognize is guilt
Her sex is easy   frank   manipulative
without a shred of mystery
                              It has
the Constitution's sweeping optimism
the brash assertion of the Declaration
a Bill of Rights for severing all ties
to feudal sex   to nature's bondage   or
to any *droit* or *jus* seignorial
*in nocte prima* or on any night

The pill is her democracy   her right
to be the same to all men
                              all who are
created equally between her legs
She has no lovers   only partners who
engage her in a ritualistic dance
which   she maintains   in any case is better
performed alone in terms of its effect
(the manuals on the subject all agree)
Even so   one tries to cultivate
healthy relationships   without demands
without those screaming shitty consequences

If she loses
            if it seems unsure
if nothing works
                  if simple quantity
fails to produce the happiness that should
be guaranteed by the pursuit
                              she knows
it can be fixed in time
                        A formula
will soon be found to take advantage of
progressive technological advance
in sexual plumbing
                    or in counselling

relationships
　　　　　and broken hopes
　　　　　　　　　　and lives
All present tense
　　　　　　　There is no history
to conquer here　and nature　as she knows
is nurture's creature
　　　　　　　　　nurture going wrong
the experts can be called to fix it up


Your body turns in space
　　　　　　　　　　　no weight　no time
A sexual walk in space
　　　　　　　　　Nothing connects
to blood and sperm
　　　　　　　　　　to death and ovulation
to stench of birth
　　　　　　　　　to anguish of lost love
to race　to earth　to pain
　　　　　　　　　　A body stretched
in space　that only wracks itself and shakes
in quick convulsion if manipulated
expertly by experts
　　　　　　　　Not in time
or history　but simply floating there
orbiting around the guarantees
the founding partners wrote into the rules
of liberation　happiness　and life


But then you creep against me in the night
after the satisfaction and the frank
and full discussion of our needs
　　　　　　　　　　　and how
the sudden pleasure can he best achieved
by slow　sequential　oral expertise
demanding nothing mutual
　　　　　　　　　　nothing fierce

no simultaneous nonsense
                    no vaginal
myths
        You curl your body into mine
and say  "I love you"
                    half ashamed
                                dismayed
admitting dirty thoughts your grandmother
had to endure in less enlightened times
of smoky kitchens
                    cabbage
                                brats
                                and sweat


I look into those slavic eyes and see
reflected in the wild green distance
                                lines
of cavalry glide on their perfect charge
toward the German tanks
                        slashing with swords
against the indifferent steel
                            So what's the use
your ever plunging into history
to know why men would die to save their young
only to have the young die in their turn
to save the women who will die to save
their young who'll die to save the women
who will die…
                    Stay out in space my love
Call in the experts   let their skillful tongues
produce your sterile spasms
                            and be safe

I shall dream of death in battle
                              or
the anguish of lost love
                         the agony
of childbirth and the death of children
                                     or
the fierceness of possession
                           or the hate
that is the kissing cousin of our loves
I'll dream
              of retrograde   archaic things
of bloody   unenlightened things
                                while you
are safe
            in space
                      inviolate
                              satisfied

# MANHATTAN SUMMER DIALOGUE: STATEN ISLAND INTERLUDE

*I am about to sacrifice the dear little divine thing from among the mountains. My friends and masters, come to the feast!*

*O Divine One, you were sent into this world for us to hunt. When you come to them, the spirits, please speak well of us and tell them how kind we have been. Please come to us again and we shall do you the honor of a sacrifice.*
"Prayer to the sacrificial bearcub"
Kyosuki Kindaiti, *Ainu Life and Legends*

*The location of the sites in remote caves, where they would be most readily concealed, indicated their reference to a cult; and so it immediately occurred to their excavators that they were uncovering the evidences of a sacrificial offering, storage places of the cave-bear skulls used in a service honoring the divinity of the hunt, to whom the offerings were rendered.*

*Such details among the contemporary Asiatic hunters as the grinding down of the teeth of the bear and leaving of two vertebrae attached to the skull, just as in the European Inter-glacial period, proves that the continuity has actually remained unbroken for tens of thousands of years.*
Herbert Kühn "Das Problem des Urmonotheismus"
(translated by Joseph Campbell)

I

He   There must be more bad guitarists per square mile
in Washington Square
than anywhere
on earth  Why do you smile?
Agree or strongly disagree? It isn't clear

She  In Staten Island Zoo there's an old bear
He's sad and grumpy  but he likes to hear
me  and me only
playing the guitar
Badly  He really is that lonely

He   Is it far
to Staten Island?   Perhaps the bear
(are you sure he doesn't smell?)
would like my conversation just as well
as your guitar  Even if I talk
badly  With bears of course one cannot tell

She  If we could walk
we'd go through Chinatown and we'd collect
(I know where they are sold)
little lanterns  red and gold
to hang up in the zoo
to please the prisoners  But I expect
that is forbidden  Most things are

He   What we could do
since we've just met and I don't even know your name
only that you
and I are no way  no way the same
is go to Chinatown and eat

She  It must be something without meat

He    O.K. Then to the zoo

She   Then to the zoo   We'll take the Ferry   Have
      you got a car?
      It really isn't far


II

She   When they take the nests to make the soup
      what do the birds do?

He    The birds have long since gone
      in a wild   wheeling   cackling troop
      to find the sun or something   Very few
      care much about their nests or what goes on
      when they have left
      They have poor memories for little things
      but memories as wide as heaven and as loud
      as the beating of their million million wings
      for distances that Caravelles can't fly
      for every star and cloud
      that in the sky
      of southern summers points the way
      to that red lantern-lighted land
      of near-eternal golden day
      And you must understand
      they don't then mind the theft
      of little nests to feed those hungry girls
      who need their strength for serenading bears

She   Is all that true?
      That garbage about birds I mean?
      About the bears I know
      They never go
      anywhere
      They live in holes alone   except
      when mating for a while
      Now it's your turn to smile
      but I have been
      in my hole alone just like the bear

He    Now you have crept
       outside to mate?

She   A bit too late
       perhaps  And yet perhaps
       What garbage
       all that stuff about the birds

III

She   They always miss—
       the ferry men  despite
       the years and years they've done it
       always hit
       the wall as they come in
       I'll blow a kiss
       to that big sad one there
       the one that looks just like a bear
       It gives him such a fright
       Is that a sin?
       I was brought up a Catholic

He    And now you worship bears?

She   No  I don't worship anything anymore
       I just don't eat meat
       and sing to bears  (it's all the poor thing's got)
       I venerate them like the Virgin Mary  not
       worship them like Christ  That's neat
       remembering things like that from long before
       I ever sang to bears on Staten Island

He    Can't be long
       You can't be more
       than seventeen or eighteen

She    Well there you're wrong
      I'm nineteen
      and it is a hell of a long
      time  a hell of a long time
      since Long Island City
      and my mother  and my sisters  and the pretty
      dresses worn to Sunday mass
      before I went into my hole
      and venerated bears
      and committed what was then
      as far as I could see the only crime—
      enjoying sex with men
      So I went mad with men  I used to pray
      I'd have two every day
      I nearly made it  Never had affairs
      You know  long-lasting stuff
      until this recent guy  and that was rough
      I liked him  but it's over  and again
      Give Us This Day Our Daily Men
      They said I'd lose my soul
      those Catholics
      But my mother was half Jewish so I guess
      I got off to a rotten start
      as far as those things were concerned  What a crazy mess
      a kosher sacred heart
      a Catholic quarter Jew
      And quit your laughing  What the hell are you?

He     God knows
      A Deist I suppose
      One who chooses to believe
      that God exists  the better for to hate
      my dear Him for his ravages  Doglike to bait
      Him the great  immortal  pompous beast
      with bestial snarls and yelps of sheer
      defiance  or at least
      to weave
      some fantasies like this to pass the year
      we seem to be spending getting off this raft

She  What garbage   I guess I should have laughed
You should take care
God just might be a bear
He did once leave
his hole in heaven to come down and mate
Just once   I think that's great
But you should venerate
the Great God Bear   This is the gate

He  You didn't bring your bad guitar
to serenade him

She  Well what was the use
the bear was an excuse
He's locked up for the night
But there is still some light
and lots of time to kill
So chase me round these trees
and if you catch me   which you will
we'll go down on our knees
with hands behind our backs and kiss
like children do in China

He  Out of breath   I'm not nineteen and I
am out of breath   But with enough
to kiss under a Chinese lantern sky
a grim polluted golden red
I couldn't miss
You let me catch you

She  Well now   Ain't that tough
Of course I did   So now let's kiss
for five full minutes   Understand
you mustn't use a hand
I am too young
to have my innocent body violated thus
So use your tongue
and gorge yourself on my young mouth
and think of us
as Chinese children learning what it's like
to kiss for the first time   Open your mouth

He   Was that five minutes

She  I don't want a quiz
       Do as I tell you
       Take my hand and run

He   Well  What's done is done
      and now I must obey
      the priestess of the bear

She  Come out this way
       and over there
       you'll see somewhere
       in the filthy  fading light
       of our Staten Island night
       if I have not
       forgotten  there behind the parking lot
       a hill  A long steep  roughly sloping hill
       That's where we'll run  where you and me will
       roll down together  locked together tight
       Have you ever rolled like that before?

He   Certainly not  and what is more
      It's bound to be against the law
      All such things are  Hills
      are not made for rolling  not these hills
      They're made as landscape features  made to ease
      the lot of weary motorists  not made to please
      bear goddesses who tease
      susceptible old deists  Merciful God
      You can't be serious?

She  Do you want to make love with me?

He   What else  Of course
      I've thought of little else for six hours now
      since we met up in town

She  Then you must roll with me and when we're down
      among the garbage   hidden from the cars
      then you can have me any way you want
      under your clumsy God's polluted stars

IV

She  You need my hand
      to lead you to the promised land?
      But first  like Pilgrim  you must climb this hill
      which will
      prove how much you want me

He  You mustn't taunt
      A pilgrimage is such a serious thing
      and if I'm to do my Pilgrim thing
      then let me do it with some dignity

She  O.K.   Then sing
      a solemn song about eternity
      and bird nest soup   and bears
      bored out of their minds by bad guitars
      Let's have few   sad   squeaky bars

He  For Christ's sake stop
      we're at the bloody top
      What now?   Do I ascend
      into a special heaven full of holes
      for timid bears afraid to mate
      with other timid souls?

She  Why no  You fall
      This is the fall of woman and of man
      the ending of my innocence
      Lie down and hold me tight   tight as you can
      Now there is no pretense
      Your bluff is called old pilgrim   Now you will
      roll with me down this hill

He   When I recall
      this day to my grandchildren
      who will ask
      "When the world trembled grandpa  what
      did you do  What was your great task?"
      I'll tell them  "Not a lot
      I rolled down hills a bit with crazy bears"

She  You talk a lot of garbage
      You talk a lot
      So let's get rolling if you want me hot

          The spinning trees  the red
          and gold revolving sky
          the frightened birds that crashed
          upward through turning
          branches as we flashed
          a barrel headlong burning
          an avalanche of legs and hair
          a long dress torn  a shattered
          watch  a sandal shed
          left lying there
          not that it mattered
          as down and round and down and round
          down round down we sped
          until we hit the ground
          among the garbage  hidden from the cars
          and all the grimy stars
          stopped spinning  and our bodies bruised
          and winded  lay there waiting to he used

She  Now  Now  For God's sake now
      Don't wait a second  Do it anyhow
      Just pound and crush me like the hill
      has nearly crushed us both  Hard  Hard  I will
      not want it in a second  Now  Now  Now

V

She  They'll hit it going this way too
      They always do
      My God that was a crazy screw
      I often have aesthetic orgasms   you know
      I come just out of joy   like when
      lighting a Chinese lantern   by its glow
      I look into the river   Or when men
      lick their lips and look me up and down
      I had one when we met in town
      and you gave me all the crazy talk
      and on the walk
      to find the crazy bear
      who I knew would not be there
      I have them when I see a sexy black
      I have them all the time when things
      are beautiful   A nymphomaniac
      for beauty's what I am
      Or a rotten sham
      Nothing rings
      true

He   Do you often do
      what we just did?

She  Hell no
      A long   long time ago
      I rolled that hill with someone just
      like you   and for the same   same reason

He   Your own form of lust
      in your own mating season?
      An aphrodisiacal tumble for a kid
      who otherwise has only superficial
      orgasms by the dozen in the street?

She Oh man   That's neat
      That's psychological
      That's really neat
      But what we did
      I did for the same reason once before
      I only ever did it once before
      I hope I never do it anymore
      And you should know the score
      the outcome   rolling lover   of what you did
      I want it beautiful   you see
      And I should know
      because to make the kid
      was beautiful   the one I'm three
      months pregnant with   And when it goes
      when I abort it as you'd say
      I want it the same way
      So thanks   You did it beautifully friend
      Now I'll wait for the end
      alone   down in my hole
      I don't think I ever had a lousy soul

# HYMN TO ISIS:
# SAN FRANCISCO SUMMER

From D. H. Lawrence, *The Man Who Died*

"I serve Isis in search," she replied.

He looked at her. She was like a soft musing cloud, somehow remote. His soul smote him with passion and compassion.

"Mayst thou find thy desire, maiden," he said, with sudden earnestness.

"And art thou not Osiris?" she asked.

He flushed suddenly.

"Yes, if thou wilt heal me!" he said. "For the death aloofness is upon me, and I cannot escape it."

## PREAMBLE: SAN FRANCISCO SUMMER AFTERNOON

> The hippie girl was pale with sickness and
> had long   uncertain hair
> I touched her shaking hand
> and kissed the flowers painted on
> her cheeks   which   death inspired shone
> through primary blue and red
> with luminous   Pre-Raphaelite effect
>
> Flowers painted on a rocking horse
> Ophelia's flowers   she being almost dead
> Flowers that Victorian girls collect
> to dry and press and torment   all of course
> to make such pretty pictures   This remorse
> is premature

She slowly lifts her head
and with my finger tips
I gently trace round purple lips
round earrings carved from oriental creeds
mandalas   wampum collars   amber beads
that hang like crystal sweat across her brow

Again she lifts her head   and now
with fingers sliding through her anxious hair
I kiss the painted stars around her eyes
while peeping through her drug-dulled stare
a childish hope discredits her disguise

She tells me how
she knows that as she lives she dies
but   she never thinks of death
despite her illness and her cough
though these remind her   Still   she shrugs it off
and hides behind a cloud of smoky breath

She tells me that the door would never lock
puts on a record   joins in with the song
She lights the incense   strokes a joint with long
uncertain fingers   serves tea and brown rice
then sits a lotus   on the floor again
and lets the music carved from hardened rock
cut like obsidian through her waking brain

Music that harsher on the spirit lies
than painted eyelids upon smoke-filled eyes

Music that strains
                    and strains
                              and falling
                                        dies

## INCIDENT IN THE UNCONSIOUS

*(with apologies to Swinburne)*


Her eyes are the eyes of hunted doe
   and I am haunted   taunted   though
by a need unspoken   a seal unbroken
   a memory hidden   a thought forbidden
a forest footfall   a frightened breath
   a murmur of blood   a whisper of death
of eyes that are mingling fear and trust
   of hands that are mangling love and lust

The loud voice screams   "You must answer her need"
   The soft voice answers   "Greed   greed   greed"
But the goddess pursuing the missing part
   finds the Maenad tearing a young god's heart
And that which was whole is rent in twain
   and that which was sundered is sought in vain
and the blood is washed from the leaves by the rain
   while the voice of the forest cries   "Pain  pain  pain"

## S.F. SUMMER AFTERNOON—CONT.

She talks a lot about herself and how
sex is for her an agreeable device
for exploring meaningful relationships
at worst quite bearable   at best quite nice
and healthy   like brown rice
not bad for you like other trips
and much the best when high
with a casual passerby
but in itself no end
a service to a friend
perhaps   to pass the time

and on and on and on
until the afternoon was gone
the San Francisco summer afternoon was gone

Then she says   (to be polite)
"You'd like to stay the night?
I get a very definite vibration
from your Victorian imagination
that I turn on to   Is it sex-and-crime—
a Jack the Ripper thing?   I'm screwing all the time

I guess I do it just to pass the time
It's like   well   good   but not great anytime
I mean   I've never had that final screw turned tight
You know   the one that might
just make me scream
but that's my dream
You're gonna stay the night?"

Loud voice   "Do it   It is right"
Soft voice   "Greed   greed   greed"

She looked at him for a moment in fear, from the soft blue sun of her
eyes. Then she lowered her head, and they sat in silence in the warmth and
glow of the western sun: the man who had died, and the woman of the pure
search.

## STATEMENT OF INTENT

No
She must be freed
Teach her to embrace pain as a friend
that she might know sex as an end
and both as means to nothing
but a meaningful relationship
of celebrants in that fierce rite
which is but an echo of the end
a shadow on a smoky summer night
a cheap rehearsal of the end
when that last   agonizing screw turns tight

So
When
floating through the amber fire of pain
(God's golden arrow through that mad saint's heart)
at last I enter   then
her frantic fingernails
I'm certain will
respond with quick   instinctive skill
clawing release from those indulgent jails
of all-too-easy sex   cancelling
the life-destroying message of the pill

The final turn   And then there is the note
of silent screaming somewhere in her throat

My torn flesh will sing
to me that all is gain
Her painted eyes
calm now beyond all pain
are smudged with stinging sweat
and yet
are penitent and wise
She will rise
moving to different music now
with certain pace
and all the oriental grace
for which she longs
and makes her like Diana of the Chase
queen of herself
and of all moonlight things
that move as underwater to the sound
of temple gongs
from cities drowned
a million years ago

When she sings
the chant will be melodious and slow
The notes will be the rain
on bars of moonlight
There will be no strain
only as from a distant height
the echo of a liquefying pain
a rainwashed forest filled with blood and pain
drowned in the moonlight and reborn again

## THE HYMN TO ISIS

Isis
now you have Osiris whole
Having found a grip
foreswear another sterile trip
into that colored fairyland
whose gainless occupation
is rhythmic   dull   ingenious copulation
Isis
let my torn body be your goal
for now you understand
love is not easy   and warm Lethe's mud
is mud despite its psychedelic hue
Isis
we have reserved for you
passage on a lengthy Stygian trip
in Charon's dark   unhurried ship
The view of death is clear
the transformation imperceptible
Isis
there   as we live   we die
and passionately try
to make the art of death perfectible
and so the art of love   and we are high
only on the acid of our blood

She turned to him, her face glowing from the goddess.

"You are Osiris, aren't you?" she said naively.

"If you will," he said.

"Will you not let Isis discover you? Will you not take off your things?"

He looked at the woman, and lost his breath. And his wounds, and especially the death wound through his belly, began to cry again…

"They did me to death!" he said in excuse of himself, turning his face to her for a moment.

And she saw the ghost of the death in him, as he stood there thin and stark before her, and suddenly she was terrified, and she felt robbed. She felt the shadow of the gray, grisly wing of death triumphant.

# ENVOI: SAN FRANCISCO SUMMER NIGHT

"You'll stay then   stay the night?"
"Well   well you know I'd like to   but you see
I've this appointment   and
I hope you understand
I can only stay an hour
Business   I must shave and shower
I hadn't planned…"

"O.K.   What the hell
an hour will do as well"

Well
It was nice
She said   "Man that was nice"
I laughed and said   "Perhaps I'll make you scream
next time I'm here"
Her eyes were dull again   too dull for fear
She took another drag   She said   "Screw that old dream
I won't be here"   She said   "I won't be here"

I got my plane
I never went again
But now at night my sleepless hours
are filled with painted stars   and dying flowers

She never wrote   but in the end
I got a letter from a friend
in San Francisco
Shit
You all know what it said

# INDIAN GIRL

(written in European exile)

What made the Mongols flee the East
the Huns to start their westward surge
the Celts to scatter 'til they ceased
their wanderings   but retained the urge?

What sent the Jews and Moors to Spain
and seaward rolled the restless herd
of Goths and Vandals   what again
in Cabot and Vespucci stirred?

What wind sent Vikings to their death
and bishops to St. Brandon's Isle
and blew them with its scented breath
to doomed Atlantis for a while?

What fascination drew each rogue
and pious pilgrim to the West
sent Ossian down to Tir na n-Og
and even now denies me rest?

What set the trireme's groping oars
to fight Atlantic waves and win
sent men from Tyre to Albion's shores—
the mere excuse of Cornish tin?

Cynics   do not call it greed
this mad desire to track the sun
it is a much more ancient need
that seizes us and makes us run

It is the voice the migrant bird
feels urgent in its blood each year
It is the call Columbus heard
it is not greed   it is not fear

not power nor the hope of gain
(though motives such as these   one finds
make it much easier to explain
the strange intent to little minds)

Whatever is the movement's source
that drove those maniacs to the sea
I only know you are the force
the magnet that is drawing me

that you were there before the ships
before the bishops   pirates   kings
and what they sought is in your lips
is in the song your body sings

is in the rhythm of your drum
is in the patience of your eyes
is in the melody you hum
to coax the rain from desert skies

For you   my Pocahontas were
princess of all   and you are still
your skin is yet the puma's fur
your breasts are each a sacred hill

your hair the trailing thundercloud
your smell the pinyon and the sage
your pride a wind-torn pine unbowed
your anger is the cyclone's rage

A towering mesa is your scorn
a colored canyon is your love
into whose depths we have been drawn
indifferent to the storm above

Yet it is shrieking overhead
a challenge to our stubborn wills
and when its snarling voice is dead
we feel the silence of the hills

We hear the mad coyote's cry
the warning rattle in the dust
The eagle's wings obstruct the sky
and fear destroys our waning lust

fear that none of this was meant
that we are prisoners of time
your body is the continent
we merely re-enact the crime

Our mutual passion comes too late
to heal the wounds of centuries
to reconcile the love and hate
inherent in such loves as these

And though I know our love is doom
(the love that drove those pirates   kings
and bishops to their watery tomb)
I crave the danger that it brings

For still you are the desert moon
that draws the tidal wave in me
towards the West   and very soon
I'll cross the inevitable sea

Four

Toward a More Perfect Dissolution

*He knows that there was once an ice age and that there will be an ice age again.*
George Wyndham on A. J. Balfour

# WHAT CAN BE DONE ABOUT SWEDEN?

*And now what shall become of us without any barbarians?*
*Those people were a kind of solution.*
C. P. Cavafy, "Expecting the Barbarians"

*Extract from a speech to the United Nations' Committee on the Problems of the Overdeveloped Countries, by the head of the UN Investigative Commission on Sweden, the Ambassador from Uganda.*

...have occupied this distinguished body for some time. But before getting as quickly as possible to the substance of my report and recommendations, I must ask for the patience of the assembly while I indulge in a little custom of my country where no one begins a speech to the "great council"—as we would call such an august body as this—without having the courtesy to tell what we would call a "little tale" or "small story." This is done—according to western anthropologists, who, of course, understand our customs better than we do ourselves (*laughter*) in order to make the assembled distinguished company feel "at home" as you would say, and less intimidated by the awesomeness of the occasion (*laughter*). The little story, as is our custom, is usually a small anecdote from the life of the speaker, and since we, that is our team of investigators, have just returned from Sweden—that unhappy, ravaged land—my story will concern my reaction to my first real view of Stockholm. This was from the beautiful dining room at the top of the tallest bank building in that beautiful city. The room had once been the apartment of the chancellor of the royal household, and our most gracious and kind hosts had pointed with pride to a window in the apartment that was bricked up and had been since the eighteenth century—the era of the said chancellor. The window faced onto the royal palace across the water, and the dis-

159

tressed man so hated his work that when he returned home in the evening he could not bear to look at the palace—hence the bricks (*laughter*) that had been left there, in his memory, ever since. But that is not my little tale. From the unbricked windows there was the most beautiful view of this "Venice of the north"—its lakes, inlets, bridges, palaces, cathedrals, parks, avenues. Even in the admittedly pale sunlight it was a superb sight. But something about it disturbed me. In the course of my peripatetic European education, gentlemen, I visited all the capitals of Europe collecting four doctorates en route. Something about this capital, however, struck me as odd, but I could not think at first what it was. At least I knew what struck me, but could not at first think why it was odd! *Everything was intact exactly as it had been built* (*murmurs*). A fifteenth-century church was still there—perfect. A seventeenth-century palace was in the same condition as when built. An eighteenth-century cathedral was there as it stood at its completion. A nineteenth-century Opera House: in pristine condition. And the thought that struck me, that tied together the "oddness" of it all? Gentlemen, I confess that I turned to my charming host and exclaimed, "Why, this city has never been bombed; it has never been bombed!" (*murmurs, some slight laughter*)

It is the custom in my country—and I was naughty not to tell you this before—that the little tale should have a moral (*laughter*) but that the moral should never be revealed (*more laughter*). In this case, gentlemen, the moral is not in need of revelation. You are all aware of the grave situation in Sweden and the reason why our intervention was required and requested. The Third World Commission on the Problems of Overdeveloped Countries has been, to say the least, overworked of late—and as you know overwork is one of the early symptoms of overdevelopment, so we must be more careful (*more laughter*)—but work we must and work we will as long as the grave situation in the overdeveloped countries persists and as long as we have the means and the will to come to their aid (*prolonged applause*).

Nor do I need to bore you with a repetition of the long diagnosis—nay the many diagnoses—that have been offered this distinguished assembly on the problems of overdevelopment. Sweden, as you know, was very special since it had been dismissed by many skeptics as a hopeless case. Social justice was perfect—both legal justice and "distributive" justice; social welfare had reached the limits of its possibilities as a result of 90 percent taxation returned largely in the form of benefits; the criminal justice system was the most "enlightened" in the world, and rehabilitation was totally substituted for retribution in all spheres; the standard of living was the highest in the world; sexual liberty was in its most advanced stages; war was outlawed and neutrality the national policy...I could go on, but these, as we all know, are the sure signs of hyper-advanced overdevelopment, with their concomitants of severe alcoholism, staggering rates of suicide and mental breakdown—especially clinical depression, and "motiveless" crimes including sexual offenses quite unnecessary in a country of such permissiveness. And this very permissiveness is indicative of the chronic nature of the problem. This did not originate as it would have done in any normal country from an overflow of natural lust (*laughter*) but derived from a puritanical thoroughness in teaching sexual hygiene to young schoolchildren such that they could not, when adult, properly distinguish sexual intercourse from good dental care, and evaluated each about as exciting as the other. Need I add that large scale epidemics of impotence have been reported and the situation is growing graver by the hour (*murmurs*).

No. I shall not bore the distinguished gathering with the details and diagnoses: severe overdevelopment is too obvious to need much analysis. When the house is on fire, you put the fire out, you do not discourse on the theory of heat (*laughter*). I shall proceed therefore to the recommendations that your commission proposed as immediate measures to be taken to "stop the rot." Whether the situation can ever be reversed is not clear, but we must always try my colleagues, must we not? We must always hope (*applause*).

The overall principle which has guided us in this as in all previous cases (our modest success in West Germany can be cited) is the introduction of a sufficient measure of social injustice and communal chaos to restore normal human functionings. Of course, this has to be attuned to the particular conditions of the country concerned, but the following are what we suggest as at least interim measures in the case of this unfortunate northern paradise.

1. The Mafia should be introduced at once and should infiltrate the trade unions and the herring industry. Gambling casinos should be opened and a number of bankers corrupted to the point

where they "make deals" with the mob. Judges and ministers should be bribed and a steady run of scandals in high places should be instituted.

2. Stockholm should be bombed.

3. About 400,000 of the Mexicans now flooding into the United States should be diverted to Sweden. They should be immediately put in charge of the postal services, and any other bureaucratic services where strict adherence to the Protestant Ethic is at present required. A bull ring should be set up in Uppsala.

4. The Swedes have already shown an admirable capacity for racist attitudes. It is your committee's feeling that these indigenous strengths should be capitalized on in all possible cases. Too often "aid" from the outside fails because it does not tap these indigenous motivations (*applause*). Thus we recommend that about two million black people should be sent immediately from some of the starving nations of the world. This will be a sacrifice for them, but their better impulses could he appealed to. Perhaps we could form an international "chaos corps?" I know my own countrymen would not flinch from their duty to the less fortunate in this respect (*applause*).

5. The above assistance would have a double effect. Not only would it introduce massive racial unrest as competition for jobs got underway, but the well-known penchant of Swedish women for black males would introduce an element of vicious sexual competition, which should cure the impotency problem overnight. The retaliation of the black women should prove an interesting experiment in its own right that might give us insights into how we might use this device elsewhere.

6. A border dispute with Finland should be provoked as soon as possible. Neutrality may not last if what has come to be known as "the territorial imperative" is threatened. If the Finnish government could be persuaded to maltreat the numerous Swedes living within its borders, this would help enormously.

7. Fornication outside legal marriage should be made a crime punishable by public flogging. Life imprisonment for adultery, and shooting for the distribution of pornography should be put on the statute books. All these sexual cases should be handled by highly vindictive ecclesiastical courts.

8. Prohibition should be introduced at once; preferably by a team of advisors from the USA to ensure maximum inefficiency.

Sufficient supplies, however, should be left intact for Mafia-run bootlegging purposes.

9. The income tax should be abolished along with most social services. A strong monarchist party should take power.

10. Ingmar Bergman should be allowed to make a staggeringly boring, highly symbolic movie of the results—with Spanish subtitles.

As with all bold moves to alleviate the problems of overdevelopment, this one has its dangers. The Swedes may already be too mentally undernourished to respond at all to these generous infusions of aid. But, gentlemen, we must try, try, and try again. Our moral obligations to the less fortunate of the world do not admit us to utter the word "impossible." Thank you gentlemen for your indulgence. I respectfully submit the commission's report and urge speedy implementation (*prolonged applause, cheers, waving of papers, etc., etc.*).

# IMAGE DE LA COMTESSE

Quand je regarde ce visage
je sais
Que je ne suis pas raisonnable
(croyance incroyable)
Ca me dérange peut-être mais
Je suis quand même un fou bien sage
au moins
Je me battrais pour ce visage

Quand je regarde ce visage
je pense
Que je ne pourrais jamais être
de moi-même le maitre
(incroyable cette croyance)
car asservi par cette image
enfin
je tuerais pour ce visage

When I look at this face/I know/that I am not rational/ (unbelievable belief)/ this bothers me perhaps and yet/I am even so a pretty wise fool/at least/I would fight for this face.

When I look at this face/I think/that I could never be/master of myself/ (unbelievable this belief)/because enslaved by this picture/in the end/I would kill for this face.

Quand je regarde ce visage
        je crains
qu'il ne soit un agent du Diable
(croyance 'peu pres croyable)
Vous vous me rendrez dans ses mains
ou ebloui par l'esclavage
        content
je mourrais donc pour ce visage

Quand je regarde ce visage
        je crois
qu'il fait des mots de Dieu une fable
(incroyance bien croyable)
Prince infernal écoutez moi
Ecoutez aussi l'entourage
        mon âme
je la vendrais pour ce visage

When I look at this face/I fear/that it's an agent of the devil/(belief almost believable)/ you give me up into his hands/where blinded by the slavery/ happily/I would then die for this face.

When I look at this face/I believe/it makes the words of God a fiction/(pretty believable unbelief) /Prince of Darkness listen to me/you followers listen too/ my soul/I would sell it for this face.

# INTUITION, STRUCTURE, AND PASSION REVISITED

## LOVE AT FIRST SIGHT

Although I never saw your face before
your image was prefigured in my mind
assuring me that one day I could draw
upon this template   knowing I would find
with instant recognition what I sought
So when you blazed into my consciousness
the golden message in my brain was caught
examined   and in milliseconds   "yes"
came back the answer   "this is she who was
and is   and always will be coded there"
I did not need to verify because
the answer was confirmed by your brief stare
        And for one terrifying moment we
        were locked in perfect mental symmetry

## STRUCTURAL SONNET

I cannot   by summation of each part
imply the living magic of the whole
That would require a logic of the heart
a limpid mathematics of the soul—
to grasp at once the juncture of green eyes
(that flash like timid emeralds in the night)
with an outrageous nose   to emphasize
the mouth when laughter sets the face alight
to witness that sharp movement of the head
so quick that it eludes the startled hair
and find for these a formula instead
to generate the surface magic there
      Then   through its transformations I would see
      the structure of my love's mythology

## SONNET OF THE DARK LADY

In search of death from gentleness   in search
of those extremes that free us from the bonds
of little life   to worship in the church
of savage flesh whose rites demand the fronds
still wet with blood from that dark forest where
your eyes are green   then blue   then vacant black
(matching the peat-pool darkness of your hair)
until the python slides across your back
and round my thighs   and tightens its embrace
with slow unyielding torture   Then your eyes
are blazing sapphires burning through your face
and we are one with serpent   teeth and thighs
      accepting pain and death with perfect trust
      crushed   and devoured by the snake of lust

## SAD SONNET

*(written in Bradley's, Greenwich Village,
with Rodrigo, improbably, on the juke box)**

Lack of you turns from numbness to despair
Neither guitars nor beer can ease the pain
With blatant sentiment that seems unfair
Rodrigo tears the guts from me again
Every female movement that's not yours
now tortures me   because I know I need
that warmth   that sensuous blindness   all that draws
my hungry mouth to fasten and to feed
My flesh irradiates the droning bar
until it drowns the gestures and the eyes
and old Rodrigo and the sad guitar
become mere adjuncts to my body's cries
     I stop my ears against these carnal moans
     and long for Satie's disembodied tones

*Actually, what was probably on the box was Miles Davis and his spooky trumpet version; but recollecting in tranquility as I sketched this out on the back of a coaster, what I heard in my head was the guitar concerto.

# DESIGN FAILURE
A Post-Tutorial Dialogue

*Metaphysics and the human sciences are made impossible by the penetration of morality into the moment to moment conduct of ordinary life: the understanding of this fact is religion.*
Iris Murdoch, *The Philosopher's Pupil*

*We have just enough Religion to make us hate, but not enough to make us love one another.*
Jonathan Swift, *Thoughts on Various Subjects*

…which leaves Spinoza and Schopenhauer with much the same position: no free will however you look at it.

A nice paper. A sound conclusion.

You agree then? Your pessimism is like Schopenhauer's; at least Spinoza had the consolation of some kind of god.

I'm not sure that agreeing or disagreeing is what I should do—in my role as tutor. I should assess your argument, comment on its logic, your use of sources…

Oh come on! We can go off the record—as it were, as you would say.

Of course—as it were.

Then we have no free will—except the contemplation of necessity. We *are* determined. What is more, we are determined to self-destruct—if you'll forgive the confusion of meanings.

Forgiven. Since we are off the record let's say "doomed to self-destruct" and have done with it.

Because of innate aggressivity?

We've gone beyond that simple-minded kind of thinking—I hope! We never had it really; it was how opponents phrased it, not us. A straw man. Innate aggressivity can be used for constructive as well as destructive ends. That's not what inspires my pessimism about Man's fate—forgive the pomposity.

Forgiven. But is there a greater justification for pessimism now than before?

Yes. Although the tendency to self-destructiveness was there, it did not previously have the means to destroy the whole species.

Is this tendency a product of modern technology, or is it endemic?

It is endemic—for reasons we can explore. But it need not have reached this pass. That it might do so was always *possible:* modern technology makes it probable. The probability increases daily.

Can science not save us?

No, because it too is at the heart of the problem. It should be what saves us, but it cannot act independently. It only acts in terms of values—judgments. These it makes very badly—a result of the design failure.

Why design failure? We were not designed.

No, but suppose we were (as some religions suppose). Would a superior intelligence have designed us the way we are? Only science fiction seems to have explored this, but it is at once our interest and our weakness that we seem to be somehow wrongly put together. God was in too much of a hurry to create in his own image. He missed.

Why did this hypothetical God miss?

Because he tried to fuse together a unique form of intelligence with a rather untried raw material—the evolving hominid. The result was a self-destructive mixture.

But if we were not in fact "designed," how did this really happen?

By an evolutionary accident. To become good at what we were doing we evolved this intelligence (or rather natural selection favored it). But having got it, it proved too powerful for its owner.

How can that be? Surely evolution does not go in for such excesses?

All the time—like the size of the dinosaurs, but not usually with intelligence—that was the error. A very different kind of feedback is set up.

How does this work to our disadvantage?

At first it didn't. Quite the contrary. The extra quality of this intelligent awareness enabled us to become top of the food chain. We should have stopped there.

Why didn't we—I mean, quit while we were ahead?

It is a peculiarity of this intelligence that it *cannot stop*. It started as simply a useful evolutionary device to help us adapt success-fully—like speed, strength, etc. But it had one huge weakness.

What was that?

It knew what it was doing and it was curious about what more it could do.

Why is that bad?

Because it changed all the rules of the adaptive game. Animals do what they have to do. This animal asked: why am I doing it; perhaps I could do it better?

But surely it isn't a mistake to do better?

Yes it is. The point of adaptation is to do just as well as is neces-sary to adapt. An adaptation does not question itself: weight does not question weight, size does not question size, nor flight, flight. But consciousness questions consciousness. That is the beginning of the end—which came rather rapidly really.

But haven't we been evolving for millions of years?

And intelligently conscious for probably less than one of those. That is a very short run in evolutionary terms. But the run is really even shorter. Until about the end of the upper paleolithic, con-scious intelligence was an adaptive aid. Then, given some unprec-edented good weather, it was able to expand. The rundown has taken at best 10,000 years.

But surely in that time we did not decline, we improved—civili-zation, technology, science, art, etc?

Not really. Until the industrial revolution nothing very basic changed. Look at the cave painting of the upper paleolithic; study the religious ideas of primitive tribes—we have not improved on these. We changed in scale and appearance, but not in skill and intelligence. It was variations on a theme.

But since the industrial revolution?

Science is the ultimate intellectual curiosity. That has made the difference. But it was only intended as a handmaiden of values, which themselves spring from the needs of survival. It was never intended to have an independent existence, and has never really had one. The problem is its very success. It is still the handmaiden of values, and these have not changed—merely become inappropriate in the new environment that they and science have created.

Are you suggesting that we should have stayed as stone-age hunters?

In some senses, yes. But here is the basic problem: the very mechanism that enabled us to be successful hunters was way in excess of its needed capacity. This is where the positive feedback came in: better brains—more intelligence—set up conditions that needed even better brains to survive, and so on. The process was too rapid. The result was a sophisticated computer built into an emotional ape.

Surely the computer could control the ape?

Not really. There was control in the sense that the ape could now do his angry (and other) things more effectively. But the computer itself did not give any directions—it only followed. And the programming had to come from the raw material of the ape in question: a volatile, aggressive, vain, sentimental, greedy, cowardly, suspicious, loving mix-up of a creature.

But if it could do ail these things better...?

Yes—sometimes it would work, but only under rather restricted conditions, namely those which it had evolved to cope with—small-scale hunting groups spread out over a rich environment. Once this scale was left behind, the great danger arose: the creature could start to design its own environment.

Why is that so bad?

It didn't know what to design. It was at the mercy of its own imagination, its own inventiveness. The computer was called upon more and more and seemed limitless in its capacity to invent more and more ingeniously. But no one knew why, except that it was worth doing for its own sake; because that is what it did.

But you said that "an animal does what it has to do." Isn't this what the human animal has to do?

Yes. Which is why we couldn't stick at being hunters. The basic design failure meant that our chief asset—conscious intelligence—would, at the service of aggression, curiosity, territoriality, xenophobia, dominance, and all the other raw material, simply run off on its own tracks. This we call imagination— *this* is what this animal does as opposed to others (some of which are intelligent enough).

So you are suggesting that the inability of intelligence to have its own values is the major design failure?

In a way. Some people have claimed values for intelligence—or its product science. For example, disinterestedness has been canvassed. But there is no evidence that it is intelligence (or reason or science) per se that is disinterested.

But surely it must suspend judgements for its operation. It cannot declare 2 + 2 "bad" and refuse to solve the equation. And surely this suspension, if brought often enough into play, would lead to a value being placed on disinterestedness?

Only in the pursuit of knowledge itself. And this knowledge, don't forget, by evolutionary fiat, is in the service of the brute raw material. It is only very recently that we have separated out certain people as pure specialists in the use of intelligence. And they are always divided in their notions of the ultimate use of their labors—usually on xenophobic grounds.

But again, if intelligence is a universal feature, cannot they claim that it should only be used for universal human good?

They can. Many have. But they are trapped. Who is to say that their evaluation is superior to that of someone who claims it should be used only for the good of the revolutionary proletariat? I told you religion was part of the problem.

You mean ideology?

O.K. Give it new and fancy names, but ultimately it is the response of the computer to the fact that it knows it exists and can articulate questions about this existence. In fact it finds it hard to operate at all without some answers to these questions, otherwise it lacks basic energy to go on computing.

Well, if it is so intelligent, why doesn't it come up with the answer?

Because there is no answer—at least not to the question as the computer feels obliged to pose it. Another design failure. But that doesn't stop it, in its ingenuity, from proposing numerous answers.

And what is so wrong with that?

Nothing intrinsically, except, for some reason, these answers seem to get hitched onto the raw material of xenophobia: we have our answer, and those with other answers are to be feared and eliminated if possible.

But what about religions of brotherly love?

They usually try to eliminate those who don't believe in religions of brotherly love. Those who believe in the triumph of the meek try to get rid of (or convert) those who believe in the triumph of the strong. And so on. The content of the ideology (if you must call it that) doesn't seem to matter. What matters is the belief in the idea—any idea.

Another design failure?

Yes. Once the computer was fully working it worked in terms of ideas (concepts, whatever). So when it began to question its own meaning it clearly assumed that the answer lay in some idea or set of ideas. Once given that it could not exist without the energy provided by an answer to its own answerless question, it clearly would become desperately attached to the ideas it had settled on. These were its engine, its motive power. Interference with them is the most damaging thing that faces the computer. Its alliance with the old xenophobic and aggressive raw material is thus fused. To threaten the idea is to threaten existence itself.

And the idea of science cannot transcend this?

Try threatening the idea of the idea of science (as variously interpreted) and see the response. Those revolutionaries who worshipped reason thought it quite reasonable to eliminate those who thought otherwise. It is the idea of the idea that rules, not the idea itself—not its content. Any idea—hence, for you, any ideology—is better than none.

Then if I understand the design failure, without attachment to ideas our intelligence cannot function, but once attached to ideas we are their prisoners and cannot function intelligently?

We can function intelligently in the sense that we can rationally adapt means to ends (try to kill the unbelievers with a knife as opposed to a lump of jello). But we cannot function dispassionately, disinterestedly, or reasonably, or even in our best long-run interests. If this is what you mean by intelligently, you are right.

I suppose I mean "intelligently" intelligently!

You probably mean what we used to call rationality—but in the special sense of having our ultimate self-preservation as a goal. If we see that short-term defense of our ideas is going to mean long-term destruction of them, then we should adjust.

Why don't we? Another design failure?

I'm afraid so. "Better dead than Red" sums it up? We lack effective long-term vision. For most people even a lifetime is too long to contemplate. In any case, it means contemplating death and we don't like that privilege the computer grants us. Also, we assume that it is the business of the computer to give us accurate information about the world. But this is doubtful. It is more likely that the thing gives us selective and optimistic information.

But surely this would have been an evolutionary disaster?

Not at all. The creature evolved to act, not to contemplate reality. The brain-computer gives us just enough information to make an adaptive action possible, then floods us with morphine to make us feel it will be possible, and adrenaline to help make it possible.

But freed from the need to act, surely it can behave rationally?

As I said before, only in a limited sphere—that of pure knowledge. Outside pure reason all is in the realm of practical reason—of action. And in this world the rational, disinterested products of science have little place except, almost literally, as tools.

And these tools, this technology, are also handmaidens?

This would be more readily agreed to, I think. But what people forget is that 90 percent of so-called science is technology. And by a queer twist, the very value of disinterestedness that science and technology pretend to, renders them the even more perfect handmaidens of the xenophobic ideas.

But surely the idea that Mankind—that the whole species—should be saved, would solve the problem; everyone would adhere to it?

As people have pointed out, this might work if we were threatened by Martians. Short of that it runs up against the formidable combination we have discussed: the alliance of the computer's dedication to the idea with the tendency to xenophobia, and the short-run vision and the inaccurate brain. People will find a way to differ about how the species should be saved and fight about that.

The xenophobia is part of the design failure? But why?

Same reason. It served a useful purpose when we were dispersed. It probably helped set the boundaries of breeding populations—language helped.

How could that be?

Has it ever occurred to you to ask why we speak so many different languages? We could all speak the same. But, given the capacity for language as such, we can develop infinite different ones.

The paleolithic "linguistic tribe" was about 5,000 (our outer limits of tolerance?). The local group about 50 (our comfortable limit?).

Was the point of this to do with breeding, then?

Probably. You don't marry those you can't talk to. Of course, you can kill off their males and incorporate the women and the children—who would rapidly learn your language. This would have worked very well as an evolutionary mechanism, again, as long as we were dispersed. The species was not threatened.

Where did it go wrong?

Ideas are couched in language. Language groups that succeeded grew enormously at the expense of others. The xenophobia got out of hand. From being a boundary mechanism it became a vehicle for the propagation of ideas. People did not have even to share the same natural language to share the same ideas and to be attached to them with xenophobic ferocity. There had been no ideological differences between tribes; they fought over real issues. But soon whole bodies of people—even linguistically distinct—began fighting over ideas to which they were attached. The confluence of these mechanisms led to a backfiring of the system.

But the tribes surely hated the ideas of the other tribes—their customs and so on. This was part of the xenophobia, wasn't it?

Sometimes they hated them, sometimes feared them, sometimes despised them, sometimes respected them, sometimes admired them. But they didn't fight because of the ideas—not to protect or promulgate them. They fought over women or territory or whatever. It was the marriage of the attachment to the idea with the tribal xenophobia, carried beyond tribal boundaries, that led to disaster. Nations, religions, movements, cults, causes, parties—all artificial entities—came to behave like tribes with ideas as totems.

So what had been a useful evolutionary mechanism backfired?
Exactly.

How can that happen? Is it unique to us?

In a sense it happens every time a species fails to adapt to changing circumstances and becomes extinct—which is the evolutionary rule by the way, not the exception. Our case is however unique.

Because we know what is happening?

Because we not only know what is happening but because the

capacity to know what is happening is also the cause of what is happening! Now that is unique—if you're after the real marks of human uniqueness!

So that is why reason, science, technology, and religion can't save us?

Yes. For what produces them is the same design failure that produces the problems they are supposed to solve—indeed they are part of the problem. They are products of the unholy marriage that is the design failure.

The logic of this is that any of our efforts to solve the problem are doomed to make it worse, is it not?

If the efforts remain within the vicious circle we have explored this must be so. Any redoubling of scientific or religious (ideological) effort is likely to exacerbate the problem. Those of us who have urged a species-centered ethic, for example, have been now classified as a cult with the marks of the devil, and all kinds of tribes with their idea-totems are ranged against us. To save the species-ethic, then, we may have to destroy a lot of the species. Scarcely the outcome we intended, but part of the logic of the system. Someone, as I said, will always differ about how the species should be saved, or which bit of it, or something such.

Because they have to?

Yes. An idea only has to be slightly different to become a point of attachment and a focus of suspicion and fanaticism.

You haven't mentioned fanaticism as such before. Another design failure?

Yes. It's an outgrowth of xenophobia. The xenophobic fanatic is a tribal chauvinist—the one who claims the world for his tribe. There were probably such: the Genghis Khans, the Alexanders. But they didn't do much long-run harm because—and we're back to this—they couldn't affect the survival of the species.

But now a few fanatics can?

Unfortunately that is the way. And they need not be foaming at the mouth fanatics. It is the degree of single-minded devotion to the idea that marks the fanatic. A seemingly cool decision that "democracy shall not perish without a fight" for example, could mean the end. This could also be a rational decision, given the premises, and one aided by all the computer information needed to augment the computer-brain. But it would be a fanatic decision, and hence a very human and very likely one. Of course, the foaming-mouth fanatics can be just as destructive—they are not usually as efficient.

And people connive in their own destruction?

Of course. The tribe is endangered—at any cost save the tribe. The idea is threatened—at any cost protect the idea. The result may be death, but without the idea we are dead anyway, so let it roll. I wonder how many realize just how ineradicably deep this is in the human mechanism? At once the reason for our staggering success and the built-in self-destruct device at the same time? Swift knew it was *the* danger—but of course he couldn't have known the evolutionary causes. But we will fight over which end of a boiled egg to crack.

People do oppose war.

Yes—and then define those who share that idea as their tribe and proceed to attack quite violently the opposition. Few people are as vicious to their opponents as the apostles of peace.

You are too cynical. What about the nonviolents?

Don't you see, we can't escape? This is another form of fanaticism (sometimes you have to be violent to do good) and it is the fanaticism that is the enemy. Every form of fanaticism (or ideology again, if you like) claims moral superiority—but what we need is an absence of fanaticism, not just another version, however pacific.

And this we cannot have?

No, because (remember the argument) the attachment to the idea is so basic a necessity (however simple or mundane the idea) that we need it to function at all. Hence we can only be fanatical in our dislike of fanatics. The Cretan liar always wins.

I'm sure that all this simply means that people have to have ideas or opinions in order to be able to act at all.

It does, but from the simple expansion of this rule comes all the paradox of our human existence. Animals don't have opinions, and they act.

They also become extinct.

But they don't know that this can happen. We do know and we let it happen anyway.

If you are right, our very knowing is what in our case causes it to happen. (I think.) But couldn't it have happened without our knowing being the cause?

Yes, of course—as with all other nonself-conscious species, including those closely related to us that are no more. But our absurd paradox is this: we should be able to avert the disaster that inevitably awaits a species since we know it can happen and can, theoretically, take steps to see that it doesn't.

But we won't?

No.

You seem confident of this. Why?

Because of my attachment to an idea.

What?

That Nature cannot be cheated. The law of extinction cannot be avoided by knowing of its existence. So Nature builds in an ingenious device: any species that comes to know of the nature of its own existence will use that knowledge to ensure its own extinction. It's quite beautiful really.

So there is no breaking out of the vicious circle? We are trapped in its premises?

I cherish a forlorn hope that some incredible change of cosmic gears might happen—some evolutionary change so profound (a quadrupling of the life span perhaps?) that it would change all the rules. But should it happen we might be forced to admit that what then existed was a successor species and not Homo sapiens at all—so the paradox would remain. We would not have become extinct, but our genes would be so changed we would be a different species. And this might more readily happen in the wake of nuclear wars with massive radiation and an astronomically increased mutation rate. From this a new species might emerge that would solve the paradox. This one never will.

I don't believe what you say, but I would fight to the death for your right to say it, of course.

Of course.

## COMING OF AGE IN JUST ABOUT EVERYWHERE*
An Ode to the Selfish Gene

This is a word of consolation
For those who fear the confrontation
Between the social and genetic

Before you all become frenetic
Let's try to figure what it means
This war of culture and the genes
The torment that provokes the colic
Twixt chromosomal and symbolic

It does not take a smart detective
To see it's all in the perspective
Pursue the symbols if you must
You then can take the genes on trust
But don't dismiss as blind or comic
Pursuit of matters teleonomic
Avoid the tediousness of faction
Through gene and culture interaction
As scientists you can wax lyrical—
The question has become empirical!

Culture ain't worth a heap of beans
If it can't propagate the genes
But if not fortified by culture
The genes are doomed to quick sepulture†
So let this question lift the gloom

"Who gives what or which to whom?"
And if you're really very keen
Try empathizing with the gene

*Except, if Woody Allen is right, certain parts of New Jersey
†Acknowledgement to R. Browning, "The Grammarian's Funeral"

The Gene is not on pleasure bent
On replication it's intent
Though sex results from its demand
The kicks are only second hand
Its puritanical devotion
To putting further Genes in motion
While organisms have the fun
Is worthy   when all's said and done
Compare the endless aggravation
Of Culture's aimless dissipation
The way symbolic systems fatten
On each unwholesome culture pattern
And try with frivolous invention
To twist the sombre Gene's intention

The Selfish Gene brooks no excuse
The inner voice screams "reproduce"
(The consequence is less complex
We hear it as "indulge in sex")
However much we symbolize
The Gene is ultimately wise
In every culture upon earth
We screw a lot   and then give birth
The Gene will never know   you see
The point of the diversity
It's ends that interest the Genes
So their concern is not with means
Choose any way you like to mate
One thing is sure—they replicate
Since replication is the game
All diverse cultures are the same
In the long run genetic view
(Except perhaps the very few
Which fail to replicate at all
But they gone beyond recall)

Of interest though we're not bereft
The only question that is left
Is fascinating   you'll allow
"So mate   so replicate   but HOW?"
It does not matter in the end
But still we can observe the trend
For in the long run   as Keynes said
We lose our interest   being dead


So cheer up social scientist
Variety's a finite list
But there to keep you occupied
(Occasionally boggle-eyed)
As ponderously you pursue
Each turn of the symbolic screw
And watch the figures weave and prance
Their patterns in the cultural dance
That goes unheeded and unseen
By the indifferent   patient Gene


# MUSIC OF THE SPHERES


Who choreographs the dance of life
God   or Balanchine?
No   Mendel and his wrinkled peas—
or something in between

Who orchestrates the song of youth
God   or Borodin?
No Jacob Monod Watson Crick—
a regulator gene

What promulgates the will to live
God   (that passer by?)
No   Mindless protein molecules
that don't know how to die

# THREE INTERRUPTIONS OF
# RATIONAL ARGUMENTS

*(These were all "interludes, " intended to comment on,
while breaking up, the otherwise heavy-going arguments
of the three papers mentioned in the introduction to this
book. The first was to have been in an article, "The
Violent Imagination." The second is from "Consciousness out of Context," published in* The Search for
Society. *This contains a critical look at Daniel Bell's*
The Coming of Post-Industrial Society, *hence the
epigraph. It may look like free verse but it isn't. It is
intended to sound like a literal translation of a chorus
from a Greek tragedy, hence "first stasimon." The last
one is from "Inhuman Nature and Natural Rights." See
introduction again.)*

THE WALL

(Christmas Eve: Jerusalem)


You scare me
      Wall
          To take me by surprise
out of the dark like that was wrong
            You draw
me on   you loom   you threaten
          Still I wear
an alien cap so I might touch you

                                        Wall
might join the pious ants who scuffle round
your ponderous stone feet   so I might mix
my fingers with their fingers while they probe
your cavities obscenely with their scraps
of futile paper     sad   mundane requests
"Please God   take care of Rachel"
                                        Put it back
I should have gone to Bethlehem but
                                        Wall
I came to you instead
                        I don't know why
Perhaps because I don't believe that myth
they seared my childhood with   but you are real
stone idol
            golden Wall
                            You are alive
You are electric   and you seem to sing
You speak not just to Jews   I hear you
                                        Wall
in some mad inner ear
                            She said to me
I saw men die so I could be here"
                                    Wall
She said that as she went to stroke your stones
said it with faith in some Judaic god
that moves me not at all
                            She came away
in tears
            I did not weep   But listen
                                    Wall
accept my infidelic touch   I could
not bear rejection
                        Let me hide in you
Your gold and throbbing stones cry out like flesh
to be embraced
                    and yet your touch is cold

I fear you
            Wall
                    for men will die again
not for their god   but you
                            And I know this
I have no reverence for that Hebrew god
that gloomy   vengeful chauvinist
                                and yet
I know that I could worship you
                        old Wall
and for your stones we all perhaps might die

## PATRIMONY FOR A POSSIBLE POSTERITY
(first stasimon)

> "...*the duplex nature of man himself*— *the murderous
> aggression, from primal impulse, to tear apart and
> destroy.*"
> Daniel Bell, *The Coming of Post-Industrial Society*

What shall we tell them?
What shall we tell the survivors?

What shall we leave them
Those who may remain?

Why should they listen?
Why should they pay attention?
We talked ourselves into annihilation
We argued our way into death
We destroyed ourselves with words
How can they learn from our experience
When our experience led to their near extinction?

We can tell them what to avoid.
That is all that is left to tell the survivors.
If there are any survivors.
We can tell them what we did wrong
If we can recognize what we did wrong
If we dare admit our mistakes
And admit them now.

But how can we admit to what we
        do not understand?
How can we tell the survivors what not
        to repeat?
Will it be obvious to them?
Will they say, "They did it badly,
        but we can start again
We can do it right this time."
And will they get it right?

Will it be so obvious what went wrong?
Hindsight has not helped us so far
Will it help the survivors?

What shall we tell them to avoid?
We cannot tell them what to construct
We do not know what to construct
Every effort at construction is a failure.
At destruction we are geniuses
We were always best at destruction
Since the first butchering
The first attack on the herds
Since the first deserts and wastelands
We have destroyed like true artists.

We can tell them to avoid destruction.
But how to tell them why they
        cannot avoid it?
How to tell them why their pleasure
        is most sweet and delicate when they destroy
Tell them to avoid ecstasy?
Tell them to avoid the delusion
        of power destruction offers?
They know the power of destruction
They will have seen the end of their
        civilization
They will have seen their cities gone
        to dust and their lakes to filth
        and their oceans to emptiness
All this they will have seen.
They will not need to be told to
        avoid destruction
They will need to be told why they
        need to destroy
Or why they cannot despite the best
        intentions avoid their joy
        in destruction.
They will need to be told to forgo
        their joy.

Is this a thing to tell the survivors?
Those few who have lived through
    the destruction?
To avoid destruction you must
    destroy part of yourselves?

Is that our legacy to
    the survivors
Torn, desperate and wretched—
A paradox?

## REASON IS, AND OUGHT TO BE, FUTILE

The function of intelligence it seems
(reflecting on the fine futility
of thinking about loving you instead
of simply doing it) is to infiltrate
confusion among the emotions—cramping and
controlling   confining and inhibiting
what otherwise might be direct   proud fierce
untroubled by concern with consequence
and prejudicial to good order and
discipline among the regimented passions.

Can I not love you and not count the costs—
foresee   foretell   predict   prognosticate—
balance the mindless consummated swift
magnetic nonsense on the one hand with
the other sentient sensible handful of
consideration consequence and cause?
Love is a feeling not an argument
It has an end but so far no solution—
a goal—but no deductive reasoning
can reach that goal or realize that end

Reason is not   dear David   as you said
slave of the passions   nor ought it to be
(and you derived an ought from something quite
so fragile—so sensational—an is?)
Reason is God's gift to man because
it makes him doubt the brutish   nasty     short
and natural   in him   and so makes him man

But that leaves me a questioner when
I want to be a lover   and the two
are seemingly at war in me   and this
is how it should be else we are not men
and would just copulate and never write
these tortured verses as a compliment
to cunning intellect that makes us men
and yet unmans us in the making   Help!

# LYRICS ON THE FEMALE ENIGMA
(again)


## THREE POSSIBILITIES

There are those women who inspire lust
for some small reason like the way a dress
clings to a limb   the mouth pulsates   the eye
droops slightly   It inflames but does not last

Some others radiate a childish mood—
a vulnerable blink   a nervous touch
a tender imploration   These can draw
but not inflame   not drive the cool brain mad

Very rarely there are those whose hurt
and restless hardness makes its own demand
that's neither love nor lust   but need to tame
the spirit's panther   yet not break its heart

## GIRLS WHO LOST THEIR FATHERS

Girls who lost their fathers   who are doomed
to drift through life like souls condemned   will stray
forever in a limbo of their own
Sealed in the past their spirits lie entombed
Their bodies meanwhile try to find a way
to hide the truth   they must survive alone

Some lacking trust in trust their bodies turn
to many lovers   intimate with none
Some desperately cling to older men
for restoration   and they rarely learn
that they are self-deceived   once it is gone
the father's love cannot return again

The lovers' contract always has fine print
The father's love seemed unconditional
Age does not guarantee a thing   but then
I do not even have the heart to hint
that all is futile   nothing will annul
the grief   however fatherlike their men

But though they lost their fathers they are not
as stricken as girls never loved at all
At least the fantasy can act like dope
and phantom fathers in a ghostly plot
endowed with other bodies can recall
a sad incestuous memory of hope

# PROSPECT OF NUCLEAR WINTER

After the desolation and the death
uprose the sun-obscuring dust   and then
the creeping cold that turned the world to ice
a smooth round shining ball   except without
the sun it could not shine   But when the dust
had cleared a little   there the beauty hung
flashing and gleaming through the shredded veil
(a youthful widow contemplating sex)

And in a galaxy far far away
an eye protruding from a stalk projecting
from a gigantic brain was pressed against
the eyepiece of a super telescope
And for a moment this superior
intelligence observed the flashing orb
and thought   in fractions of a nanosecond
that it would call it – <' #+˜%_& *˜{:+–!˜
"crystal(ine) planet-the"   then turned away
to its far more important work   the planning
of the ultimate war made necessary
by the discovery of a logical
contradiction in the arguments
between galactic ideologies

And in a parallel universe   a far
far far superior intelligence
noticed this blip in time   and since for it
time was running backwards (at the time)
it saw the end result and named it thus
(I translate roughly   for they spoke in math)
"consciousness = crystal universe"

# BULLFIGHT AT ALTAMIRA: THE SEA AT SANTA MARTA

(Colombia, 1981)

> *La vaca del viejo mundo*
> *pasaba su triste lengua*
> *sobre un hocico de sangres*
> *derrarnadas en la arena,*
> *y los toros de Guisando,*
> *casi muerte y casi piedra,*
> *mugieron como dos siglos*
> *hartos de pisar la tierra.*
> Federico García Lorca, *Llanto por la*
> *muerta de Ignacio Sánchez Mejías*

> *I do not find*
> *The Hanged Man. Fear death by water.*
> *I see crowds of people, walking round in a ring.*
> T. S. Eliot, *The Waste Land*

## ALTAMIRA DE COELLO, TOLIMA, AUG. 8

Conquistadores brought the name that tells
it all   if you can break the code   It was
Altamira   They added (Portuguese)
de Coello   but all was in the name
The paleolithic brain that painted bulls
is the same brain that manufactures rockets
to send brains to the moon to play at golf
But here we're free of such banality
inheriting direct through Mithras and
the cult of Minotaurus to the roots
of Indo-European mysteries

And here at Altamira de Coello
we free ourselves from all the tinselled pomp
that troubled Spaniards weave around the bull
to pacify their Catholic guilt when in
their pagan hearts they feel participation
in things that mock their Christian piety

Because we know we die   that all things die
so we can make a cult of death   (or love
or food or self-denial or compassion)
We are nature's cultists but the cult
of death defines us most—not ritual
The animals perfected ritual
before the first australopithecine
had ever chipped a stone—we ritualize
as easily as we digest   But cults
are products of our pure imagination
and gorge upon the ritual tendency
to feed the cultic appetite
                              The bull
does what it has to do to be a bull
At Altamira in old Spain a man
painted a bull   So simple   Yet consider
*he did not have to*   Nor do we today
at Altamira de Coello have
to dance the dangerous dance   And yet we must
We do not have to   yet we have no choice
We need not make a cult of death   but how
to face the fact of death without a cult?
So we transfer it to a cult of life
and Mithras and the bleeding bull become
(through Persian soma like our own?) a death
changed into life
                          The cycle turns
The bull must fertilize   the god must die
the bull-calf lives   the god must rise again
to fertilize and die eternally

Old Altamirans killed both bull and horse
and did not live with them or dance with them
But they did paint them   and the first remove
from ritual to cult was realized
That painter was the universal man
Both bull and horse were tamed   and in the herds
of some Caucasian mob was born a race
that lived upon the anvil of the earth
forged from the fury of the fire of heaven
the rivers   plains   the horse   the sky   the bull
the restless movement and the endless wars
til it became a fierce particular
of that old Altamiran universal
And even when the matriarchal plot
had rendered them as fat and slow as oxen
and made them cautious tillers of the earth
there still were those—those brains of Altamira—
who never did   who never could forget
the bull that was their life   As more than meat
but as the thing sent down in fire and thunder
to test their manhood and to make them men
(For men must make their men   There is no way
that nature makes a human male a man
A rigid penis is no use unless
its owner's arms can turn aside a bull
or paint it on the walls of Altamira)

Here we are at the heart   at Altamira
the place where when the bull and he together
perform their ritual   the matador
stands in the sun and sand alone   appalled
at being (without knowing) at the source
of all that makes him his particular kind
of human creature   and that makes him man
Here there are the bulls   the sky   and us
We do not fight   we dance   and in the dance
so little intervenes   (a curious crowd
of visitors   paisanos   Some are high
on soma—sister of the bull itself—

and some   the friends of Dionysus are
a little sacred with aguardiente)
Stark in the dust there is the rough wood ring
the sun   the sky   the bulls   and in the ring
waits symbol-sodden man   drunk only with
the mystery of loving perfect death

And so despite the mother goddess they
continued with the ballet of the bull
and with the passage of the years forgot
except in some intuitive recess
of racial and of species memory
the meaning of the dancer and the dance

But here at Altamira we remember
because there is so little to distract
And I   novitiate   careless with the cape
invite the charge with casual invasion
of that enchanted circle which the bull
has claimed as his   And when he turns and when
with lowered horns starts on his sudden charge
and I too numb for fcar yct drunk with truth
turn him aside—a hundred thousand years
of history are frozen in the heat
and swirl about me in the sand   and enter
my nostrils from the mingling of our sweat

And when I turn too slowly and our bodies
crash in a mad embrace of man and beast
my brain explodes with mysteries too intense
for verse or science or philosophy
I only know the bull and I must die
and that together we can make it perfect
and in that making   in that calm perfection
something is fulfilled that at its root
is what makes me a man and him a bull
and is as necessary to our beings as
the blood that we each spill   that we both share

## SIERRA NEVADA DE SANTA MARTA, RIO DON DIEGO, AUG. 20

The waves at Santa Marta charge at me
and throw me to the sand   and when I try
to gain the shore they suck me back again
I can't believe it is impersonal
so fierce and so particular the fury
the sea affronts me with   I am afraid
of death by drowning   Nothing has endowed
the waves with instinct   Death   you say   is death
But I will take death from the bull   and he
will take it from me also   With respect
Because we share so much   Not so the sea
that alien idiot ferocity
Canute   old Dane   there with your cape of words
you taught a lesson deeper than you knew
One cannot turn aside the charge of waves
A death from drowning has no meaning and
one cannot make it meaningful   it is
"an accident"   a misery of chance
The bull death is a mystery of choice
a bullfight a memento mori   so
I choose   therefore I am   therefore I choose
the beauty of the bulls of Altamira
and shun the mindless danger of the sea

Protestant   alone and without God
the universe is only what I make it—
this curious cosmic accident   and yet
I'm caught in the inevitable flow
of nature   and if then I must impose
a meaning on the accident I claim
a death of my own choosing   (since my birth
was yet another accidental quirk)
As I was born through semen   blood   and pain
so let me die the bull death and complete
the circle   and with one symbolic stroke
impose my meaning on the natural

and yet cheat nature by cooperation
because what I impose is nature's will—
we struggled he and I   and he survived

How human thus to die by paradox
and in that death assert humanity
flinging a cape at accident and mocking
the imbecile indifference of chance

# PSALM ONE HUNDRED AND FIFTY-ONE

*nulla fugae ratio, nulla spes: omnia muta*
*omnia sunt deserta, ostentant omnia letum*
—Catullus

*How is it possible to expect that Mankind will take*
*Advice, when they will not so much as take warning.*
—Jonathan Swift

Thou holdest in thine hand, O child of man,
    the power to destroy thyself: and who shall
    save thee? Who shall stay thine hand?
Shalt thou save thyself: Look into thine own
    heart; multiply thy vision a billion times
    five;
Does it shout salvation? O miserable echo:
    it whispers—help!

Shall thy great leaders save thee, child of heroes?
Shall Gandhi, Churchill, Stalin, King?
Shall Begin, Khomeini, Roosevelt, Ho?
Shall Kennedy, Sadat, Qaddafi, Jesus?
Shall Moses, Akhenaton, Joan of Arc?
The fanatics of strength: the megalomaniacs of
    Peace?
With the fateful formula: xenophobia plus
    fanaticism plus the instinct of the
    herd equals power—for me, my children,
    my likenesses, my ideas.

Shall ideas save thee, child of mind?
Shall empiricism, idealism, nominalism, racism?
Shall romanticism, pacifism, feminism, positivism?
Shall predestination, reincarnation, transubstantiation,
    verification?

Utilitarianism, pragmatism, relativism, pantheism,
Anarchism, humanism, creationism, scientism,
Behaviorism, stoicism, nationalism, solipsism,
Evolutionism, rationalism, structuralism,
    Marxism, progress or original sin?

Shall thy philosophers save thee, child of
    knowledge?
Shall thy men of science man the breach
    and save thee, child of the experimentum crucis?
Shall thy physicians heal thy sickness, child
    of flesh?
Shall the knowledge of thy teachers save thee,
    child of learning?
Shall the conscience of the rulers of earth?
Shall the meekness of earth's inheritors?

Shall religions save thee, child of faith?
Shall Catholicism, shall the Polish Pope,
The Anglican, Unitarian, Baptist, Presbyterian,
Lutheran, Orthodox, Methodist, Congregationalist,
The Maronite, Copt or the Countess of Huntingdon's
    Connection?
Shall the Buddhists, the Hindus, the
    Confucians or Taoists,
The Swedenborgians, Christian Scientists, Mormons
    or Shakers,
The Church of God in Christ, the Church of Christ
    in God,
The Bahaists, the Sunni, the Sufi, the Judaic,
The Shiite, the Holy Rollers or the Peculiar
    People?
Shall Shinto, or Zoroastrians or the Old
    Believers?

Shall religion save thee or divide thee
    O thou quivering, devoted faithful?
Turn to it for Truth; it gives thee truth;
    so choose thy Truth and die for it;  thou
    splendid martyr!

Shall patriotism save thee?
My country right or wrong:
The jingoistic, xenophobic high?
Pursuit of our manifest destiny?
Recapturing our sacred national territory;
Regaining our sacred national freedom;
Exploiting our sacred national wealth;
Protecting our sacred national borders;
Restoring our sacred national virtue;
Destroying our sacred national enemies;
Defending our unimpeachable national honor,
Revenging the insult to our beloved national flag;
Reviving our virtually unspoken national language;
And above all having our uneconomic national
    airline.
To spend more than we earn; borrow more
    then we can repay;
To equip our national troops for all the
    above purposes with weapons we cannot
    afford;
To raise the standard of living of our people from
    terrible to tolerable with luck;
To be a light to lighten other nations with
    our proud example.

And the little nationalisms—shall they save
    thee, child of the tribe?
The heartland of the xenophobia, fanaticism
    and instinct of the herd?
Shall Basque, Catalan, Provençal, Breton,
    Corsican?
Shall Ukrainian, Georgian, Serbian, Croatian,
    Montenegrin?
Shall Palestinian, Kurdish, Baluchi, Québecois,
    Biafran?
Shall Welsh, Zionist, Bugandan, Punjabi,
    Assamese?
For as thou prophesiest their decline, so
    shall they rise, feeding the tumor
    of xenophobia, fanaticism and the
    instinct of the herd.

And fearing thine own superstates thou
    sayest:
"Yea, this is good: the people are returning
    to their sense of identity; of place:
    this is more human."
And indeed it is, child of the tumor that feeds our
    humanity;
And even as thou sayest, another child dies
    shouting slogans for the tribal crusade.
For will the tribes in their folk wisdom
    fail to perfect the weapon which is
    their god?
And will they shrink from using it if the
    tribal honor is affronted, its lands
    possessed by strangers?
Yes—give them back their spears!
At least in savagery we are safe from
    ultimate destruction, child of the weapon.
But remember, child of the pogrom and the
    massacre, to carry thine own spear,
    and lock thy door at twilight, and put
    thy trust in no one.
And remember the knowledge of the weapon
    that will end forever the enemies of
    the tribe;
Remember the knowledge, child of progress,
    that thou canst not take away;
And remember that knowledge is the tumor's
    slave.

Where shalt thou turn?
Shall technology save thee, child of ingenuity?
Shall science save thee, child of intellect?
Shall computers, electronics, optics, polymers;
Plasma physics, micro-chip information storage
And retrieval; nuclear fission and fusion?
Shall gene-splicing, solar water pumps;
Robots, artificial intelligence, space shuttles?
Shall green revolutions, herbicides, pesticides;
Defoliants, synthetic fertilizers, dams?

Shall cybernetics, systems theory, multiphase
Analysis, multidimensional scaling, feedback?
Shall linear programming, Markov chains,
Stochastic processes, topology, field theory,
Quantum mechanics, quarks, quasars or
      red dwarfs?

Where shalt thou look now God hath deserted thee?
Thou hast nothing but these mirrors of thyself:
Art thou safe from thyself, child of fantasy?
In the hollows of thine heart hast thou not
      destroyed us all a thousand times in
      thine omnipotence?
And are those who hold the power to destroy—
      children re-born to real omnipotence—
      more than thou art, bastard child of Cain?
Look upon them, see thyself, and weep.

You demand guidance, you ask for advice; be not cynical
      be constructive you cry.
You ask for advice, children of necessity; I say
Remember the Manicheans, they gave you advice; I say
Remember the Shakers, they gave you advice; I say
Remember the Albigenses; I say remember all the sages
Who thundered "Abandon Sex!" "Abandon Procreation!"
That was advice. Why did you not take it? I am the
Shaker/Manichean/Albigensian of ideas. I cry unto thee
"Abandon Nationalism" I exhort thee "Abandon religious zeal"
I plead "Abandon hatred of the stranger, your giant bureaucracies,
Your greed for power, your lust for progress" And I cry
With the same result as they. Did you abandon sex? If I cry
Will you listen? Will you abandon this eroticism of the soul?
Do not ask for advice you know you cannot heed.

Thou hast built incredible engines of travel
      and manufacture; of pleasure and of
      science.
Thou hast extended thy memory with machines
      and improved the speed of thought with them.
Thou hast probed the nature of matter with

thy machines down to the machinery
of life itself.
But nowhere hast thou probed thyself, child
of invention.
Nowhere hast thou probed the tumor that
lives on thee and by which thou
art forced to live.
Nowhere hast thou discovered why thy
genius for machines leadeth
inevitably to engines of ultimate
destruction.

Thy most perfect thinking machines cannot
answer thy most simple, most desperate
question: what shall we do to be
saved?

Where shalt thou search?

Shall thine assemblies save thee, child of
rhetoric?
Shall parliaments, dumas, dáils, assemblés
nationales?
Shall senates, congresses, cabinets, caucuses;
Disarmament conferences, arms limitation talks;
Leagues of cities, leagues or unions of states
or nations;
Cominterns, central committees, United Workers
of the World in conclave?
Shall thy parties save thee, child of faction"
Shall conservatives, liberals, socialists;
Radicals, centrists, slightly left of center?
Shall radical social Christian democrats;
Christian democratic radical socialists?
Bolsheviks, mensheviks, narodniki;
Popular fronts, national fronts, coalitions;
Progressives, reactionaries, single issue parties;
Mugwumps, know nothings, monarchists
or whigs?

Shall thy teachers save thee, child of learning?
Shall colleges, lycées, universities, foundations;
Polytechnics, gymnasia, institutes of
Advanced study for the solution of everything;
Career development grants and genius awards?
Shall faculties of arts, science and humanities?
Shall presidents, vice-chancellors and deans; shall professors
Emeritus, regius, distinguished, adjunct
    and part-time?
Shall causes save thee, passionate child of
    faction?
Shall anti-war, shall anti-waste, shall
    anti-pollution?
Shall C.N.D., shall S.D.P., shall Solidarność;
    The Hitler Youth, Young England, the Young Turks;
Children's crusades, the Green Party;
Zionist Leagues of Youth, Young Communists?
Shall Boy Scouts, Weathermen, Gay Liberation;
The P.L.O., the Ku Klux Klan, The League of Women
Voters, the Young Republicans, the Red Brigade;
The A.C.L.U., the National Front, Save the Whales;
The Moral Majority, the Provisional or
    Official I.R.A.?

Shall capitalism save thee, child of affluence?
Ever afraid of boom and slump and the
    skeletal rattle in the trade cycle
    cupboard of stagflation, unemployment,
    currency collapse, bank failure;
The cartels, trusts, multinationals, monopolies,
    oligopolies and O.P.E.C.;
Protectionism, laissez-faire, tariff controls
    and agreements?
Shall Texaco and U.S. Steel, B.P., United
    Fruit, Royal Dutch Shell;
General Motors, I.B.M., I.T. and T.(that was);
U.A.W.U., the Central Banks, the I.M.F.,
The E.E.C., the I.L.O., the World Bank, I.A.T.T.?

Shall the celebrities save thee, child of the
    stars?
In their narcissistic whirl around the galaxy
    of mega-admiration, the adulation of
    the herd?
Do the old gods go down giving way to:
    Grammies, Oscars, Emmies, Platinum discs;
    Gold medals, Nobels, Pulitzers, National
    Book Awards, literary luncheons, O.B.E.s
    Prix de this-and-that?
And when they join the causes and the parties
    and the religions, child of factiousness,
    dost thou feel safer when they twinkle there?

Shall the strong save thee, child of weakness?
Shall the will of the proletariat embedded
    in the party and its leaders give thee
    comfort with the promise of the withering
    away of the state when there shall be no
    purges, gulags, martial law, interrogations?
Shall the will of the people embedded
    in its always benign protectors, lull
    thee to security unless as an enemy
    of the State thy disappearance is
    deemed necessary for the public good
    until the next coup and the
    next round of disappearances?
Put thy trust in strength and thou shalt
    feel that strength undoubtedly, child
    of fear.

Shall thine institutions save thee, child
    of liberty?
Shall the separation of powers, one man one
    vote?
Shall due process, habeas corpus, judicial revue?
Shall cabinet responsibility, the single
    transferable vote?
Shall they? So thou hast believed, child of
    optimism.

There is nothing we can point to as worth saving
That has not sometime been an instrument
   of crude destructiveness.
To try to save it is at best a gamble.
Dost thou not see, child of paradox,
These lists of the agents of thine own destruction
Are the glorious creations of thine intellect?
(Add art and music, but these serve any masters.)
These powerful products of thine imagination
Are all that raiseth thee up to bring thee down.
The beast does what it must; we do what
   we imagine.
What price the outcome, child of the
   imagination; name the price?
The imagination runs riot like
   vegetation in a jungle.
We are nature's most incompetent
   gardeners.

As children we labored lovingly to build
A castle in the sand—a fairy palace
Of intricate and fragile beauty, knowing
That we built it to anticipate the
Wide-eyed awe, the thrill, the terror and
The pleasure, the sadness and the ecstasy
Of seeing its quick obliteration by the waves.
Adults learn to lie and say—"The waves
Will never come. We have a formula
(Consult the lists) to hold them back."
But children know—and that is why
They build. The children lie not neither
Do they spin webs of ideas to hide their
Gleeful sorrow at ultimate destruction.

But thou, bright educated child of hope
   still criest, "Yes, yes this one shall save
   us, this is the truth/he is the truth/they
   are the truth."

Shalt thou protest, child of indignation,
     "But yes, these are good/she is good/
     this movement is good"?
Shalt thou insist, O child of righteousness,
     "But yes, let them listen unto us/him/
     her/them; let them hearken unto us,
     unto *our* words, and they shall be saved"?
And when the other answereth, child of
     conviction:
     "Nay, for it is *our* truth/his truth/
     the truth; so hearken unto *us* and
     learn the real truth," what wilt
     thou say, O child of contradiction?
And if I say unto thee, "There is no truth
     but there is every truth and the
     truth of truths is the war of all
     truths against all, and in this
     war there is no victory for truth
     but only the destruction of all truths"?

What wilt thou answer—or hast thou already
     begun to hate the question?
"I still have my truth, plague me not old
     man with thy cynicism; drink thy
     wine and be silent;
"For my truth shall triumph, shall redeem
     the world, shall stay the destructive hand."

O Blessed Child! How beautiful it would be
     to believe thy truth if only for the opium
     of hope.
But I have believed too many and the wine
     of conviction is vinegar in my mouth.
Once I would have said: "Better the flame
     of thy useless passion than the timid
     turning to the self."

But now I know not such consolation.
The tumor that we feed on and that feeds us,
The xenophobia, zealotry and gullibility
     of man
Runs rampant through our billions.

No, child, it is not so easy now.

Once, in those days when it was very
     joy to be alive and young, the choice
     was easy: pick a cause, a simple
     truth—life, liberty or country,
     justice, freedom, love—and live
     and die for it. And if thou diest,
     if thousands died or hundreds of
     their thousands, no final harm was
     done, and always hope, hope, hope
     for better things to come made
     even life worth giving up.

To die now is to contribute to nothing.

The interglacial cometh to its end.
The ice looms waiting for its turn;
And that is our best hope, child of the ice.
If any of us stay to face the ice, perhaps
     we'll face it well; we'll be ourselves again.
If any should remain after the cold-eyed
     children of the survivors of the first
     ice have sent their terminal spearheads
     singing the final death song into the
     camps of their enemies;
If any should survive, the ice may cleanse;
The tumor may freeze into inactivity;
The children of the ice will walk the earth
like gods...

As it was in the beginning

Glory be to the power of the idea;
Glory be to the hatred of the stranger;
Glory be to the lust for domination;
Glory be to the conviction of the leaders;
Glory be to the gullibility of the mob;
Glory be to the tumor that feeds us and
      on which we feed for it has left us
      in its greed for self-annihilation
      with the cruelest legacy of all;
It has robbed us of the chance to cheat
      our unbearable knowledge that we
      must die by dying to some purpose,
      and in that moment of death
      saying, "I died for better things to come."

Child, when nothing is to come, we have
      left thee nothing worthy
      of thy death.

Amen.

# Five

# Daughters of Earth/
# Sons of Heaven

*I am not so lost in lexicography as to forget
that words are the daughters of earth, and that
things are the sons of heaven. Language is only
the instrument of science and words are but the
signs of ideas.*
Samuel Johnson, *Dictionary*, 1775 *(Preface)*


*As it will be in the future, it was at the birth of Man -
There are only four things certain since Social Progress
   began:-
That the Dog returns to his Vomit and the Sow returns to her
   Mire,
And the burnt Fool's bandaged finger goes wabbling back to
   the Fire;
And that after this is accomplished, and the brave new world
   begins
When all men are paid for existing and no man must pay for
   his sins,
As surely as Water will wet us, as surely as Fire will burn
The Gods of the Copybook Headings with terror and slaughter
   return!*
*Rudyard Kipling, "The Gods of the Copybook Headings," 1919*


*And why is it, that still
Man with his lot thus fights?-
'Tis that he makes his will
The measure of his rights,
And believes Nature outraged if his will's gainsaid.*
Matthew Arnold, *"Empedocles on Etna," 1852*


*General, der Mensch ist sehr brauchbar.
Er kann fliegen, und er kann toten.
Aber er hat einen Fehler:
Er kann denken.*
Bertolt Brecht, *"General, dein Tank," 1938*

# JUVENILIA

## Schoolboy Poems

### FROM CATULLUS: "TO LESBIA"

Let's live my Lesbia and let's play,
Despise what senile rumors say
(They count less than a servant's pay).
Suns can rise and suns take flight,
But once we've burned our tiny light
We sleep through a perpetual night.
Give me a thousand kisses, then
A hundred, then a thousand more,
A second hundred, ceasing when
A hundred thousand are in store.
Then, with many thousands made,
We'll mix the count, and stay confused,
To fool the envious, who'd invade
What our uncounted kisses fused.

---

Vivamus mea Lesbia, atque amemus,/Rumoresque senum seviorum/Omnes unius aestimemus assis./Soles occidere et redire possunt;/Nobis cum semel occidit brevis lux,/Nox est perpetua una dormienda./Da mi basia mille, deinde centum,/Dein mille altera, dein secunda centum./ Deinde usque altera mille, deinde centum./Dein, cum milia multa fecerimus,/Conturbabimus illa, ne sciamus,/Aut nequis malus invidere possit,/Cum tantum sciet esse basiorum.

## FROM VERLAINE: "CLAIRE DE LUNE" (FÊTES GALANTES)

Delightful dance and dancers range
The chosen landscape of your soul,
Yet they, beneath disguises strange,
Despite the lute, are sorrowful.

Singing of life and conquering love,
Their song takes on a minor flight;
Their aspect does not fortune prove;
The song melds with the pale moon's light.

Moonlight, lovely, calm and sad,
That sets the tree-bound birds to dream,
And sobbing water-jets seem glad
When marble guides their slender stream.

---

Votre âme est un paysage choisi/Que vont charmant masques et
bergamasques,/ Jouant du luth, et dansant, quasi/ Tristes sous
leur déguisements fantasques.

Tout en chantant sur le mode mineur/ L'amour vainqueur et la vie
opportune,/ Ils n'ont pas l'air de croire a leur bonheur,/ Et
leur chanson se mêle au clair de lune,

Au calme clair de lune triste et beau/ Qui fair rever les oiseaux
dans les arbres/ Et sangloter d'extase les jets d'eau,/ Les
grands jets d'eau sveltes parmi les marbres.

# Undergraduate Poems (1955-57)

## NEW PHILOSOPHIES

> *The new philosophies call all in doubt.*
> John Donne

We, like all good sinners everywhere,
Had called upon the righteous to repent,
And so we had our contract with despair
Sealed, signed and witnessed by our discontent.

The righteous said that we would come to grief
And went about their business.  We had taught
Belief in nothing but our unbelief,
So we surrendered long before we fought.

We called this absurd world a human hell.
The modern school looked sadly on and sighed.
"Although," they said, "you seem to ring a bell,
Such propositions can't be verified."

Paralyzed, scarce daring now to think,
We stand bewildered, but not at a loss
For an escape; when one is on the brink
There always is the river, or the cross.

## MAUVAISE FOI: Hommage à la Rive Gauche

The river rats have stripped our flesh
and left us here
a heap of whitened bones
to decorate the dragnet's slimy mesh

All our fancies
mock us in the filthy water's
obscene  indifferent tones

Those that sought us
favor us with sympathetic glances
Spectators feigning horror
rush to cinemas and dances

And our lost chances?
Of what could we be sure
we who were no more
than echoes of forgotten aspirations
patchworks of unrealized desires?

Yet we felt complete
and in our self conceit
proclaimed that freedom was our only sin
and gloried in
our moral suicide

But freedom found no voice
and our uneasy pride
choked on choices in the hostile air
of this sane wilderness  this ordered world

and we  unable to commit were hurled
into the deadly waters of despair

## SUBURBIA: Inauthentic Lives

I think that hell will be
a suburbia of well-cut lawns
stretching to a green eternity
where tiny automatons  respectable souls
clip clip at non-existent hedges
survey with pride
a fantasy of little red-brick houses
(something such
houses a life's promethean attempt
not to be nothing  but to be nothing much)
all the while protesting at the fact
that the sun with a deplorable lack of tact
is blistering the varnish from their lies

So here with bright
striped awnings they deny the light
from room conspicuous
for their meticulous
tidiness  Where ideas
are carefully dusted every Sunday
and values neatly ranged
along a marble mantelpiece
with an admirable solidity that proclaims
"All which is ordered thus shall never cease"

Who knows  they could be right  and hell will be
a neat  suburban  green eternity

## TAME KILLERS

The hooded falcon on the glove
    in his imagination hears
screams of the pinioned bleeding dove
    —indifferent to human tears

The boarhound straining at the trace
    drags at the earth with urgent paw
ignores the anti-hunting case —
    anticipates the ravaged boar

The ferret in the poacher's coat
    snugly thinks of warren holes
and razor teeth in rabbit's throat -
    not the stuff for squeamish souls

The colonels in the silo wait
    the order to insert the key
No scruple makes them hesitate
    to wipe away humanity

## OUR LADY OF THE TEACUPS: Hommage to Prufrock

Across the frozen tundra of my mind
pressing without haste
hurrying without impatience
the shaman phantoms
having plundered my memory
commence their ritual
play their mystery
and I am the helpless observer of it all

Drums conjure to life
bird  bear and fish
to mask the human dancers
hide the human hates
conceal the barely human cravings
send them on their spirit travels
drive them deep into the frozen
places of the subsoul
places of jurassic fear
places where the permafrost of guilt
leaves no soulprints
leaves no spookspoor
leaves no trail for the hungry image hunter

So meanwhile I must improvise

Here on the edge of the cliff
in the picturesquely ruined
marble theatre
of a forgotten god
high above the petulant seas
thundering against sullen rocks
in the haughty summer heat
we lounge and make clever conversation
we sit and sip our tea
from tiny china cups
and my eyes meeting yours
on the edge of the cup
as they so often met
on the edge of happiness
see nothing
but beauty
and remembering the night
I worship this tangible

But I cannot hear our clever
conversation for the noise
the waves are making
and the sound of fish
chanting in the stunted olive trees
and the seals clapping
on the marble benches
and the screaming birds
sitting on your elegant hat
and the polite bears
waiting watchfully in the background
to clear the table
ready for the masque
we have been promised

And I am the helpless observer of it all
frightened of the too-polite bears
hearing drums in the waves
seeing smiles on the seagulls
rattling the delicate china teacup
terrified that the mummers
will appear without their masks

Then you tell me
that we are the mummers
and we are the masks
and there is no escape
So meanwhile have more tea
indian china camomile menthe
milk or lemon or nothing
nothing at all

Sometimes the preparations
take a little while

## NEATLY ROLLED UMBRELLAS

We're the School's* hand-tailored students,
    we stand out in a crowd,
Our blazers are superbly cut,
    we're very, very proud
Of the tiny, well-tied Windsor knots
    that decorate our ties
But the Neatly Rolled Umbrellas
    are the things we really prize.

Our accents have been radio trained
    by Snagge, Alvar Liddell,
The Sunday morning critics
    and some lecturers as well.
We like to sip our coffee,
    but we loathe excessive noise,
And the Neatly Rolled Umbrellas
    are essential to our poise.

They'll turn us into commies here,
    at least that what we're told,
And when the workers run the country
    as we did in days of old,
We'll support the revolution,
    as discreetly as we can,
If the Neatly Rolled Umbrellas
    are within the Five Year Plan.

*London School of Economics

## POPULAR SONG: with redeeming social content

Two different worlds,
    that's what we're from;
two different notions
    of right and wrong.
You go to college, and I drive a bus,
'cos I never passed my eleven-plus.*
    O yeah, yeah, yeah!
Two different worlds.

Two different worlds,
    that's what they are;
two worlds so near
    and yet so far.
There's no way of solving this status riddle,
'cos I'm lower-lower and you're upper-middle.
    O yeah, yeah, yeah!
Two different worlds.

Two different worlds,
    that never meet;
two different houses,
    a different street.
I'm the despair of the social planners,
'cos your Mummy don't like my table manners.
    O yeah, yeah, yeah!
Two different worlds.

Two different worlds,
    such an abyss;
but we will bridge it
    with a kiss.
Your Ma will agree and your Pa say OK,
when I get you in the family way.
    O yeah, yeah, yeah!
Two different worlds.

*The U.K. public examination, taken at or after the age of eleven, that used to determine entry to public secondary education leading to college preparation possibilities.

**225**

# NEW SONGS OF INNOCENCE AND EXPERIENCE

> *There is a Grain of Sand in Lambeth that Satan cannot find*
> —William Blake, *Jerusalem*

## Three Love Conceits

### THE CHILD IS MOTHER TO THE MAN

Because you touched me with your innocence
I grow  like Merlin  younger every day
But when I reach the child-world of pure sense
You  in your wisdom  will refuse to play

Since I cannot be a child with you
I'll crawl into your aching womb and wait
to be reborn with features grave and new
that innocence and wisdom generate

## LADY IN A PARACHUTE: MAN IN A HANG-GLIDER

My mind cannot embrace
your slow fall through the sky
The intervening space
conspiring to deny
my reason its pure peace
seems always to remain
the same  not to decrease
and ease me of my pain

But where my reason fails
my love will intervene
and rise on silken sails
to fill the space between
my passion and your flight

Suspended thus in air
ethereal and light
we'll float above despair
and some raptorial breeze
will hold us in suspense
to chill  and then to freeze
our weightless innocence

## LAST REQUEST

If they came to me and said
the world will end tonight how
will you go?
I'd say in bed
with you   I have no
hope of heaven so
I'll take it now

In their short while
they only have
love and each other
But love is fragile
and
they do not understand
each other

So let us be glad
that our love beams
like the infinity of Pi
mysterious constant
of a constant mystery

And for those instants
understanding gleams
let us be glad

# Four Daughter Poems

'Φεῦ, φεῦ, τί προσδέρκεσθέ μ' ὄμμασιν, τέκνα;' — Medea

## TO KATIE—WHO LOVES MUSIC AND MOUNTAINS

I wish  Kate  I could see
the mountain through your eyes—
that seeing  I could be
as innocent and wise

I wish that I could learn
the music through your ears—
that learning  I could turn
indifference to tears

I wish that I could feel
emotion through your heart—
that feeling  I could heal
a memory torn apart

I wish  Kate  I could find
that unremembered thing—
that finding  I'd unwind
and hear the mountain sing

## KATE'S EYES (From The French)

If I had your eyes Kate
I'd be afraid
that should I cry
the brilliant cascade
of burning tears
would inundate
my soul  and I would die
innocently drowned
in that calm stream of tears
sad and profound
that no words could abate

## MEMO TO DR. OEDIPUS

My daughter with the golden hair
(so worldly wise and so aware
now in her twelfth engrossing year)
had left me to the freezing beer
I sipped because the day was hot
and sauntered through the parking lot
I watched her from the noisy bar
reach out and stroke a rakish car
Alfa-Roméo  fresh from Rome
a gigolo in red and chrome

Sensations hit me with a rush
to see her girlish fingers brush
this object so caressingly
for almost simultaneously
my mind in an electral whirl
went spinning to my other girl
(the dreamy one with nut-brown tress)
to when I saw the long caress
she planted once and then again
upon her favorite horse's mane
and fiercely told me "Oh papa
j'adore mon cheri Mustapha!"
(for being Arab  then his name
appropriately was the same)

It was  I thought  by some mischance
an odd result of school in France
But no  it was true love  and she
shared love between the beast and me
with tenderness for me of course
but passion lavished on the horse

I tell you  grave psychologist
there is a phase that you have missed
From father (Alpha) they must go
not straight to pimply Rómeo
but to a horse  or to a car
or anything that stops the jar
they feel when hormones activate
that heady pre-pubescent state
of shy  uncertain womanhood

They hear the whisper in the blood
but still cling to the father's hand
because they do not understand
that jolting  elemental force
They touch a car  or kiss a horse
and stroke each young mammalian thing
yet wander  even while they cling
to that paternal certainty
which will  without condition  be
there to indulge the horse  the car
there to adore  however far
they must  so soon  decide to go
when magnetized by Rómeo

What fortune thus to rationalize
to be so calm  urbane and wise
So then  dear doctor  tell me why
despite the beer my throat is dry
despite the heat my skin is cold
and why I suddenly feel old

# A TEARDROP WRAPPED IN AN ENIGMA—TO ANNE

I have a fear that renders me perplexed
I do not understand the fear  and yet
I know that it will plague me when I next
see your brown eyes with lashes long and wet

Wet with the tears that very rarely flow
for you are brave and stubborn  won't admit
so easily to sadness  yet I know
that there is sadness at the heart of it

The heart that yearns for something I can't give
Is that my fear?  fear of incompetence
fear that I don't know how to help you live
fear that I can't tell feeling from pretence?

Fear that I do not know you  little one
that something never grew between us  that
you do not trust me?  Yet when you are gone
away  my life is empty  dull and flat

And do I know you little brown-eyes?  Do
I understand that stubborn  self-contained
delightful little person that is you
or is there something missing  something strained?

(What answers has a child?  I cannot ask
such questions as I ask myself  and these
I cannot answer  Such a hopeless task
defeats our normal sensibilities)

And yet we share  share an amused delight
in all things natural  in ancient things
You know my pride in you because you're bright
and brave  and funny  like a cat with wings

But hidden in it all you have a fear
a fear that trembles on a bitten lip
and lingers on your lashes in a tear
and tightens in your fingers as they grip

I do not know your fear my little love
but I can feel my fingers close round yours
and in the grip my hand is like a glove
that warms cold winter hands  a sun that thaws

That thaws and melts the little heart of ice
the heart that froze its meaning from the sun
and now runs free with tears that are the price
for melting stubborn pride  my little one

So when you grip my hand  smile through the wet
long lashes  and with all your ten small years
are brave again  I am relieved  and yet
I feel the chilling sadness of our fears

**233**

# Four Poems Of Disillusion

*A brooder of an Evil Day, and a Sun rising in Blood*
—William Blake, *Jerusalem*

## AMERGIN'S SONG REVISITED

I am a usually reliable source
I am a source close to the President
I am an unindicted co-conspirator
I am an innocent bystander caught in the crossfire
I am an unregistered voter
I am an unidentified source
I am a juror empanelled for lack of obvious bias
I am a member of the control group
I am a spokesman who asked not to be identified
I am an undischarged bankrupt
I am the witness who was afraid to come forward
I am the suspect released for lack of evidence
I am the man in the picture who could not be identified
I am a source which asks to remain anonymous
I am one of those who fled the scene of the crime
I am a spectator at a rape who did not intervene
I am the evidence heard in camera
I am the body that could not be identified
I am the undecided voter
I am the homeless person who refuses shelter
I am one of those who stays in the closet
I am the alleged serial killer who was never apprehended
I am the man who is helping the police with their enquiries
I am an undisclosed source
I am the resumé with the embarrassing gaps

I am the body burned beyond recognition
I am the anonymous phone call
I am John Doe and Jane Roe and Baby X
I am a pseudonym for an actual person
I am a ghost writer for an illiterate celebrity
I am the alleged victim
I am the alleged perpetrator
I am all of the above

Any resemblance to persons living or dead
      is purely coincidental

## THE MIND'S I

I smell with the mind's nose and the smell
   is pungent and acrid like dry urine in an alley
      or discharged gunpowder after a battle

I hear with the mind's ear and the sound
   is sonorous and loud like Tibetan chanting
      or a stag's bellow during rut

I taste with the mind's tongue and the taste
   is smooth and bitter-sweet like chili and mole
      or roasted human flesh sucked from the bone

I cannot see with the mind's eye  the view
   is blurred and two dimensional
     like a winter sea in rainfall
       or a grief after loss
  or the flat metallic lake of purgatory
     where no daffodils dance on the banks
        nor by the fishing pool behind the gasworks
          slick with motor oil and metaphors

I feel with the mind's skin and the touch
   is blistered and rough like a leper's blanket
      or the deceitful tongue of a rabid dog
       licking before it bites

I think with the mind's brain and the thoughts
   are nothing but a string of stupid similes
      like forgotten charms on a lost bracelet
  or rusted trade beads on the rotting necklace
     of a Seminole skeleton oozing mud and snakes

I weep with the mind's tears  and leave it at that

## THE LEGACY (Belfast 1997)

We laud the selfsame God and praise
His bloody  sacrificial son
then put our bibles down and raise
the barrel of the loaded gun

With this religious argument
we settle questions which the years
have so obscured  besmirched and bent
not much is left but primal fears

These are enough though  quite enough
to overheat the fevered brain
and cook to boiling point the stuff
the xenophobic cells contain

We do not need excuse to fight
we are not them  they are not us
which is sufficient to invite
the musket and the arquebus

the Uzi or the bombe plastique
to make sure that the children die
who otherwise might try to seek
a place of safety from our lie

For though we rationalize and preen
our leaders and our prelates prate
the shabby truth by all is seen:
our one solution is our hate

So join us in our hatred child
it's all we offer  all we've got
praise gentle Jesus meek and mild
then grab the gun and take a shot

Shoot father  mother  neighbour  son
shoot priest and clerk and dominie
shoot every which and every one
Their death's your immortality

For when the shooting's done you'll say
"I did my part  I shot them all"
and then you'll kneel to him and pray
"God bless the Cause for which I fall"

And when you fall  as fall you will
the Cause will linger  so will you
Comrades will chant the songs that thrill
but none will sing the song that's true

Your death was pointless child  the Cause
will be forgotten  truth to tell
a footnote  a scholastic clause
no reason why you lived or fell

But do not fear  your legacy
will live beyond you  future years
will find us at our hate  and we
will cry again your dying tears

In places different  costumes strange
causes stranger  you will thrive
and die again  nothing will change
The hatred will keep you alive

That hatred is your legacy
inheritance and testament
your fated human destiny
inevitable sad lament

Each generation learns anew -
since wisdom does not cumulate -
not to put hatred in review
just change the objects of its hate

## WHERE WERE YOU WHEN KENNEDY WAS KILLED?

Leaving a suburban London train
the slamming doors like heavy rifle shots
that echoed in some hollow of the brain
where premonitions fester  and the plots

of dull assassins plan a pointless dying
Walking along that bland suburban street
the garden fences lined with people crying—
people who otherwise would never meet

It broke the barriers as it broke our hearts
and left us feeling useless  empty  dry
clinging to strangers for what that imparts—
a sense we are still real  we can still try

to keep ourselves convinced  although we've seen
a bullet cancel out democracy
and votes made meaningless  and law obscene
and all the sense that order makes to be

a plaintive irony for those who say
"heaven is but a ballot box away"

# ONE MORE HOOP FOR THE TIGER: THE ALLEGORY OF THE CIRCUS

It has recently been discovered that the versions of Plato's REPUBLIC that we have are in fact later distorted versions produced by Idealist philosophers—so-called neo-Platonists, and that Plato himself was, like his pupil Aristotle, much more of a naturalist than we could have known. The discovery of fragments of the original REPUBLIC in jars buried under the Acropolis, and which the academic establishment tried to keep hidden from us for fear of wrecking centuries of scholarship, has caused a complete re-evaluation of our ideas of Platonism. Here, as an example, is a first translation of the opening of Book VII, the famous Allegory or Parable of the Cave, as it appears in Fragment #317 of the original text. Readers may wish to compare with Francis Cornford's excellent (if a little terse) translation of the accepted version (Oxford: Clarendon Press, 1941), on which I have depended for those portions of the text that indeed overlap. Socrates, of course, is speaking, and the ever agreeable—not to say obseqious—Glaucon, is the straight man.

\*\*\*

Next, said I, here is a parable to illustrate the degrees in which our nature may be enlightened or unenlightened. Imagine the condition of men living entirely under the big top of a grand circus.* Here they have been since childhood so that all they know is what they see in front of them.

I see, said he.

---

*The word actually used is *kirkos* — literally "a ring"—as in Latin "circus." The internal rings of the circus itself are *mikrokirkos*. This is the only known such reference in Greek.

Now in the three rings of the circus the animals are performing various elaborate tricks: the horses and zebras are standing on their hind legs and walking backwards or turning in circles; the elephants are making a line, with each elephant's front feet on the back of the one in front, and they too are walking on their hind legs; the clowns are walking on their hands with hats on their feet. The spectators are impressed and amused.

Naturally so, said he.

The acrobats meanwhile are attempting the world's highest human pyramid, and finally, the tiger is jumping not through one, but through two hoops of fire. Now remember that for purposes of our parable, we, the spectators, have never seen anything else.

It is a strange picture and a strange sort of prisoners.

Like ourselves, for we also take for granted what we see happening as being all that can happen.

We do indeed.

You are getting positively irritating. However, to continue with the parable. Suppose it was thought that the tiger could only be persuaded or trained to jump at most through two hoops of fire and this was positively accepted as a fact of nature.

Let us so suppose.

Leave it, Glaucon. Now suppose that the trainer announced that he intended to prove that the tiger could jump though three or even more hoops of fire. Would not the spectators think this the most significant and marvellous thing in the world?

They most certainly would! Well you asked.

O. K. Glauc. Now consider what would happen if their release from their chains and the healing of their unwisdom should come about in this way. Suppose one of them were released and taken into the outside world where he he saw the natural habitats of the animals, and even of the human performers.

241

What do you think he would say if someone told him that what he had formerly seen was totally unnatural and that what he now saw was nearer to reality and a truer view of life? Would he not be perplexed?

Yes, truly perplexed. Sorry, it gets to be a habit.

Presssing on. Suppose he were to be dragged to the top of a hill and shown the panorama of nature, with the animals running free on four legs and the men on two legs (with hats on their heads) chasing them, and the whole assemblage forming into families, tribes, troops and herds with complex social hierarchies and relationships. Would he not be astonished and disbelieving until his eyes told him what he saw was not an illusion but was indeed reality?

Yeah, yeah, yeah. Most truly astonished, etcetera, and so forth.

There's hope for you yet Glaucon. But let us then suppose that our released prisoner thought back to his fellow prisoners and what passed for wisdom in his former dwelling place. He would surely think himself happy in the change and be sorry for them, and not envy their enjoyment knowing that they mistook the circus for reality. Don't answer.

But . . .

Now imagine what would happen if he went back to take his former seat in the circus and told the spectators that he had seen the real world of men and animals and that it was quite unlike the world they judged to be real. What is more, what if he told them that what they regarded as dangerous and unacceptable behavior in the animals was just what he had seen in the real world outside the tent? They would laugh at him and say he had gone out only to come back with his sight ruined; it was worth no one's while to make the attempt. If they could lay hands on the man who was trying to set them free and lead them out, they would kill him.

Yes they would. And who would blame them?

Glaucon, you're stepping out of character. Every feature of this parable, my dear Glaucon, is meant to fit our analysis. The circus, my boring little sycophant, is HISTORY. The spectators are those of us trapped into being unable to see beyond the bounds of historical contingencies. The escaped spectator is one of the few who has seen nature whole and uncontaminated by history.

When do we get to kill him?

(Here the fragment breaks off, carrying with it the irony that the otherwise patient Athenians did indeed kill Socrates. Blame the messenger!)

# ALPINE EXCURSIONS

## ALPINE INTERLUDE

You are a fragment of a fleeing moon
    seized by the mountain in a wakeful age
before this tedious god began to dream
    of beasts that dance to his transhumant tune
destroying pagan flowers his hot rage
    would wither were it not for your cool beam

To say I fell out of God's nightmare  there
    to find you on the mountain with the flowers
the gentians and the orchids  and to say
    you are the flowers and you are the air
that stuns my senses in the sun-born hours
    and in the moments when the wind-borne spray

from clamouring cascades alerts my brain
    this is to say  not all that could be said
nor can be said  nor ever I can say
    and if I try then metaphors again
will trap my thoughts and leave my feelings dead
    If one plucks flowers in the heat of day

the flowers die   If I love you I'll break
    the magic of an ancient mountain spell
woven of flowers and the songs of birds
    that only works when God is not awake
and in the nightmare of his mountain hell
    I trample flowers with his bleating herds

You are the thought the patient mountain took
    a million milllion years to formulate
and then expressed as flowers and as air
    that breathes wild wisdom  I can only look
out of God's dream  knowing I am too late
    to steal the flowered wisdom breathing there

## THE MOUNTAINEER

(A poem in the Romantic manner, written in a state of
exhaustion on the Col de Granon)

I am too close to heaven here  The stars
dazzle  In the day the sun will press
down on my back until it weighs like bars
of molten gold  The glaring snow will stress
my eyes with silver whips  Incongruous bells
astound my ears in the diminished air
Discordant music from the torrent swells
and bursts into my head and clamours there

Dear God there is no further I can go
up these mad mountains  I am yet too near
and there are warnings  like the falling snow
that I have tried too hard to conquer fear
that I have gone too far into the night
too near the singing stars  too far away
from plain and valley things  into the white
indifferent peaks that even in the day
stare back with glacial malice at the sun
Yet they demand I scale them with my pack
of heavy sunlight  silver stars  I shun
the white road forward  but I can't go back

Last night we were fierce lovers in the snow
our passion making tolerable then
the hostile cold  A thousand feet below
we did the same wild thing and that was when
my head slipped from your breast and gently fell
setting my lips against a smooth hard rock

What in that moment happened I can't tell
but passion was arrested by the shock
—the lust-destroying shock inside my head—
to feel the same sensation as I felt
when by his coffin  he being three days dead
I kissed my father's forehead as I knelt

I've left you now my snowy lover  and
I must climb on  You are forgotten  All
I know is that I will not understand
until I reach the peak  or else I fall
and one way or another join the dead
who tried to search for fathers in the sun
but found that mother ice was there instead
and that the mountain claimed them one by one

## LA FEMME QUI ADORAIT LA LUNE

Ton corps et la lune
pour moi insepérable
lune corps étoiles montagnes
paysage incomparable

Tu es de l'étranger
on m'a dit  mais je sais
que tu n'est pas d'un pays
que tu n'est pas la mienne
que tu n'est pas de la terre
non  tu n'est pas d'ici
Tu est une femme de la lune
reine  fille  mâitresse  mère
de la lune du paradis
de la grande lune du mal
de la vielle lune féminin
de la lune folle sensuelle
de la lune de toute sagesse
maitresse  sauvage mâitresse
de la lune triste  éternelle

Parmi ces montagnes  si étranges
tout est confus  et en même temps clair
Clair parceque tout était décidé
par la lune  il y a une million d'années
au ciel froid  loin d'ici
ou les étoiles étaient
une fontaine de feu gelé
Confus par les choses mondaines
et leur tyrannie

---

Your body and the moon/for me inseparable/moon  body  stars mountains/incomparable
landscape

You are from abroad/they tell me  but I know/that you are not from a country/ that you are not
mine/that you are not from the earth/no you are not from here/you are a woman of the moon/
queen  daughter  mistress  mother/of the moon of paradise/of the great
moon of evil/of the old feminine moon/of the mad sensual moon/of
the all-wise moon/mistress  savage mistress/of the sad eternal
moon

Among these strange mountains/all is confused and at the same
time clear/Clear because all was decided/by the moon a million
years ago/in the cold sky far from here/where the stars were/a
fountain of frozen fire/Confused by worldly things/and their tyrrany

Moi et cette mouche  nous sommes
également confus
Lui  parceque ma lampe remplace
la nuit par le jour
Moi  parceque ton corps remplace
la lune encore

Tu m'a dit
au fin d'un autre jour
tu m'a dit
"Il faut faire l'amour
pendant le passage de la lune
entre ces deux montagnes
ces deux seines de la terre
il faut le faire
tranquille  pas trop rapide
sans cesse mais sans orgasme
jusqu'a l'aube  et puis
après ces heures avides
tu dois me poignarder
comme une vierge de sacrifice
désemparée
sur la pierre de sacrifice
sur la pyramide de la lune"
Et tu m'a dit
"fais lentement l'amour  ami
et regarde bien la lune
car mon corps va mourir
et encore vivre quand mourra la lune"

---

This fly and I  we are/equally confused/He because my lampreplaces/day by night/I because your body replaces/the moon still/
  You said to me/at the end of another day/you said to me/ "We must make love/during the journey of the moon/between these two mountains/these two breasts of the earth/we must make it/calmly not too quickly/without stopping but without orgasm/until the dawn  and then/after these greedy hours/you must stab me/like a sacrificial virgin/helpless/on the stone of sacrifice/on the pyramid of the moon"/And you said to me/"make love slowly friend/and look well at the moon/because my body will die/and yet live when the moon dies"

C'était vraiment comme ça
Ah oui  c'était comme ça
et quelque chose était
sacrificié
et j'ai peur
qu'il ne soit mon coeur
et pas ton corps
qui est mort

Ton corps est un paysage
naquit sur la lune
il y a longtemps dans
les montagnes de la lune
et maintenant je ne peux pas dormir
car le clair de lune
inonde ma chambre  et ainsi
lorsque je regarde la lune
je sens ta bouche et j'écoute
ton chant étrange
moitié d'une femme
et moitié de la lune

---

It was truly thus/ah yes  it was like that/and something was/sacrificed/and I
am afraid/it is my heart/and not your body/that is dead

Your body is a landscape/born on the moon/a long time ago
in/the mountains of the moon/and now I cannot sleep/because
the  moonlight/    floods my room  and thus/when I look at the moon/
I sense your mouth and I hear/your strange song/half a woman/and half the
moon/

Je vois les montagnes et je sens
dans ces cimes et ces vallées
ton corps étrange
éclairé par la lune
et je ne peux pas dormir
parceque ton chant de la lune
brille dans ma chambre comme
une cascade d'étoiles entre la lune
et les montagnes et mon lit
ou tu dors comme la lune

et ne dors pas
J'ai de reste la lune
et mes restes mortels
sont seul avec le corps de la lune

---

I see the mountains and I feel/in these peaks and valleys/your strange body/
lit up by the moon/and I cannot sleep/ because your moon-song/shines in
my room like/a waterfall of stars between the moon/and the mountains and
my bed/where you sleep like the moon

and do not sleep/the moon remains for me/and my mortal remains/are
alone with the body of the moon

# CHANSON DU VAMPIRE

> *Voici le soir charmant, ami du criminel;*
> *Il vient comme un complice,à pas de loup; le ciel*
> *Se ferme lentement comme une grande alcôve,*
> *Et l'homme impatient se change en bête fauve.*
> —Charles Baudelaire, *"Le crepuscule du soir"*

Je suis maintenent un vampire de l'âme
je dors le matin et je travaille la nuit
Dans les mondes blancs aux images égarés
des ombres puissantes je vole l'essence
Des corps qui encombrent les grands lits de l'esprit
je bois tout le sang des idées virginales
J'arrache les coeurs de leur pâles fleurs du mal
Le soif tout gorgé  l'intellect bien calme
mon cercueil secret doucement regagné
je m'endors le matin d'un sommeil innocent

---

I am now a vampire of the soul/I sleep in the morning and I work
at night/In the white worlds of bewildered images/I steal the
essence of powerful shadows/From bodies which litter the great
beds of the spirit/ I drink all the blood of the virginal ideas/I
rip out the hearts of their pale flowers of evil/The thirst satisfied
the intellect very calm/my secret coffin sweetly regained/I go to
sleep in the morning  an innocent sleep

# NEW JERSEY LANDSCAPES

> *Hence, as more individuals are produced*
> *than can possibly survive, there must in*
> *every case be a struggle for existence,*
> *either one individual with another of the*
> *same species, or with the individuals of*
> *distinct species, or with the physical*
> *conditions of life.*
> *Many cases are on record showing how complex*
> *and unexpected are the checks and relations*
> *between organic beings which have to struggle*
> *together in the same country.*
> —Charles Darwin, *On the Origin of Species*

## SPRING: EARTHWORMS

These are the days God sends to fool us  He
in his air-conditioned heaven knows
that summer will descend and blanket us
with itching sweat and nasty biting things

But while they last we're willing to be duped
and to imagine cool eternities
of dogwood bright and white  a springtime snow
peopled with colored birds and floating petals
pointillist paradise of dabs and specks
that gush and shudder into tenuous life
bloom blossom burst—a sly magician's flowers—
into sprays and bunches overnight—
forsythia  azalea  rhododendron
daffodil  crocus  tulip  cherry  plum—
and just as quickly don their uniform
and heavy green to meet the dank
humidity of soporific summer

Farmer Ralph tells me that he won't plough
the back field this year  only harrow it
because he doesn't really want to waste
the earthworms' earnest handiwork   Each hole
lets air out  water in   Their excrement
is our free soil food   Let them do their job

I noticed sea birds last year following
the plough  Says Ralph  they came in thousands for
the worms   Once worms are turned they only have
five minutes to dig back  and that gives time
for greedy gulls to strike and gobble down
worm upon worm in avian holocaust

Ralph sometimes shoots a gull and strings it up
behind the tractor—scares some birds away
and gives our frantic earthworms half a chance
to make it back to sanctuary  But this year
yuppies from the new development
protested at the carcass of the bird
said it would traumatize their little ones
to see the mangled corpse   They ought to take
their little darlings' hands and dip them in
the birdie's blood and rub it on their faces
Let them know that corn has to be fought for
that one bird has to die to save the worms
that without death their lives are meaningless

I tell Ralph of that far-off frosty morning
surrounded by the blood-bespattered hounds
of how they rubbed the mangled fox's brush
across my forehead   how the still-warm blood
came trickling down from nose to lips  and so
even as a child I tasted death
(We were Diana's people  Dionysus
bade us tear the flesh and drink the blood
ingesting the real presence of the wild)

I didn't tell Ralph this  but told him of
the care that Darwin lavished on his earthworms
amazing all his neighbours  Was he mad?
He knew  we know  and they know not who only
know supermarket  freezer  plastic wrap
The moral's getting heavy—let it go

But we agree we can't have bad relations
The yuppies are a fixture now  we have
to live with them as with the worms and birds
No gull need die  We will not plough  The crows
will get a few  but crows are local birds
not alien gulls  It's hard to like the gulls
If they're so hungry why don't they eat fish?

No.  We won't plough  Earthworms will be saved
and little darlings never be exposed
to messy death  Next year  I said  I'll walk
behind the plough and shoot above the birds
scare and scatter them a bit  enough
to give the worms at least an even chance
Who knows perhaps we'll print a bumper sticker
proclaiming "Save the Worms!" and get some help

Who knows?  Perhaps the back field then
will be a supermarket  Flesh and corn
will come all sanitized in plastic wrap—
tasteless  but undisturbing to the kids
who dream of Superman and Disneyworld
and Ninja Turtles playing games with death

## SUMMER: CROWS

No one can tell us we weren't patient with
our crows  Lord knows we let them gobble worms
and stood their crazy dawn cacophony
and even didn't mind some ears of corn
The deer were worse offenders even when
we put transistor radios in the corn
low  on twentyfour-hour news  The soft
murmur of human voices scared them off
but hunger was more urgent  Human hair
hanging in cast-off socks had some effect
but otherwise the price of corn was constant
vigilance  or electric fences  too
expensive  too exhausting  What the hell

We fenced the sweet corn patch to save a bit
leaving the feed to radios and hair
The deer went elsewhere  but the bloody crows
ignored our volts and amps  flew down among
the growing ears and springing tassels  fed
with insolent impunity while we
were kept away from them by our own fence
Autumn loomed with harvest prospects bleak

But Farmer Steve is an old hand with crows
He calmed us down  talked tactics  not to waste
futile energy on noise and scares
(they use the scarecrow as a lookout perch)
I told him of my father's memory
(his earliest perhaps)  when as boy
dressed in smock and hat of woven straw
went out with water bottle  piece of cheese
to spend whole days with rattle  stick  and stones
in heat of English lost Edwardian summer
scaring crows with other farmers' sons

What goes round comes around said Steve  but you
are not your father  and you have a gun
and I know how to beat them at their game
(So Steve explained  and so we listened  rapt)
The crow's a clever bird  more so than most
the cleverer for being sociable
The crows are not haphazard  they've a plan
They have a leader-bird  a lookout-bird—
wise old crow who knows the countryside

The secret is to spot this leader-bird
before he senses us  Creep up on him
He won't be with the mob but in a tree
You'll see his head in fast neurotic jerks
scanning the human country round the corn
Should we dumb sapiens appear he'll squawk
and set the whole flock rushing skywards like
a vision from van Gogh  (that's me not Steve)

The secret is to zap the leader-bird
to use our social skills to combat his
One gun won't do it  but we'll ambush him
Suppose the first shells miss  the second two
will bring him down
                                Now here's the cunning bit:
it takes the crows about two weeks to find
another leader-bird  meantime their raids
are more haphazard  more disorganized
We don't know why it takes the birds two weeks
or what strange things go on in conclave there
among the colony  Do females vote?
Do males compete?  Is there a Crow Apparent?
Are females a reward for taking risks?
Whatever is the scheme we can be sure
in two weeks time there'll be another leader
sitting with his beady  crazy look
and shifting up and down along his branch
like some old clergyman about to spot
a choirboy reading comics in the sermon

Steve and I have popped two leaders now
Our corn has had its four-week crow reprieve
and flourishes towards its harvesting

I tell Steve how the Indians when they kill
have some ritual apology they make
Steve doesn't seem impressed   He doesn't see
the need to say he's sorry to the crows
That would be dishonest  Them or us
he says  it's them or us  And anyway
we keep the killing down   We don't just blast
away like maniacs  We take out leader-bird

Yup  There he lies   His glossy feathers limp
his beady eye glazed over  red on black
Illusion of a smile across his beak
suggests he understands his servile crows
will still be at the corn when we are all
mere rotting carrion  potential food
He mocks our cleverness  our weak attempt
to beat the birds   His black intelligence
knows wisdom deeper than our ambush reigns
in Crowtown as they cackle at the dawn
and send another leader to distract
our sapiential ingenuity
which cannot overcome  and never knows
the stern collective wisdom of the crows

### CROW INVICTUS
Crow is become the inviter of death,
Cackling rake who had all the female crows.
God substitute, mocker of men and metal,
Crow feels intimations of immortality.

Crow is dead.
                    Long live Crow!

Crow offers his slick breast to the cowardly guns,
Draws them with death-black magnet eyeballs,
Flaunting, sneering, offering his feather robe arrogantly
To the gamblers at the foot of the world tree

He is the rack of bone and feather,
From which will hang an infinity of crowlings.

Crow waits impatiently for the sun to burst.
He has already planned the opening of another galaxy,
A reception by white angelic crows,
with God serving sun-dried human carrion for appetizers.

Who is lord of corn and men?   Death.
Who is lord of gods and galaxies?   Death.
Who is lord of Death?   I am, apparently.

Pass Crow.

Ah! But he did not pass our blazing guns
to soar immortal through the cosmic suns
King of the colony   the king must die
His flock survives to make another try
No Trickster he   I hate to tell you Ted
King Crow has had his day   King Crow is dead

## AUTUMN: TREES

The colored skin  that bright disease  falls from
the trees like drying scabs  until
they stand as slim white skeletons against
the grey-washed sky   Except that when
on dismal days  one sees them on the hill
they look like silver spray  or drifting smoke—
more mist than bone    But we know that they are
hard at the core  and patient for the spring
when ruthlessly green flesh will re-appear

For now our fields lie reddish brown and neat
Their rows of straight-ruled furrows tame the ground
(*nomos* the allotted pasturage)
an ordered clean demand that nature wait
the springtime impact of a planned invasion
by nurtured seed   to mingle with the flint
arrowheads of long-dead shamans  knowing
something more is planned than germination

A sulky adolescent sun picks out
the brutal gleam of massive metal struts
earth movers  grabbers  shovels  all the grim
impedimenta of development
From wilderness to neat suburbia
without a nod at barbarism and
savagery  long buried in brown earth
forgotten  never hoping to re-form

Climate conditioned shopping malls and chic
town houses planted in a wilderness
How can the earth accept such things as it
accepts the rough cooperation of
plough and harrow?   These things dominate
and ask for nothing fruitful in return

The skeletons are not impressed  they have
their own agenda   We're no more to them
than scattering leaves to an enchanter clinging
They know the green is waiting

                                    In the sky
an updraft sends a vulture looping round
(the shaman's totem-bird defying time)
its cold indifferent eye looking for death
among the alien dwellings by the trees

# WINTER: VULTURES

Midwinter  like the carol says  was bleak
Earth hard as iron  water like a stone
The deer were dying in the woods  they bled
thin  watery blood  and gave us little meat
The rodents froze to death under the ice
so desperate hawks were savaging the birds
they usually left in peace  the robins
blackbirds  bluejays  cardinals and grackles
Mobbing did not deter them  and the flocks
of frightened blackbirds hit the house like hail
in wheeling desperation to escape
As many died from crashing into walls
as from the slashing talons in the air

A starving buck came staggering from the woods
fell in the back field there among the stalks
of long-dead corn we left to fertilize
the now unwilling land  They cracked like twigs
as he first blundered  stumbled to his knees
then dropped  a weary heap  onto his side

It didn't take the vultures long to come
The vulture is a territorial bird
          (How odd the image of the bird as freedom
          Imperative territorial commands
          the dinosaurs' descendants just as surely
          as it constrains their earthbound cousinry)
I estimate some twenty-five square miles
supports a pair with  in the spring  one young
But when a bigger mammal ends its days
particularly in a hungry winter
they come in dozens  Boundaries be damned
Our local pair were first of course  they started
to rip the belly open  peck the eyes
get all the good soft stuff (it's hard to strip
the muscle off the bones)  The other birds

guided by an air traffic control
that told them twenty miles away that here
in our back field a buck was dying  dived
in swooping circles  looping through the wind
graceful as eagles as they found the thermals
drifting round each other like a bunch
of black sky-diving acrobats  to land
within a few feet of the dying buck
already disemboweled by the first
(our neighbours whom we'd christened Fred and Ethel)

You note that how in telling you this tale
I'm passing on the cute poetic things
Few similes  few striking images
Because its all too brutal  Elemental
It's too damn cold for metaphors  The cars
are frozen in the snow  The rain flows round
the fields of ice without a place to sink
and builds up into waves that roll across
the tundra and then quickly freeze again
This is the ice world  Ice and death are king
and queen  both unenlightened despots
They crush us in their autocratic grip
That's bad  That's getting too poetical

These birds that are so graceful on the wing
they make you want to cry from joy of watching
are  on the ground  about the ugliest things
in all creation  scaly snake-like necks
and stiff unwieldy bodies  folded wings
They look like (yup  here comes a simile)
linebackers draped in academic gowns
mad hunchbacked priestly things of some crazed cult
their cobra necks engaged in swift debate
on points of gruesome sacrificial detail
that avian theology requires
(You see  the cold can't freeze out images)

But lord are they efficient scavengers
They do their garbage work with ruthless skill
ripping at flesh and snipping through the muscles
gulping down the carcass skin and all

I think that vultures are misunderstood
at least these turkey vultures (wrongly called
buzzards by those who know not Peterson
Buzzards are migrants  vultures stay year round)
There is a curious order to their work
They do not swarm obscene across the kill
the way you see in films of Africa
(or rats across a carcass of a dog
the way I've seen them on a city street)
One pair at a time rips at the buck
and then is challenged by another pair
They flap their useless wings and do a dance
like crippled witches at a winter sabbat
stick out their necks and hiss and hop about
until the feeding pair gives way  The others
wander round about  waiting their turn
to play king of the hill  while some of them
seem totally distracted from the task
that you would naturally assume demands
their whole attention—getting at the meat
They walk away  backs to the buck  until
they reach a seemingly set distance where
they stop and slump  as if against the cold
Sometimes they all seem frozen in the act
as though a leader bird has shouted out
"Simon says!"  and all go statuesque
then just as suddenly resume the feast
the walk  the wait  the shuffle and the slump
There are some principles of order here
A rudimentary contract is observed
but what goes on inside the vulture's head
is locked away like dead flesh under ice
It doesn't take them long to finish it

and one by one the pairs go lumbering off
and thrash their clumsy wings until they find
the upward thermal and begin to soar
as gracefully as eagles once again
to all points of the compass whence they came

The skeleton is whitening in the field
I took the rack  eight points  a pretty thing
to decorate a wall  Memento mori
Winter is its own best hunter still

Farmer Ralph said we should leave the bones
Next spring he'd scatter them and plough them in
They'd give the soil much needed minerals
(Calcium and phosphorous at least)
He said to take a few and bury them
beneath the ornamentals and the firs
But when I tried I couldn't pry them loose
They'd frozen to the stubborn earth and she
refused to give them up  I left them there
There was no profit in this 'til the spring
The stony icemad earth was in control
We mortals could just shiver and observe

Looking at the rack up on my wall
I think about the vultures and the buck
and how my Will says I should be cremated
My world to end in fire  but what if I
instead should end my world out on the ice
falling into that sleep that comes with cold
and being eaten by the turkey vultures
with all their clumsy ordered expertise
My flesh flown high above in all directions
My bones left in the ice to fertilize
the cornfield with their human minerals

I would have died by ice and beak and plough
yet not have died at all  I need not cite
Frazer in my defense  you get the point
(about the vegetation god I mean)
The Parsis do it  Mortuary towers
receive their bodies  birds do all the rest
Perhaps I should convert  claim first amendment
But sure as hell there'd be an ordinance
that tells me there are ways I cannot die

Yet I could do it surreptitiously
For should they ever give me weeks to live
let it be winter  and a vicious one
Then I will tie the horns onto my head
(like that old dancing shaman at Trois Frères)
and go out naked on the icy field
to lie among the debris of the corn
Grant that my last sight would be the birds
circling and dropping to their task
as humorless as any bureaucrats
and twice as serious as any priests

My wife read this and turned the heating up
commenting that spring was overdue
and what we badly needed was a break
in Florida  to watch the pink flamingoes

# WHAT THE SHAMAN SAW

(Incident at Lascaux, circa 15,000 B.P.)

*The great release, the breaking away*
*which is our uniqueness, came during the*
*Upper Palaeolithic. Futhermore, the release*
*is not something that happened in times out*
*of mind, in an interesting but essentially*
*irrelevant past. From the standpoint of a human*
*lifespan any change dating back 30,000 or more*
*years must indeed seem like ancient history. But*
*it is the blink of an eyelid ago on the evolutionary*
*time scale. We are very young, an infant species*
*just beginning to wonder and observe and explore.*
*The process which gathered momentum among the*
*Cro-Magnons continues to accelerate in our time.*
*The same forces which drive us today drove our recent*
*ancestors underground with paints, engraving tools,*
*lamps and notions about their place in the scheme*
*of things.*
—John Pfeiffer, *The Creative Explosion*

*"What I want to know is: if everyone was so smart,*
*why didn't they know what would happen?"*
*"They did."*
—Neville Shute, *On the Beach*


Coolness of the spirit cave
spluttering oil wicks  ochre  soot
spread and stencil  line and grave
cold wet floor-clay underfoot
twang of bowstring  bison gut
dead painted deer
good hunting year
a walking protein glut

Song by lamplight  frightened eyes
strobe-like flickers  frescoed bulls
    boys to men through shaman cries
scars and paint and bear-cult skulls
        twittering lads like nervous gulls
                seize the spear
                stab painted deer
        Magnetic manhood pulls

    Yet all must make the female sign
and stroke the pregnant bison cow
    leave handprint and a male design
so culture will not disavow
        the natural union  but allow
                cult-making man
                into the plan
        that Nature must endow

    Nothing severed  all is joined
boy to man and man to maid
        nothing natural purloined
only borrowed  then relayed
        through ritual and magic aid
                with calm recourse
                back to the source
        that started the cascade

    For what is killed is born again
and what is born again must die
        The round of metabolic strain
that shaman seeks to signify
        while searching with his inner eye
                tracing on walls
                of painted halls
        that never see the sky

Emerging from the painted dark
savage sunlight sears his eyes
a blazing flash  a sudden spark
a spike of terror and surprise
unfolds the future centuries
in vision sought
now dearly bought
as penalty and prize

He sees the wheel and then the cart
and then the metal car of war
the stirrup and the lancer's art
the cloven bodies by the score
the thousands and the tens and more
of thousands lying
twisted  dying
on his valley floor

He know that warriors fight and die
for he has fought and he has killed
but never has he seen the sky
with blackened smoke of bodies filled
and lime-white pits with corpses spilled
like reindeer pinned
but dressed and skinned
by ranks precision drilled

He used to hear the drumming feet
of star-drawn herds on summer nights
but now he sees a crowded street
and human herds and city lights
that overwhelm the hunting sites
deny the space
the ungulate grace
requires for its delights

Neon flare blocks out his moon
while spreading towns obscure the grass
　　This transformation came too soon
yet he intuits it will pass
　　　this anti-nature reel en masse
　　　　　beneath the need
　　　　　of its own speed
　　　surpassing to surpass

　　Fanatics rage and millions die
while millions more are born and scream
　　Their birth song is a hunger cry
a lifetime is a pointless dream
　　　as driven to a mad extreme
　　　　　they quicken pace
　　　　　reduce the space
　　　pollute the human stream

　　The herds are gone　the forest felled
the tribes are scattered　few survive
　　The trampling billions have expelled
the hunters　and the cities strive
　　　like cancers mindlessly to thrive
　　　　　consuming that
　　　　　sustaining fat
　　　they need to stay alive

　　Yet still they shout the shining hope
(a hope the shaman does not share)
　　that science will expand its scope
and ingenuity will spare
　　　the victims from that final scare
　　　　　its bag of tricks
　　　　　a magic fix
　　　the ultimate repair

They craved the tyranny of things
worshipped the icon of ideas
deified and destroyed their kings
embalmed  entombed  despoiled their fears
and yet could never stop their ears
against the sound
from ancient ground
of faint  forbidden tears

The shaman sees the fabric rent
the contract broken  nothing gained
the treasury of Nature spent
the sacred lake of Nature drained
the seething numbers uncontained
the losing race
the shrieking pace
that cannot be sustained

He turns in sorrow to the cave
the vision gone  the darkness deep
The painted world he cannot save
he leaves to its extended sleep
We of his vision now who peep
with awe and fear
can faintly hear
the phantom of him weep

# THE HEDGEHOG AND THE FOX

*The Fox knows many things, but the Hedgehog knows one big thing.*
Archilochus of Paros (c.650 B.C.), as quoted by Isaiah Berlin

The fox who knew many things, knew very little about hedgehogs; they were not a part of his diet. Of course he knew they were mammals of the family Erinaceidae, and hence related to porcupines, but not to spiny anteaters which were monotremes. Otherwise he had little need to bother with them. On the few occasions he had sniffed at one, the result had been a stinging snout. He decided they were best left alone. But when his friend the tiger (they were friends mostly because they didn't compete for resources; the tiger was after bigger stuff and wasn't interested in the rabbits and chickens that the fox spent his time chasing) told him about what Isaiah Berlin had said about the hedgehog, he was certainly intrigued. For the fact was he did indeed know many things, perhaps too many. Sometimes he felt his brain was on overload.

How nice it would be, he thought, if instead of being in command of so much information he too knew just one big thing. But he was always put off by the thought that this, on the one hand welcome, simplification, might be, on the other hand, very dangerous. It would surely simplify life to know only one big thing, but what if that thing were wrong? At least knowing many things meant you could try them out and find out what worked and discard what didn't. Except that isn't how it seemed to happen at all. Things just piled up; they accrued; they multiplied. They didn't get discarded, they simply cluttered up the mental space available for them, competing for time and attention. But they didn't seem to add up to anything. They just complicated everything further and further.

The fox had come more or less to accept that this was the way of the world: information accumulated while mind decayed. He was rather pleased with his word play on the best-known line of Oliver Goldsmith. He knew about eighteenth-century poets among many other things. He was concerned at the time to decide between the merits of Swift and Johnson as the best prose writer of the century. Johnson somehow epitomized the era while wasn't Swift, for all his talents, something of a hangover from the seventeenth? Now what a strange century that was, mused the fox, as he trotted aimlessly through the woodland paths. James I was writing the definitive work on witchcraft (and Shakespeare was writing the witches into *Macbeth* to flatter him) while Bacon was writing the *Novum Organum* and founding modern science. And what was all this stuff about the Puritans being behind all progress? They might have been responsible for capitalism (although the Catholic Italians were doing pretty well it seemed, while the Geneva Calvinists were positively anti-capitalist) but there weren't any Puritans among the scientists. Look at the Royal Society, with Charles II playing jokes on the members and all having a jolly time with plenty of high living going along with the high thinking. Not many Puritans in that company. It seemed to be the people who liked life that liked science. The fox shook his head hard to stop the ideas tumbling about. He thought that perhaps this was something the hedgehog with his one big idea could settle.

(We should explain, gentle reader, that in this world of the future, sentience and consciousness had been extended through genetic engineering to all God's creatures. Once it became possible to do it, the animal rights people had insisted. So the gift was benignly bestowed on what little was left of the animal kingdom - which wasn't much after the depredations of the industrial civilizations, and the third world countries' desperate depletion of their own natural resources. So far the experiment was in its early stages and the animals were not in any seeming hurry to join the forward march of progress. Perhaps they had been on the receiving end of it for too long to be eager, or perhaps it was something else, something to do with having been given consciousness and not having, as it were, earned it through evolution. But we have to make this state of things clear, because it was one of the many things that puzzled the fox, and otherwise this would just be a kind of soppy Aesop's fable wouldn't it?)

So the fox decided he would seek out the hedgehog and find out what he knew. What was the one big thing? Archilochus, bastard son of the leader of the Parian colony to Thasos (the fox knew this) and renowned elegiac poet of his day, now known to us only through fragments, had not said. Perhaps it could even be a formula that would tie together all the things the fox knew; the grand theory of everything that Hawkings was supposed to be working on but which even the fox, with all his information, couldn't figure out. It was all probably to do with time he thought. Was there really time at all for photons for example? And time for inert matter was surely different from biological time with its inevitable sense of future, and both from the time of sentient creatures with both a past and a future as well as the eternal present. It all seemed to end up in mysticism. The fox gave his head another hard shake.

But surely hedgehogs were not mystics. They seemed rather mundane and down-to-earth creatures, and even if they did know one big thing it might be of the order "grubs are nice to eat." That would be one big thing for your average hedgehog perhaps, but it wouldn't do much for the fox's problems. But obviously intellects of the order of Berlin and Archilochus (and the tiger for that matter) must mean something more. They were surely thinking of some kind of Ur-hedgehog who had got the handle on THE one big thing, otherwise why would they get so excited about it and bother to raise the issue in the first place. Well, there was only one way to find out. Try it on the dog... er... pig... whatever. Find him a hedgehog (rather, find the Hedgehog) and ask. How hard could it be?

Harder than you might think. They were elusive creatures. In the old days they had been a favorite food for gypsies. (Another piece of whimsically useless knowledge the fox had casually acquired.) The gypsies used to catch them and bake them in clay. The wet clay was pressed into the spines and then all around the body and it was put into the fire. The clay hardened. It was raked out, allowed to cool, and then when broken and pulled off, the spines all came out with it leaving a succulent ball of spineless hedgehog meat behind for the gypsy supper. The fox knew this as he knew so many things. And as with so many things, he couldn't remember when and how he learned it. It wasn't from the gypsies. There weren't any around now. The society of men didn't like gypsies wandering freely about. They were a little loose end that couldn't be accounted for. So they had either been extermi-

273

nated or settled—which amounted to the same thing. Once settled they ceased to be gypsies. They didn't speak their Romany language any more (an old Indo-European tongue, the fox knew, probably related to Sanskrit and hence suggesting that they originated in India not Egypt as their popular name implied.) Their customs disappeared apart from the odd bout of fortune telling by old ladies. Certainly they stopped that unhygienic baking of hedgehogs and bought their food in supermarkets like other humans.

This had probably led to a growth in the hedgehog population mused the fox, just as the prohibition on hunting had led to a similar rise in fox numbers. The fox knew this. But he couldn't help thinking that it didn't solve his problem if what was involved was some wise old hedgehog who somehow or other could get his thoughts above grubs and rolling up in balls for protection. Most of the foxes wasted their new found sentience on the more cunning pursuit of chickens—to the point where the humans were seriously considering re-introducing fox hunting except that it would give pleasure to the hunters and for some reason the humans found this distasteful. He couldn't think why. He certainly got pleasure from hunting rabbits and stealing chickens. Depended where you were on the food chain. But then the human philosophers were all hung up with the newfound sentience of animals. Could you hunt creatures with minds? The philosophers had a terrible time with this one, while their politicians blithely continued to kill off other humans who, if not always using their minds wisely, certainly had minds. The fox knew this. But it didn't seem to help. Find the hedgehog with the secret.

Several tries with very unwilling hedgehogs who just rolled up into balls and refused conversation were beginning to discourage him. Who could ever imagine that these stupid little creatures had any kind of secret worth knowing? And if they had, they seemed stubbornly unwilling to share it. What did Archilochus know anyway? Perhaps the tiger was just having a game with him. But he persevered. At last, one older, more savvy hedgehog poked out his little snout and snuffled an enquiry.

"Whod do you won foxy?" he semi-articulated.

"I'm looking for the old wise hedgehog who knows the one big thing," said the fox trying to keep his patience.

"Why din' you say so?" snuffled his spiny companion, "he's

nod here."

The fox was almost losing his temper.

"Look," he said,"you prickly little pest, tell me where he is or I'll..."

"You'll what?" jeered his diminutive but impenetrable adversary. The fox tried politeness once again; the fox knew many things, don't forget, and one of them was to be realistic in such situations.

"Could you possibly tell me where he is?"

"Thad's bedder," said the snuffler, and gave perfunctory directions.

Following the trail indicated, the fox indeed came upon a large, old and therefore, *prima facie*, profoundly wise hedgehog, sunning himself on a bank whereon the wild thyme grew and where there were clearly bugs and beetles in profusion: hedgehog heaven. The fox knew that J. B. S. Haldane, when asked what a study of nature revealed about God, had replied that the Almighty must have an inordinate fondness for beetles. Perhaps it was really a fondness for hedgehogs and a concern for their food supply; perhaps this was why they knew that one big thing: favorites of the All-knowing? Whatever. The fox decided a polite cough was perhaps the best approach, and to his surprise the old one did not instantly curl up at all. He blinked a lot (hedgehogs do that) and said with equal politesse:

"Ah! I've been expecting you. You must be the fox who knows many things. This is indeed a great pleasure for there is much I would like to learn."

Any statement as to the degree of the fox's astonishment would have been a gross understatement. But he had decided on a tone of imperturbable politeness.

"Au contraire," he said (the fox liked to cultivate expressions in foreign languages), "I have come to learn from you. I am a student of the *Ding-an-Sich*. I have come to find out the one big thing that you know."

"Oh dear, oh dear, oh dear,"sighed the hedgehog, "that wretched tiger has been spreading rumours about some Greek and a man called Berlin; isn't that so?"

"Mais certainment," said the fox. "You are famous for that one bit of wisdom, hedgehog, and I think you should share it with the world, or at least with me."

"But you see," said the hedgehog shyly, "I'm not sure I know what it is. My problem is that I have such a little brain; such a simple brain. Things come in but they don't stay. I'm fascinated with them while they are there, but then they are gone."

"Well", said the fox, who of course knew about these things, "that is probably due to the lack of sufficient neo-cortex, and hence a paucity of storage space. Although whether memories are stored in specific areas, or holographically, or somehow distributed throughout the neural network and subject to elaborate means of recall, we are not sure yet. Do you dream?"

"Very little," said the hedgehog. "I've heard about it of course, from the likes of you bigger animals. But I only seem to have dreams of bugs and beetles."

"That could explain it," said the fox. "It seems to be well established that neuronal gating in the hypothalamus during rapid eye movement sleep is responsible for dreaming which is in fact a clearing house for both short- and long-term memory. Of course, in lower mammals such as yourself, REM sleep is still wholly tied to theta rhythms which would explain your bugs and beetles."

"Oh dear," said the hedgehog, "you see you've lost me already. I just can't keep all that information in my little brain at once. So how could I possibly know anything that would be of use to you?"

The fox mused for while, and then replied:

"It must be something that you know instinctively, not something you have learned. That raises a problem though because it suggests that there are such things as innate ideas, and as good empiricists we usually resist that idealistic notion. However, since we animals have only recently acquired sentience and language, it is possible that you have become able to articulate an instinctive wisdom. What do you think is the most basic thing you know?"

"Oh dear, well, I know to roll up into a ball when I sense danger. I know to look for food when I am hungry."

"But these are not ideas," said the fox, a trifle impatiently. "The big thing you know must surely transcend mere instinctive activity that would have existed before your metamorphosis?"

"Does it for you?" asked the hedgehog.

"Does it what?"

"I mean do you do anything differently now that you have these abilities? What do you do with your day?"

"Well," replied the fox, "I hunt rabbits and steal chickens."

"Yes," said the hedgehog, "and when rutting time comes round you search out lady foxes."

"Of course," said the fox, blushing slightly, "cherchez la femme. Naturellement."

"And then you talk about it a lot?" the hedgehog added quizzically.

"Indeed," replied the fox.

"But then you are little different from myself. You are still a fox, but a fox that talks about what it does. The only difference is that you remember things, and so you know many things. But what you DO is chase chickens and the other stuff."

The fox was a little huffy.

"Bien sûr. But what is the point of having mind, and intellect and language if one does not use them?"

"I suppose I'm just a simple creature," said the hedgehog, "but somehow it doesn't seem that much of a help to me. I still have to get grubs when I'm hungry, and curl into a ball, and hibernate, and in the spring look for a lady hedgehog and make some little fellows that she takes care of anyway. Quite honestly, I think I could do without a mind."

"This," said the fox, "is not promising. How are we going to find the one big thing that is in such mind as you do have?"

"How do you know I have a mind?" asked the hedgehog modestly. "You know so many things, perhaps you could reassure me on that."

This threw the fox a bit, but he did indeed know so many things and was equal to the question. He decided to bypass Bishop Berkeley and the problem of other minds, which would probably only confuse the old fellow, and get to the cutting edge.

"There exists," he said, "an infallible test: the Turing test."

"I'm hopeless at tests," the hedgehog began nervously, but the fox cut him off.

"It's not that kind of test," he explained, "no right or wrong answers and all that. It was designed to see if machines had minds. Do you know about computers?"

"The tiger told me," said the hedgehog, "but I've forgotten. He told me if I had one I could get females. But I have them already, so I didn't really follow."

"He probably said E-mail," suggested the fox, "but never mind, let's stick with computers."

"Aren't they the things that can do sums very quickly?"

"They can, but they do much more than that."

The fox decided to skip the explanation about binary logic, graphic interfaces, digitalized information, operating systems, RAM capacity, and hard drives. He somehow had a feeling the hedgehog would lose it as soon as he delivered it.

"They are very complicated machines that do thinking much faster than humans," said the fox,"and the Turing test—called after its brilliant but unfortunate inventor—is intended to determine at what point they have the right to be credited with minds—with intelligence and consciousness, that is, for all practical purposes indistinguishable from human minds."

"How on earth do they do that?" asked the hedgehog, more out of politeness than real interest. But the fox was in full swing now and continued on inexorably.

"Suppose the human is on one side of a screen and does not know what is on the other. He can pass messages and ask questions to the Other and receive answers. Now suppose that on the other side there really is a supercomputer and it gives back answers that are indistinguishable from those a human would give. Voila! It has passed the Turing test. We have to admit that it has a mind, consciousness, or whatever."

"Is the computer ever sad?" asked the hedgehog

"No," said the fox irritated, "computers have no emotions."

"Was Mr. Turing ever sad?"

"Yes, I think he was, but..."

"Can the computer change its mind?"

"Only if it is programmed to do so."

"Can the computer say: I think this is all very boring, let's do something else?"

"No," said the fox,"but that isn't the point..."

"I think it is," said the hedgehog, "if that is the kind of mind the computer has, I'm not sure I'd want it."

The fox was getting confused.

"What is the point of having a mind if all you use it for is to do the things you did without it anyway?" he retorted angrily.

"Because I'm a hedgehog. What do you do except chase rabbits, steal chickens, and mate? What does the computer do except those things the humans have told it to do? What do the humans do for that matter?"

"But that is the point," said the fox angrily. "Look at what the humans do. They do whatever they want!"

"They do what humans do," said the hedgehog. "These are at bottom the same things we do, but they talk about it a lot, and they elaborate on it a lot."

He was warming to his point. Contact with fox-the-curious had inspired him.

"How did humans get that way in the first place? It doesn't seem to have done them a lot of good. They've certainly spoiled things for we animals. Why didn't your kind become like humans?"

"The canids?" asked the fox a bit startled

"Yes. The tiger told me it was something about being pack-hunting animals that did it to the humans. Well, foxes and tigers don't hunt in packs but the others do—the lions and the hyenas and the dogs. Dogs seem ridiculously fond of humans. Why didn't it happen to dogs, or wolves?"

The fox really did know about this, and like a punch-drunk boxer came out fighting when he heard the bell ring.

"Eh bien! The hominids—that is, the ancestors of the humans, if you like—had a peculiar evolutionary trajectory. They were vegetarian primates living in the forests, like most of the present monkeys and apes, but the forests shrunk and they found them-selves out on the savannah—the grasslands. Their usual food was not available, so they took up scavenging and then hunting for meat."

"But that makes them just like you."

"Hélas! Not really. We were carnivores who had honed our hunting skills over millions of years (not that I am suggesting some Lamarckian inheritance of acquired characteristics you under-stand, this was all a result of random mutation and natural selec-tion) and we lived entirely on meat. They were omnivores now, with the old vegetarian gut, but a new need for meat. However, they lacked the basic skills and natural weapons that we had built into our bodies and behaviors."

"So what did they do?" asked the hedgehog, genuinely inter-ested. This was a story, and he liked stories.

The fox was almost rapturously warming to his theme. "They had quickly to develop ways of surviving that we (the canids and felines that is) had taken those millions of years to perfect. They made tools and developed these into weapons. They had to use their basic group-living skills to become efficient hunters and gatherers and processors and sharers of food. Human scientists think it was this enormous pressure over a relatively short evolutionary period that led to the growth of their large brains, language, consciousness, and all those other things that make them humans— that make them able to do whatever they want."

"All well and good," said the hedgehog who was working at the top of his small-brained capacity to take this in, "so why do they insist on making such a mess of things? There are very few of us left, you know, and there are so many of them that they get in each other's way and become very nasty about it."

This floored the fox. For while he knew many things, this thing had always eluded him. All the things he knew did not add up to an answer to this thing. The hedgehog persisted.

"If humans can do anything they like because of intelligence and consciousness and all that, then why don't they do things that will make a nice safe world for all of us?"

"Well they do try," said the fox a bit lamely. "It just seems that there is something about them that gets in the way of their doing it consistently."

"Ah! Yes, yes, yes," said the hedgehog, sighing heavily and nodding a lot.

"What?" said the fox, dripping with curiosity, for the hedgehog seemed to be sitting dreamily on the edge of some revelation. Was this the One Big Thing?

"So, like the rest of us, after all these millions of years, they came to be what they are?" asked the hedgehog.

"Of course," said the fox, "but that is obvious, n'est-ce-pas?"

"The one big thing is always obvious," said the hedgehog.

"Then for heaven's sake what is it?!" the fox almost shouted.

"It's the only thing I think I really know," said the hedgehog, "so it must be it."

"What?!!"

The hedgehog sighed again, rubbed his little snout with his paws, blinked a few times, and answered as sonorously as he could manage, since obviously the fox expected something profound:

"THINGS ACT ACCORDING TO THEIR NATURES."

"That's it?" asked the fox incredulously.

"I really can't think of anything else. I'm so sorry to disappoint you Mr. Fox. But I must attend to these grubs, and if you get really angry with me I shall roll into a ball, and soon I must hibernate. I feel the cold weather coming on. I shall dream but a little and when spring comes round I'll look briefly for a lady hedgehog. Meanwhile, you'll go off and chase rabbits and steal chickens and the rest. And with our new-found skills we'll talk about it endlessly. And the humans will go on doing what they do and talk about it even more to the point where their overburdened brains will probably explode. All this talk is making me dizzy. But thank you for your conversation. It has been a great pleasure to meet the fox who knows so many things. Unfortunately, I won't remember most of them tomorrow. Good day."

And quite exhausted by this unusually long speech he shuffled off, his tiny snout pushing up the dead leaves, the beetles scurrying in panic.

The fox (who knew oh so many things) felt cheated. So much for Archilochus and Berlin and that meddlesome tiger. The damned hedgehog had turned out to be nothing more than an Aristotelian naturalist after all. Clearly he (the fox) could solve nothing without knowing so much more. But he was distracted by the sight of an unguarded chicken coop and a rabbit within striking distance. That night in his den he dreamed of sad gypsies and Alan Turing crying and giant chickens and the stupidity of hedgehogs. The next day he meant to engage in the ultimate deconstruction of the concept "natural" and put that to rest once and for all—after, that is, snagging a nice fat bunny for breakfast and rousting a few nesting grouse in the high copse. Then perhaps he would find a pleasant site for a new den; this one was getting too full of fleas.

# HEROES, POETS, AND OTHER WAIFS

## WHERE HAVE THE HEROES GONE?

Oedipus stands dumb before the Sphinx
Hannibal has a war of words with Rome
Alexander sees the knot and shrinks
Achilles packs his bags and sails for home

Jason takes the Argo for a cruise
Theseus starts a fund for Minotaurs
Leda takes the swan to court and sues
Hercules gets the nymphs to do his chores

Aeneas sets up house with Dido  kids
litter the Carthaginian marble halls
The Roman enterprise is on the skids
Horatius knows he hasn't got the balls

Orpheus finds his inspiration gone
Pegasus is kicking down his stall
Great Ceasar paddles in the Rubicon
and builds a summer home in southern Gaul

Anthony and Cleopatra find
they don't have much in common and split up
The Gorgon likes her hair piled up behind
Cerberus is just a friendly pup

Dracula is now donating blood
Samson has his hair trimmed once a week
Noah bought insurance for the flood
and sold his livestock tanker to a Greek

 Midas is a leveraged buyout guy
Jokannan has married Salomé
Judas is hidden by the FBI
(He says he didn't do it for the pay)

The Essene scrolls have got a big advance
Paul's gospel program gives them rave reviews
David before the Ark forgets to dance
P. Pilate grants occasional interviews

Great Pan is dead!  The funeral was nice
Anansi let the flies go that he trapped
Loki has won the Nobel Peace Prize twice
Trickster reformed and helps the handicapped

Krishna gave the maids their clothing back
and preached a sermon stressing safer sex
Maui got his penis back on track
by lecturing it on balances and checks

Parsifal has pawned the Holy Grail
A CAT-scan showed that Amfortas was clear
Arthur had Lancelot released on bail
They live ménage-à-trois with Guinevere

Roland and Oliver have three boutiques
Cuchullainn was elected for Sinn Fein
Ivan and Ghengis smuggle Slav antiques
Ulysses is on lotuses again

Quixote dodged the windmills (kept it quiet)
Don Juan is doing well in men's apparel
Gargantua is on a fiber diet
Diogenes is auctioning his barrel

Siegfried winced and called the fire brigade
Brunhilde threw a sulk   In Avalon
King Arthur jogs and drinks his Gatorade
Lohengrin has fallen for the swan

Jefferson does tours of Monticello
John Adams makes his litigation pay
Franklin remains a jovial decent fellow
Arnold is working for the CIA

Washington won't budge from Valley Forge
Padraic Pearse calls off the Easter Rising
Holmes dodges Moriarty at the gorge
Columbus drops the jaunt—too enterprising

John Wilkes goes in to business with Tom Paine
Lenin decides that Finland is too cold
Bismarck plays soldiers with his Lionel train
Shaka waits 'til opinion has been polled

The Venusburg gives condoms—short or long
The Gods eat McAmbrosia and drink Coke
Disney acquires Valhalla for a song
Dionysus doesn't get the joke

Nelson made up with Hamilton   And while
he and Emma try  they don't get on
Dick Burton works to unpollute the Nile
Oh Valkyrie!  Where have the heroes gone?

## OEDIPUS DENTIFREX

Old King Cadmus went to Thebes
and sowed the teeth of discord there
So his descendants—lords and plebes—
had problems with their dental care

The Spartoi—dentoids to a man—
deploring Cadmean attack
joined Hera's Hellene dental plan
to counteract Semitic plaque

King Laius never could get used
to Delphic brushes—straight or flex
He rinsed and flushed and then abused
young Chryssipus with anal sex

King Oedipus refused to floss
(The toothless Sphinx was too banal)
He showed his daddy who was boss
then drilled his mother's root canal

The Gods at Colonnus cut short
the tale of Oedipal adventures
Theseus and the Athenian court
inherited the Holy Dentures

Tough King Creon D.D.S.
extracted seven at a killing
Antigone in great distress
tried hard to fix her brother's filling

Experience shows whoever wins
eventually fades away
Decline and fall always begins
with moral or with tooth decay

Sly Socrates concealed the truth
(hard enamel—rot beneath)
the problem's not corrupted youth
but tartar on neglected teeth

The Ideal Forms  as Plato knew
(spit and rinse and open wide)
The Good  The Beautiful  The True
are Brush and Floss and Fluoride

So heed the wisdom of the Greeks
(the wisest of the Aryans)
chew carrots  olives  beans and leeks—
chocolate is for barbarians

## THE LONG LINE

I have this friend the lyric poet (so he proclaims himself, I
     didn't make this up) who was much praised for his skill at
     the "free verse long line" (I quote).
The critics—those who liked his work—were unanimous about his
     consummate skill and delicate artistry in the admittedly
     difficult business of writing "the long line."
He, naturally, fed on the praise and saw this as a definite
     strength on which to build all his poetic effort in the
     future, namely: "the long line."
So he began to write lines longer and longer than the previous ones;
     lines with intricate punctuation and much matter in
     parentheses (which of course lengthened the line even more)
     designed to "preserve the tension without losing the integrity"
     (as one delighted critic put it) of "the long line."
In the end his lines were so very very long that even for him—
     and he was not usually one to question his own skill at
     prosody—they began to pose a very very uncomfortable and
     even debilitating question; one that crept up on him and
     forced itself into his perceptual field as he lengthened
     his lines still further to achieve the maximum effect of
     "the long line"—namely:
When does a long line of free verse become a paragraph of prose?

     Well, you tell me.  He had no answer and
     he went quite mad.  They tell me in the home
     he sits there writing letters to the dead
     in strict blank verse, five measures to the line.
     But even so his paragraphs iambic
     tend to a length that would make Browning blush.
     So is he better for the discipline?

**287**

Who knows?  The doctors won't release him and
the editors of all those magazines
take blank verse paragraphs as evidence
of sheer poetic lunacy.  So what's
a man to do?  He says he would write prose,
but that would cost him his integrity.
Perhaps he's better where he is.  The strain
is certainly too much, and we conclude
"the long line paradox" has done for him.
Who knows:
perhaps the dead enjoy pentameters?


## A DOROTHY PARKER MEMORIAL

"And spoil a page with rhymes" she said
yet we continue  now she's dead
and cannot make us wince with shame
to carry on the pointless game

So poets  rhyme to end your clause
indicative  poor dinosaurs
who unlike her lack guts to face
the terror of subjunctive space

Yet should I be so hard  for she
was still a rhymer such as we
who  while she scorned prosodic crime
found it imperative to rhyme

And what she knew that made her sad
was  even if the rhymes are bad
when desperation makes us scrawl
they're better than no rhymes at all

# HIPPIES AND LOST LOVES

## HIPPIE GIRL

There is no image that can capture you—
    except  perhaps  a shivering guitar
(electric) in an ecstasy of sound
    throbbing into distance like a star
(galactic) in its fierce expansive round
    It is not false  but then it is not true

There's no experience that recalls you quite
    unless  perhaps  the feeling that a doe
is quivering an arrow's length away
    unseen yet palpable  waiting the blow
that seals the bond of predator and prey
    It is not wrong  but then it is not right

There's no sensation makes you manifest—
    and yet  perhaps  an incense yet unburned
would have the chanting odor of your hair
    sacred and sensuous  drowning all that's learned
by reason with its dense hypnotic prayer
    This is better  but it's not the best

These images are words  and lacking flesh
    cannot convey you    No experience
can match the wild reality we know
    only by straining every desperate sense
to reach that agony  exquisite  slow
    old as the flying star  yet always fresh

## TIREDNESS

I grew tired of those waves
of soft brown bodies breaking
warm and shallow over me  then
disappearing softly in the sand

tired of sleeping among graves
sleeping and waking
only with the lovely dead
murdered by my own indifference

tired of the corpse inside my head
rocked in the tepid water
where it rotted without consequence

tired of the sharp and brittle shell
my crabbed and hermit tongue
maneuvered with sickening skill
against soft creatures with such slaughter

tired of the pressure on my eyes
always turned inward where
the hailstones of suppressed despair
fell from the shining clouds of clever lies

Images are not
enough  but Ill try this
Aphrodite coming from that sea
alive and giving life with every kiss
refusing to let unwilling corpses rot

No  They are not
Enough that I am free

If I am tired now
it is the tiredness of one possessed
so much by love  so often  he must rest

## PRIMATOLOGICAL FLIBBERTYGIBBET

Life  liberty and the pursuit
of happiness  Lie flibberty
and the escape from death
Does liberty hang gibbeted in a suit
of seriousness  while you
purr at the gibbet's foot and I pursue
undignified and very out of breath?
Life  is too short  a gibbet's rope
and liberty too scarce for hope
However heavy was its purse you'd spend
it fast enough  my gibbety
flibberty  love of liberty
laughter shaking  play-face hooting
gibbet sentence quick commuting
logico-primatic woodland friend

> *troglodytes* genus *Pan*
> peering with suspicion on
> willful woman  reckless man
> sapiential semblance gone

So let's throw caution to the apes
(for we like they are nature's dupes)
pursuing happiness as only flib
berty gibbets know  Other people's lib
erty is their concern  Let's see a smile
We are released from seriousness awhile
Life is too short  Pursuit takes far too long
So let us be the singer  and the song

## MR TITMARCH

(only slightly edited from my
great grandmother's diary, 1881)

July 16

I doubt that I shall ever marry, but
if all else fails there's always Mr Titmarch.
He may not be as suitable as some,
(a bank clerk is not of much consequence)
but Mr Titmarch would, I do believe,
be somewhat of an interesting man.
I don't know why I say this; there is just
something in his manner that attracts.

July 29

It now has been two weeks since anyone
has heard a single word from Mr Titmarch;
but I cannot complain about neglect,
since, after all, I had no expectations.
All the same, I fear I must confess
that I had entertained some little hope.

August 13

We're all abuzz!  The word has just come in
that Mr Titmarch has been "apprehended."
It seems he's guilty of embezzlement.
The bank he worked in nigh on twenty years
has been relieved of thirteen thousand pounds.

Well, surely they were right and he was not
the best of matrimonial prospects, but
I feel I may take comfort in the fact
I too was right: he was most interesting!

Dec 29

The probability of marriage fades
with every passing month.  I often think
of Mr. Titmarch in his prison cell,
and how I would have written every day,
and sent him cakes, and visited each week.
Oh! such a loyal little wife for such
an undeserving villain!  One may dream.


## UNBORN SONNET

So  You want me dead  I understand
I feel your anguish  and I hear you cry
You do not hate me  but I was not planned
Your life is ruined  so I have to die
Oh  I'm not bitter  Since I've not been born
there's nothing of the life out there to miss
I'll never know oppression  hunger  scorn
or failed ambition  or a lover's kiss
I might have been a Mozart  or might not
Mahatma Gandhi  Michelangelo
Perhaps a Hitler  Stalin or Pol Pot
It doesn't matter since we'll never know
    Through this warm fluid  echoes of your voice
    convey me your last message "choice  choice  choice"

# KINGS, SOCIALISTS AND OTHER FUTILITIES

HAIKU (engraved on a medical bracelet)

> If you are starving
> and I die  eat my flesh  I
> have no use for it

EPIGRAM (on the problem with the nineties)

> We saw the sixties come and go
> We thought that they had gone to stay
> But this thing we have come to know—
> The sixties never went away

## KISSING YOUR SISTER

It's honorable to die
your life a scoreless tie
at least you didn't lose
But was it such a sin
that painful need to WIN?
Which would you choose?

## THE END—R. Frost meets O. Nash

Fire
would be dire
But ice
might be nice

## EXISTENTIALIST CLERIHEW

A drunken Albert Camus
told Sartre he was "pflammu"
which Sartre  dazed with wine
challenged him to define

## HIGH LIVING

In Aspen  Colorado
the sophisticate will find
intellectual bravado
and a mercenary mind

Here the mental elevation
does not match the altitude
but amidst the meditation
the business sense is shrewd

Narcissistic self-obsession
fights with fashionable doubt
but an instinct for possession
quickly puts the doubt to rout

All this splendid isolation
helps the mind to cultivate
a refinement of sensation
and a feel for real estate

but the rarefied endeavor
brings them little satisfaction
and the straining to be clever
soon provokes an abreaction

With degrees of desperation
they attempt a sad retreat
into jungles of sensation
where they languish in the heat

Yet in their lucid phases
their thoughts are elemental
each lovingly appraises
the coming Christmas rental

They pursue with dedication
their adulteries and trips
and the earnest cultivation
of mature relationships

But the cynic from the city
who is only passing through
does not need to waste his pity
for at least they have the view

We should spare our condescension
for is it so absurd
this sad but brave intention
to do better than the herd?

And when our world is ended
all the cities gone to dust
maybe here they'll live suspended
with our knowledge in their trust

They'll be writing  painting  skiing
in their languid Shangri-La
while we stragglers are fleeing
the destruction of our star

## SERIOUS OLD SOCIALISTS

When I was young and anti-socialist
I sneered at them  their threadbare suits  their gray
and ill-cut hair  worn pullovers  their list
of grave complaints on issues of the day

They smelled of stale tobacco and thin beer
and taught the young in Fabian Sunday schools
the hurt of buying cheap and selling dear
instead of equal distributive rules

When mentioning Kier Hardie  Ramsay Mac
a twitching smile would touch the careworn face
Engels and Marx brought shrugs  the forward track
was signified by Owen and his race

The Webbs were quoted much  so Shaw and Wells
and Fabian factions lovingly dissected
The General Strike was Marathon  the cells
of suffragettes were often resurrected

But oh  and most of all  the march from Jarrow
was their Trafalgar  when the working classes
invaded mammon  eagle mobbed by sparrow
with claims of jobs for working lads and lasses

They saw a fairer world where everyone
might well be gray and threadbare in his soul
but cleansed of envy  competition gone
pursue a stern egalitarian goal

They reach us from that book-besotten age
when men read Comte and Ruskin and Carlyle
and Edward Bellamy was thought a sage
not crackpot worth a condescending smile

Russia was still a subject of debate
though some thought Stalin went a bit too far
But could you criticize a socialist state?
and anything was better than the Czar

They got their government  it didn't work
While others compromised  they never said
the fight was over  (not their style to shirk)
But they and their ideas are stiff and dead

I sneered back then at their naivety
but now  I kind of miss them in a time
when greed is elevated to divinity
and no one can distinguish trade from crime

I look at so-called socialists today
a bunch of Scandinavian welfare weeds
and in a purely secular fashion pray
for serious old socialists in their tweeds

## LE ROI S'AMUSE

> *Puisque règne aujoud'hui la hache*
> *Que venez-vous parler au nom de raison.*
> —Louis Aragon, *"Le regard de Rancé."*

The liveried servant stumbles and drops
the porcelain soup tureen  Oh the noise!
So loud!  with the stuff flying everywhere
The courtiers  startled  sniff  say "Oh!"
"My goodness!"  Servants bustle and clean
  But the king does not notice such things
  Lesser people take care of such things
  The king does not notice  It does not exist

The petitioners crowd in the palace yard
some kneeling  some crying  some raising their arms
"O pardon my son  sire  he stole from hunger!"
The courtiers  startled  sniff  hurry by
Officials collect the petitions and burn them
  But the king does not notice such things
  Other people take care of such things
  The king does not notice  It does not exist

The beggars reach out  they clutch and grasp
at the silk and lace  Their cries are loud
and pitiful  and they stink and shuffle
The courtiers  startled  sniff  call the guards
The dragoons disperse the beggars like chaff
  But the king does not notice such things
  Little people take care of such things
  The king does not notice  It does not exist

The mob is armed and opens the prisons
The soldiers refuse to fire on the mob
The mob yells loudly "Death to the king!"
The courtiers startled sniff pack valises
They all are seized as the mob storms the palace
  But the king does not notice such things
  Someone else takes care of such things
  The king does not notice  It does not exist

A figure is standing alone in the dock
head raised above the abuse from the crowd
of inquisitors screaming for death and revenge
"Acknowledge your guilt" the inquisitors yell
"your own and your ancestors'" Thus he replies:
  "We  the king  do not notice such things
  You people take care of such things
  The king does not notice  It does not exist"

A figure is mounting the bloodstained steps
stumbling  filthy from weeks in prison
A blindfold head is laid on the block
where the blood of the courtiers stinks like offal
The frenzied mob cries "Off with the head!"
  But the king does not notice such things
  Strange people take care of such things
  The king does not notice  It does not exist

# THE GRAND MARQUIS TO HIS EXECUTIONER

I am the Grand Marquis  you see
and it is clear you envy me
(one's bound to be a little vain
when one descends from Charlemagne)
but there is nothing you can do
to alter this  It will be true
if you relieve me of my head
for though I'll certainly be dead
    I still will be
      the Grand Marquis
  and you  a nobody

# THE EXECUTIONER REPLIES TO THE GRAND MARQUIS:

Your argument  seigneur  is just
But mine is new  sharp  free from rust
And when I've used it  I'll be vain—
I squashed the spawn of Charlemagne!

# FORM AND CHAOS

## SNOWFLAKES AND SIMILES

A snowflake is a frozen memory
of thirty thousand random drifting feet

That long descent  so slow  so intricate
so infinite in its particulars
of influence from all the elements
could not  could never be the same for each
minuscule droplet  so there never will
be any two alike  though all observe
the laws of symmetry and branching trees

This is an endless source of similes
that fall (like snowflakes) through a mental void
no two the same  but when they incarnate
in words  then each is forced to start
with a comparative conjunction  and
to follow rules of syntax  Form Is All

## MANDELBROT SONNET

Small initial differences (*a blink*
*so nondescript it might have passed unseen*
*had mild intention not produced a wink*)
can have gigantic outcomes that had been
unknown at their inception (*how predict*
*the mild flirtation  pregnant with design*
*would spawn a dynasty that would inflict*
*misery on millions?*)  with no sign
of their impending order (*yet contained*
*within the gesture consequences down*
*to final victim*) lawfully constrained
(*imagine if the wink had been a frown*)
       both unpredicted yet determinate
       exquisite fractal geometry of fate

# Six

# The Jesus Tapes:
# We Are Not Alone

*Who say ye that I am?*
—Matthew: 16:xv


*Thou hast conquered, O pale Galilean*
—Algernon Charles Swinburne, *"Hymn to Proserpine"*


*By the term Beauty are properly signified two things. First, that external quality of bodies already so often spoken of, and which, whether it occur in a stone, flower, beast, or in man, is absolutely identical, which, as I have already asserted, may be in some sort typical of the Divine attributes, and which therefore I shall, for distinctions sake, call Typical Beauty; and, secondarily, the appearance of felicitous fulfilment of function in living things, more especially of the joyful and right exertion of perfect life in man; and this kind of beauty I shall call Vital Beauty.*
—John Ruskin, *Modern Painters*, II:3:1:iii, 1846


*A patient and conscientious reading of the gospels will always destroy any explanation which we devise. If it makes sense, it is wrong. That is the only reliable rule-of-thumb which we can use when testing the innumerable interpretations of Jesus's being and his place in history.*
—A. N. Wilson, *Jesus*, 1992


*First, there were the miracles.*
—Morton Smith, *Jesus the Magician*, 1978


*Formerly it was possible to book through-tickets at the supplementary-psychological-knowledge office which enabled those travelling in the interests of Life-of-Jesus construction to use express trains, thus avoiding the inconvenience of having to stop at every little station, change, and run the risk of missing their connexion. This ticket office is now closed. There is a station at the end of each section of the narrative, and the connexions are not guaranteed.*
—Albert Schweitzer, *The Quest of the Historical Jesus*

# THE JESUS TAPES

Zygon Y-2737451 (of Zygon 3) speaks to his friend Zygon
AA-2341 (of Zygon 2) using, for practice and mutual
amusement, the linear form of communication he learned
during his first incarnation on Sol 3, commonly known
as Earth.

## THE MESSIAH MISSION

After the crucifixion and the tomb—
the three-day sojourn with myself They forced
upon me—before making me take up
the futile pageant—why?  Well  Their excuse
was re-assessment of the project  so
They re-assessed and i was shuffled out
to do the resurrection number—why?
Surely by then it was quite obvious
the whole Plan was a failure—why?  because
those hopes They pinned on hopeless hominids
were doomed by hominidic hopelessness
There was no way and well They knew it  Had
not one experiment already gone
awry when Zygon X had played his part
as—what was it now?  'Buddha' the name
he ended up with—no THE Buddha  not
enough to be what he proclaimed himself—
the mere exemplar of a common way

And that's the point if only They would see
These humans turn exemplars into Gods
as easily as they digest their food—
and once that's done by God there's no way out
The whole 'religious' circus starts again
and factions breed like roaches  sects and schools
are at each other's throats—but why go on?
It's all too boringly well known

                           In my
report ("On project M"—the 'M' stands for
'Messiah'—i'll explain that later on)
i stressed the overall futility
of 'working with the system'  (how that phrase
makes my mind tremble  sanctimonious rot)
But still They try—because They cannot face
the grim alternative  the fact most feared:
admission that the whole thing is a fraud
OK (i learned this slang just recently)
OK  perhaps 'fraud' is too strong  'mistake'
should be preferred  but even then why not
admit the damn mistake?  But no  They must
interpret it as serendipity
that left them with the choice of leaving it
alone and seeing where the error led
an error glossed as happy accident
which led to an experiment of sorts
but one which all our scientists agreed
was far from canons then acceptable
of carefully controlled experiment

That was the point—it was out of control
At first it was not obvious  but when
it started with the God thing then They should
have known to shut it down  There was no way
to roll this back and keep it under wraps
(you will admit i've 'licked' the idiom)
you cannot—as They should have known—endow
matter with mind and not expect the stuff
to stumble on the secret of itself
however clumsily  and then begin

to arrogate those features to itself
that don't belong to it—or only half
belong to it—but thereby hangs a tale
(the idiom again—i have it pat!)
And what a tale! But no  that was Their plan
'work with the system: change it from within'
take the very faults and turn them round
use them to change the elemental forms
of thinking so the creature would not change
but still the outcome would be passable

Ever since They in Their wisdom thought
by binary fissions twice to amplify
the brain size of their precious hominid
the creature was devoted to ideas
and by ideas it lived and loved and erred
But if with our superior techniques
we could but generate some new ideas
out of those already there in place
why then we could continue with The Plan
without admitting we had erred ourselves
Much better!  We had found a clever way
to make a virtue of necessity
thus adding to the stock of interest
in our already boring universe

The human flaw was obvious  but ours
was worse  for we knew better  but had not
the courage to admit to our mistake
And so the Guardians decided that
the one supreme impossibility
was 'direct intervention'  That must be
the very last resort  and before then
we must exhaust the possibilities
of 'working with the system'  Lovely plan
for those who merely planned it  for the rest
who had  like me  to take up human flesh
and pander to their idiocities
(is that a word?  i sometimes miss a beat)
it was a torment none of us deserved
(although I always thought that Zygon X
had had it easy with his Buddhahood)

## THE INCARNATION PLAN

After the incarnation and the cross
i pondered for three days  while They in council
decided what the next stage of The Plan
would be   Should i expire and let it die
as I myself had "died"  or should we try
to resurrect The Plan as was expected?
(And thus 'roll back the stone' and let me out)

The ever hopeful Guardians assumed
that if we gave the gullible a chance
to re-assess  then they would understand
"you all are sons of God" (you idiots!)
"Christ is in all of you  you can attain
Christhood and Christian kingdom here on earth"
Why should they understand?  Poor Zygon X
had told them all these things of Buddhahood
and had they listened?  Not a bit of it
Within a dozen years the walls were up
the factions and the sects  the wars  disputes
the splitting of the hairs  the hate  the words
Caught in their web of words  poor hominids

If i seem harsh sometimes  forgive me friend
i liked them in a way  as only one
who was one of them (in a sense) could like
i even envied them their total lack
of any sense of what their situation
was  or how it came to be that way
Within their limits these converted apes
had found some solace  and a kind of joy
was possible for them that is denied
to creatures of pure mind like you and me
i know that we experiment with form
and translate mental substance for effect
but we can never know as from 'inside'
a creature that has moved from form to mind
where matter is the substance of the thought
and not its temporary habitation

During the incarnation i was torn
because i never could assimilate
this earthy (if you will forgive the pun—
i can't resist these word games as you know)
this matter-bound existence of the spirit
Although i tried 'twas all dissimulation
They never knew  They thought i was 'aloof'
Found me abstracted  not like one of them
which was alright  i was supposed to be
'divine' which in the idea system means
aloof  so nothing caused them to suspect
But then what was there to suspect?  The Plan
called for a 'God' to take on human flesh
and in a way  though modesty forbids
that is what happened  If there was deceit
it only lay in the identity
of 'God' which in their system means a thing
so far removed from us it's quite absurd
That petty  vengeful  tribal  thunder god
that Moses fabricated from the pure
idea he learned from our most promising
of pupils called—Akhenaten  was it?
Another dismal failure of The Plan

But then The Plan called—as with Zygon X—
to take a fertile doctrine of the times
and meld into it  thus transforming it
Why  you have often asked  pick on the Jews?
i asked myself  and having been one  still
i ask myself again  But there was method in
The Plan  i must admit  Why not pick Rome?
you often ask  but i suppose that They
found Rome too rational  too like the Greeks
and added to it power  self-satisfaction
Rome thought herself eternal  there was need
to find a people striving to achieve
an end yet unaccomplished  one that we
could turn to our own uses  propagate
and spread it to the hominids at large
to try to strip the flesh from the idea

and make them like ourselves  if not exactly
then somehow more devoted to the Forms
than to the substance  as we told the Greek
the one who almost got it—there we go
lamenting our mistakes  Where was i then?

The Jews were ripe  but our miscalculation
was unforgivable   Their root idea
was not amenable to transformation
Oh we tried  They drummed it into me
"plug into Messianic expectations"
that was The Plan  then once in place
the scion of the House of David would
set out to de-messianize Messiah
move them from the God-idea to the
'Christ within you all' idea which
would make them closer to our own condition
partaking as they did of mental grace
(i fall occasionally back into the slang
i picked up so much from them)


## THE FOLLOWERS


                          So you ask
"whom did you like the most?" accepting that
the concept of a 'friend' or 'liking' cannot
be that of ours where only minds in tune
—quite literally in tune—can claim that state
Our minds have always trembled tunefully
in quite exquisite harmony and so
i call you 'friend'  But there on Earth
where bodies do the trembling it was hard
to find that harmony without excess
of glandular and hormone interference
Of all—i think that Judas was the best

So much maligned  poor man  by those who sought
some hominid excuse for cowardice
for mental failure—never did 'betray'
was all part of The Plan of course  but some
who envied him his seeming understanding
of what the 'message' was  sought to malign
his character—the humans are like that
Well  Judas was the nearest to a pure
intelligence among them  so I felt
the closest  felt a quiver of a mind
(They couldn't even get his nickname right
and lumbered him with that 'Iscariot'
a meaningless perversion  As we knew
he was 'sicarius' from the little dagger
he always kept concealed inside his cloak)
He knew that i was playing at 'Messiah'
He never knew the truth  until the end
But still he knew that all this was about
something other than the restoration
of petty kingship and a nation state
He also knew the concept was too hard
for any of his brethren  they must
convert it into godhead  sacrifice
salvation and the blessed life to come
The Plan said 'let them have the sacrifice
there is a lesson in it  they should learn'
But did they learn?  NO—not a bit of it
i died to purge their sins  to expiate
the very knowledge that their legend saw
(with dim perception of the awful truth—
one reason why the Guardians picked them out)
was basic to their incapacity
to handle their own lives now that ideas
not instincts ruled their poor mentalities

Their dimwit God  according to the story
that they cooked up in Babylonian jails
forbade them out of bloody mindedness
to eat the quinces growing on the tree
that held the juicy secret of the Forms
of 'good' and 'evil' (notions that i must
when we have leisure try to explicate)
So then their legend hooked into the truth
that consciousness of crude morality
was of the very essence of their minds
and that forbidden juice had poisoned them
and made them more than apes yet less than gods
and trapped them in a struggle with the flesh
that they tried to resolve with groveling
to that same 'God' who did not know himself
what his taboo was all about   But i
digress (a human failing  please excuse)

## JUDAS AND THE TRUTH

This Judas  what of him  you ask  the end?
i must admit that in exasperation
i did reveal to him—yes  a mistake—
the part that i played in the cosmic plan
i told him of our life on Zygon 3
where  though we were pure minds and without form
(at least as known to his perception) we
could take on shapes for pure aesthetic needs
(such needs being all we had)  in complex forms
diverse and intricate  supplying what
for mere material creatures are supplied
by drives  desires and instincts  and the like)

These shapes  as best I could describe to him
were like transparent floating jelly fish—
square  or slightly rhomboid  quivering
continually as they floated through
the Zygon atmosphere—unique to us
and one that can support a form of life

so alien to his imagination
i told him how the forms communicate
whole patterns at a time  the quivering
giving off bell-like sounds and radiating
shifting color patterns on the surface
that in conjunction with the sounds gave meaning
that we descried in different degrees
of pure aesthetic value—as the sound
and color combinations came towards
a pure perfection of communication.

His constant question was "what is your truth?"
(as Pilate after him demanded too—
the hominids are much possessed by truth)
and he could not accept that truth for us
was simply  solely  elegance of form
the perfect marriage of the elements
Thus—i tried to find a metaphor—
the greatest music held the greatest truth
by virtue of its perfect harmonies
and these in turn mysteriously produced
the greatest works of plastic art  as if
music and art spoke with one voice and were
mutually self creating  That was truth
(Remember friend how puzzled we have been
that though we have decided to reveal
the systematics of this truth to one
called Ruskin  how the earth's philosophers
have treated *Modern Painters* with disdain?)

While Judas was enthralled he could not grasp
a notion of the truth so alien
But he (i had suspended disbelief
in him for purposes of intercourse)
enquired how such beings as we were
could take an interest in human things

i tried then to explain the interest
and how our major pleasure was to solve
such puzzles as the universe evolved
and like a gardener to prune and trim
the growing or declining cosmic plant
(i'm falling into metaphor again)

How in particular we were intrigued
by forms of life that took material shape
and through developments like DNA
could consequently reproduce themselves
That this was fascinating to a race
as timeless and as static as ourselves
i added—while he goggled gasped and shook—
that we had taken pleasure in the fact
that on one planet of a distant sun
a group of living creatures had evolved
and happened on the unsuspecting edge
of something that appealed to our aesthetic
sense of wonder joy in the unique
They could (and this was thrilling to our minds—
the quivering and the music were intense
producing symphonies of sound and light
that sent us into transports yet unknown)
they could produce from matter simple minds—
not minds that were pure mind you understand
(i told the hapless Judas as he gaped)
but minds *evolved from matter* (emphasis
is mine) this *in reverse* from all we knew

Matter made conscious of itself! A push
was all the little hominid would need
And so we pushed And so the game began
And you dear Judas (him i still addressed)
are the one human privy to The Plan
and also to the planning's fatal flaw—
mind still entrapped in matter mind indeed
that draws its substance from that matter must
be always partial in its operation

We  on Zygon  separate the modes
of 'music' and of 'color' but we know
they are one substance differently expressed
And so for you   dear Judas  and your kind
matter and mind are not two things apart
But yet you think they are  think you can live
solely by mind's dictates  You have a gleam
of insight into liberated mind
You see the Zygon world in dreams and glimpse
the possibilities of unmaterial thought
But we were wrong to tease you mortals so
to let you think you ever really had
the pure-mind option even for a moment
(At least that's my opinion  They will not
admit  as we already have observed
that it was a mistake  aesthetically
it could not work  was not harmonious
a constant discord in the flesh-bound soul)

When I had finished Judas was so stunned
i could not leave him thus and so erased
the memory of all that I had said
But Judas never was the same  and when
The Plan demanded that he speed my "death"
some distant echo sent him to his own
"And Judas went and hanged himself" they wrote
not knowing that he could not bear to know—
in some recess he thought was deity
speaking in dreams or trance—the awful truth
(as he would understand it) that he was
one of the playthings of a cruel race
and all his brethren the chorus in
a tragedy that had no denouement—
that they would go on playing in the hope
that i would someday—deus ex machina—
return to make them whole

## THE CLEANSING OF THE TEMPLE

Oh Judas  friend
when simulating 'sorrow' for the pleasure
of savoring 'emotion' i remember
how close we came to partnership  There is
a twinge of that regret that humans feel
when loved ones leave them  Ah  but I digress
You  Zygon double-A cannot imagine
what these 'emotions' are   I had to try
I tried out 'anger'—which for us of course
is an extreme of bright vermillion
crossed with diminished fifths and quivering
of quite unusual severity
provoked by some distasteful combination
But there on Earth the body has to shake
the chemicals inside to circulate
with more than usual rapidity
and mind  such as it is  reverberate
with 'hate' or 'indignation'  honor scarred
desire thwarted  piety reproved
i tried it on the brokers in the temple
(In fact they were a useful crowd because
only Jewish coins could be accepted
in tribute by the priests  and pilgrims came
from many lands with different currencies
The brokers  for a reasonable fee
would change their coins to shekels—or whatever
and make their offering acceptable)
But still i raved and threw myself about
"My father's house become a den of thieves!!"
and all that kind of thing   Quite an effect
The crowd liked that—assertion of my rights
in my own father's house   But i was bored
i never liked this playing with emotion
i did not 'feel'—but They demanded it
"You must be human and be seen to be
or it won't be convincing when you die"

## THE MIRACLES

And so to garner their attention  i
was forced to walk on water  still the storm
feed thousands with a morsel  heal the sick
raise poor bewildered Lazarus from the dead
(i hesitated there  but then succumbed)
and "cast out devils" from the wretched souls
who could not tolerate the grinding strain
imposed on them by their material minds
and sought a refuge in bizarre behavior
This always pained me since i found it best
to leave them locked in their illusions where
they could take temporary refuge from
the glimpses of the truth they could not bear
But on it went  the wretched 'miracles'
that were demanded if i was to prove
myself material for Messiahhood
But oh those endless  boring 'parables'
Can you imagine  Zygon double-A
the mental agony those put me through?
But that was how the teachers reached the crowd
along with healing and the little tricks
to keep the crowd's attention  So i preached
with borrowings from Hillel i'll admit
but i was improvising  Yes i know
never apologize  do not complain!

## THE TRANSFIGURATION

Sometimes in desperation i departed
from the appointed script  Once in a fit
of extreme loneliness (as we would know
when in a moment of rejuvenation
we must withdraw and shut out other minds)
i took three of the blockheads up into
a mountain where i showed them my true self
and even called two lesser Guardians
to witness for me what i really was—
my dazzling whiteness  purity of mind
But Peter  John  and James—dear simpletons
cried out "Elijah" "Moses" "Let us build
altars for offerings" i wrapped them in
a cloud of merciful forgetfulness

i knew by then that it was hopeless  all
would be distorted by the chroniclers—
except i really did perform the tricks
and all those later 'modernists' were wrong
with their assertive 'demythologizing'
Popped out the tomb too  right on time as planned
once our noble leaders had decided
to go through with the farce  i always think
that that sly devil Thomas 'in his heart'
suspected something of the truth despite
the quite convincing evidence of 'wounds'
(He knew i was an incorporeal thing
Some of the humans had a sense of it
but put it down to godhead or the like)

## PILATE AND THE TRIAL

What of Pilate?  Well  the chroniclers
anxious to appease their Roman lords
and new-found Roman converts  and to dump
the blame onto the Jews (who were to blame
in one sense since they did arrest me) forged
a 'trial' in which Pilate—Lord of Rome—
is pressured  bullied  yes and shouted down
by hate-filled Jews who yodel for my death
and ask for some fictitious Zealot's life
(Bar Abbas—'I who am my father's son'
Who were they kidding?  Ah!  That idiom!)

That Pilate would have suffered any such
indignities from Jews is ludicrous
He was a man of some intelligence
and very little patience with the Jews
But  Yes  he did demand to question me
and though officially we did not speak
a common language  through interpreters
(their Aramaic wasn't very good)
he asked me who i really thought i was
to satisfy his curiosity
i gave the answers that the part required
which was a pity since i think that he
saw something was not square with those reports
that painted me a Zealot  even if
Simon and Judas in my entourage
(i had to have the Zealots on my side)
had made me guilty by association

For a moment i was tempted to suspend
the tiresome illusion  and in Latin
as good as Virgil's let the procurator
('Arma virumque cano  Troiae')
into the secret for a little while
i felt some resonance  some common bond
with this high Roman set the sordid task
of keeping order in this frantic land
But since this was impossible  he told
some minor flunky to dispose of me
to Herod  who then promptly bounced me back
(too hot to handle)  Some centurion
bored with all this dithering indecision
decided I was due for execution
along with any other sicarii
who had been caught  So I was crucified
(a kind of bureaucratic afterthought)
along with two of Simon's 'patriots'
after being beaten  mocked  and all
the stuff that is quite faithfully recorded
and that The Plan had faithfully prepared
so that the ancient prophecies would seem
fulfilled  The sacrificial lamb of God
went to the slaughter  and he played his part
down to the last words on the dreary cross
reciting psalms and crying out to God
"Why hast thou forsaken me Eloi?"
to make the thing convincing  all the while
remembering to be magnanimous
"Forgive them  Father  for they are misled"
"Mother  behold thy son  Son  mother thine"

## THE MOTHER

Oh that poor woman who was forced to be
my 'mother' yet who never knew me  She
convinced herself that 'God' had done the deed
and i was heir apparent to the throne
of her exalted  distant ancestor
(that wife-collector David  with the harp)
Oh she was such a snob  Her husband though
was quite a decent man who never held
mysterious origins against me and
pretended to believe the fairy tale
she and Elizabeth had fabricated
accounting for the stranger in her womb
(a story I might say she quite believed
 after a thousand tellings  let it pass)

i must have been a sorry disappointment
as son  or king  or even human being
by her sad simple standards  Did i not
reject her in a vain attempt to show
that all the hominids should free themselves
from these gonadal ties?  Should aim to be
like creatures of pure spirit  fit to live
in a non-material kingdom of the mind
 with no allegiance but to the eternal
not having their ideas the slaves of flesh
"Not of this world  my Kingdom!"  Yes  i tried
but all they heard was some apocalyptic
call to a ringside seat at Armageddon
(Those Essenes with their Zoroastrian
excesses have a lot to answer for)

## THE MAGDALENE

Such a charade!  And anyway the plan
was only partial  for they shut me out
from that most human humanness  the thing
that links them still to life on Earth
however near to godhead they aspire—
participation in the round of life
and death and life again   that my own death
and resurrection was to symbolize
What was the point of all that humanness
if i was not to reproduce myself?
The Plan could not begin to contemplate
such an outrageous possibility
A temporary sojourn in the flesh
for creatures of pure mind is possible
but since we do not reproduce ourselves
there was no way that we could enter into
a pact of more than momentary union
But need I must remain a celibate?
In fact i always felt it as a flaw
for as a Rabbi i deserved a wife
and without one was suspect  rather odd
which brings me to the priestess of the doves
which brings me to the case of Magdalene
which brings...

(Here the tape breaks off, and the other tapes have
yet to be transcribed)

Seven

Epilogue:

Fire of Sense/
Smoke of Thought

*Therefore they shall do my will*
*Today while I am master still,*
*And flesh and soul, now both are strong,*
*Shall hale the sullen slave along,*

*Before this fire of sense decay,*
*This smoke of thought blow clean away,*
*And leave with ancient night alone*
*The steadfast and enduring bone.*
—A. E. Housman, *A Shropshire Lad*

## REGRETS: FROM THE GAELIC

Two Donegal Folksongs

> Oh Lord, such artful grace
>   going down the glen last night;
> Escaping through the moss,
>   and a calmness in the light.
> Darling one, such sweetness,
>   but our loving all in vain.
> Oh King of heaven's brightness
>   give us last night again.

---

Is a Rí nár lághach an ealadhain/ ag gabhail síos an gleann
aréir;/ Ag ealodh fríd an chaonach,/ agus ciúnas ins an spéir./
Rún mo chléibh nár mhilis,/ ach a'súgrudh croidhe nár ghoirid,/
Is a Rí na glóire gile/ tabhair arais an oidhche aréir.

> O sweetheart, O love, don't wed the old man with
>   grey hair,
> But marry a young man like me, though he last but
>   a year;
> Or you'll be in the end without grandson or son for
>   your care,
> In both evening and morning a-weeping the heaviest
>   tear.

---

A chuisle 's a stór ná pós an seanduine liath,/ Ach pós an fear
óg, mo leó, mur' mairidh sé ach bliadhain;/ Nó beidh tu go fóill
gan ua ná mac os do chionn,/ Sileadh a'ndeór tráthnóna nó'r
maidin go trom.

## EPITAPH ON AN INTELLECTUAL MERCENARY

My reach was always well within my grasp
 (No hope of heaven now or heretofore)
My manhood bid me do the usual things
 (Less said the better  no one's keeping score)
I aimed at something lower than a million
 (Ah the orgy of self-justification)
I apologised and I complained
 (Then bored the world with earnest explanation)
I was a borrower and a lender both
 (Returns were negligible  debts unpaid)
I loved my neighbour as I loved myself
 (My neighbours knew they ought to be afraid)
I did not live an unexamined life
 (The final grades were pretty mediocre)
I played the hand fate dealt me well enough
 (It lacked a trump  I never got the Joker)
I strove for there were many worth my strife
 (I just can't quite remember who or why)
I did not kill nor loose the dogs of war
 (But then again  I didn't really try)
I was true to myself well  more or less
 (What was I being true to after all?)
I took a modest pride in objects scaled
 (Never such heights as risked a nasty fall)
I gave a fair day's work for likewise pay
 (Who's ever fairly paid?  I punched my card)
Just criticism never did offend
 (Since none of it was just I took it hard)
My upper lip was almost always stiff
 (The tendency to whine I found invincible)
I didn't mind the message all that much
 (But I deep-sixed the messenger on principle)

# GROWING OLD GRACELESSLY

An aging brain accepts
    the boring body's lot
Yet fearfully rejects
    the mind's relentless rot

Tormented dreaming crams
    the shrinking space of sleep
soft nightmares ulcerate
    the porous skin of fear
unsummoned insight dams
    the toxic stream of thought
unwanted memories clear
    the lazy censor's gate
old mouldering guilts revive
    the feuds no longer fought
crazed conscience renders cheap
    the will to stay alive

Why protest fight or cling?
    the end is plain to see
Oh life where is thy sting?
    the grave is victory

## THE DREAM-MAN

I was a fish-thing  floating shoaltide seawards
sometimes stranded  terrified in tide pools
scraping sharp seashells  moving among mollusks
leaving life to fathom its own fragile future
squirming  squirting  groveling in gravel
gasping  grasping  shoveling in shallows
lung sac swelling  flailing finlike fingers
living longer landward waiting for weak water
amphibious  amorphous  mutant of mixed margins

I was a reptile  resting in cold corners
waking with the warming  poised perfect predator
moving machinelike  through ferns feather fronded
sudden swiftness striking  vulnerable victim
deliberate digestion  eventual elimination
in time appointed  sensing suitable stimulus
weaving and waving  making meticulous mating
deadly dancer  contriving complex copulation
efficient  effective  mindless minus mercy

I was a frightened  furry furtive tree-thing
creeping in canopy  darting in deep darkness
grasping and grooming  constantly companioned
then bursting through branches  brilliant brachiation
chirping and chattering  foremost in the forest
nursing and nurturing  deadliest of dreamers
powerful and playful  plentiful of paramours
cunning and curious  perpetually puzzling
teasing and tempting  sight of sparse savannah

I was a man-thing  wobbling and wavering
learning long leg-lope  stilt shanks for stalking
forced from fond forest  fearing fresh fierce foes
half hunted  half hunter  researching rich reversal
seeing scenarios  vague vanity envisioned
dreamwork weaves deed-world  thought thrives as thing-like
forms freely fashioned  sound sanctioned as symbols
babble of brotherhood  hand heavy hafted
proud  preening predator  laughing loud  lunging

I am the dream-man  doubting my dark deeds
pursuing perfection  boundlessly building
rushing with reason to limitless lodestars
I am the dream-man  fish-free in future
farewell firm forest  reject rigid reptile
huge head hurls headlong  no past plying pressure
I am the dream-man  unlimited license
slate safely scoured  willing words waiting
numberless narratives  ready for writing

But in secret silence  noting naked nightmares
senses of serpent  drive dreary dreamworld
fears of forest fur-thing  create archaic action
pride of pack-thing powering  motives mainly murderous
symbols slaves to senses  fixing freedom firmly
I am the dream-man  knowing nothing novel
I am the dream-man  natal nightmare neutered
I am the dream-man  buried beneath birthright
I am the dream-man  Do not disturb me

## About the Author

Robin Fox was born (1934) in the Brontë village of Haworth and raised in the Yorkshire Dales, and, as an army brat, all over the British Isles. After education at the London School of Economics and Harvard, he did anthropological fieldwork with the Pueblo Indians of New Mexico and Gaelic-speaking islanders in the west of Ireland. He taught at the universities of Exeter and London until 1967 when he founded a department of anthropology at Rutgers University and has been there ever since, with stints as a visiting professor at Oxford, Paris, Cambridge, Los Andes (Bogota), and California (San Diego). For twelve years he was a director of research for the H. F. Guggenheim Foundation, together with Lionel Tiger, co-author with him of *The Imperial Animal*. He has published thirteen books and hundreds of papers and essays; his *Kinship and Marriage* (1967) is reckoned to be the most widely used anthropological text in the world. He has three daughters and four grandsons, and lives with his wife Lin—a teacher of health sciences at Kean University—in Princeton, N.J., just up the road from Ashley Montagu, and has a winter retreat on Sanibel Island, Fl., where he indulges his interest in Gulf Coast archaeology. Apart from poetry his interests include playing and writing music, fishing and cooking, college football, and wine. He is currently University Professor of Social Theory at Rutgers.

## About Ashley Montagu

Ashley Montagu is an anthropologist by profession and a polymath by vocation. He is one of the foremost public intellectuals of his age, which spans most of this century. He was, for example, one of the architects of the great UNESCO "Statement on Race." Born (1905) in England, he has spent most of his life in the USA, where he taught at a number of universities and medical schools. He is best known for his books, some sixty volumes, including *The Natural Superiority of Women, Man's Most Dangerous Myth: The Fallacy of Race,* and *The Elephant Man* which was the source for the play and film of that name. He lives, with his wife Marjorie, in Princeton, N.J., just down the road from Robin Fox.